The American Marathon

Sports and Entertainment
Steven A. Riess, *Series Editor*

The American Marathon

Pamela Cooper

 Syracuse University Press

The paper used in this publication meets the minimum requirements of American National Standard for Information Sciences—Permanence of Paper for Printed Library Materials, ANSI Z39.48-1984. ∞™

Permission to reprint the following is gratefully acknowledged: Pamela L. Cooper, "The 'Visible Hand' on the Footrace: Fred Lebow and the Marketing of the Marathon," *Journal of Sport History*, Winter 1992, 244–56; Pamela Cooper, "Marathon Women and the Corporation," *Journal of Women's History*, Winter 1995, 62–81.

Library of Congress Cataloging-in-Publication Data
Cooper, Pamela (Pamela Lynne)
    The American marathon / Pamela Cooper. — 1st ed.
      p. cm. — (Sports and entertainment)
    Includes bibliographical references (p.   ).
    ISBN 0-8156-0520-X (alk. paper)
    1. Marathon running—United States—History. 2. Runners (Sports)—United States—Biography. I. Title. II. Series.
    GV1065.2.C66 1998
    796.42'52'0973—dc21 97-45156

To John J. Kelley and H. Browning Ross

Pamela Cooper received her Ph.D. in history from the University of Maine, with a specialty in twentieth-century U.S. history. Formerly assistant professor of history at Texas A&M University—Corpus Christi, she currently writes articles for, and serves as historical advisor to, *Runner's World* magazine. She has published articles on the marathon footrace in the leading academic journals on sports, such as the *Journal of Sport History* and the *International Journal of the History of Sport.*

Contents

Illustrations

Acknowledgments

I owe my greatest scholarly debts to the advisors who guided me throughout my university career. Richard Judd of the University of Maine gave invaluable advice and criticism when this work was in the dissertation stage; this book is a tribute to his efforts. Richard Blanke, William TeBrake, Stuart Bruchey, and Henry Munson are other University of Maine faculty who contributed significantly to my development as a scholar. The books of Allen Guttmann determined the way I would look at sport; he continues to be a major influence. Through the North American Society of Sport History I met Melvin Adelman, Steven Riess, and Stephen Hardy, whose writings helped me interpret the history of the marathon footrace. Mario Bick of Bard College encouraged me to pursue sport history when I was an undergraduate; Wilfrid Hamlin of Goddard College helped me progress on that path. The University of Maine Graduate School three times awarded me the University Graduate Research Assistantship, enabling me to publish three articles while I wrote my dissertation. Harvey, Tricia, and Gretchen Kail gave me a loving home for all six years of my doctoral studies; Kenny Brechner and Ann Atkinson were my friends from our first graduate class together.

I could not have written this book without the collections and librarians of the New York Public Library; to quote Richard Mandell, "I shiver with awe when I enter its doors." The Boston Public Library, the Port Chester Public Library, and the Yonkers Public Library provided the details of each city's marathon. Individually I would like to thank

Brad Hart of the Amateur Athletic Union, Charlotte Fisler of Muhlenberg College's Trexler Library, Lucy Kortum of the Petaluma Museum Association, and Fiona Bayly of the New York Road Runners Club. I am especially grateful to Betsy Beattie, Libby Soifer, and others on the staff of Fogler Library at the University of Maine.

Before I was a historian, I was a runner. Stephen Clapp, editor of *Footnotes*, Michael Chacour, of *Track and Field News*, and Susan Marcus of the New York Road Runners Club were the first to validate my interest in marathon history. I became a writer the day Steve accepted my first article, "How the AAU Suppressed the Marathon," for publication in *Footnotes*, the newsletter of the Road Runners Club of America.

John J. Kelley, ever the teacher, affirmed my plans for graduate study. Ambrose Burfoot of *Runner's World* and Kathrine Switzer of the Avon Running Program have done everything they could to help me finish this project. Edward Levy, Browning Ross, Ann and Nat Cirulnick, and Jacqueline Hansen Sturak were most generous with their time and reminiscences. James Dunaway of *Track and Field News* read this manuscript critically and made many important suggestions.

The first time I met John J. Kelley, he talked to me about Jack Kerouac and the cultural influence of early rock and roll. Was he the one who turned me toward social history? The idea of this book was born, I think one autumn day in 1983 when John, Amby Burfoot, and I visited a little square in Stamford, Connecticut, and looked for the plaque that marked the starting line of the first American marathon. Years later, when I was an unemployed Ph.D. with a book contract and few job prospects, Amby offered me freelance work at Rodale Press.

Amby also brought me into the vibrant running community of the Lehigh Valley Road Runners. Bernadine Pongracz, Catherine Akridge, Christiane Torchia, and Nancy Hofmann ran with me regularly; their goodness and good sense were my mainstay during the arduous months of writing this book. Michael Prokup always had positive comments about my manuscript. Other members of the club who encouraged my work are Ilene Prokup, Anne Povenski, Ernest Pongracz, and Jack and Elaine McCambridge. And I am grateful for the expertise and unlimited patience of our coaches, Jane Millspaugh Serues and Megan Othersen Gorman.

There are many old friends who do not run but who have always been there for me. Laura M. Ohanian, Amy Baranow Stone, and Philip Stone ask nothing in return for years of long-distance telephone friendship but the occasional race T-shirt. And there are those who by being part of my life enabled me to get on with my work: Akira Fitton, Lynn Friedman, Zeva Herman, Michael Marder, Nelson Novick, Julius Shulman, and Charles Stacy.

Most of all, I thank my aunt Eleanor Cooper, my brother Arthur Cooper, and my fellow marathoner Murray Melnick.

Abbreviations

AAU	Amateur Athletic Union
ARRA	Association of Road Racing Athletes
BAA	Boston Athletic Association
BDE	*Brooklyn Daily Eagle*
BDG	*Boston Daily Globe*
BET	*Boston Evening Transcript*
BG	*Boston Globe*
BP	*Boston Post*
CORE	Congress of Racial Equality
DN	*Detroit News*
IAAC	Irish-American Athletic Club
IAAF	International Amateur Athletic Federation
IOC	International Olympic Committee
IRC	International Runners' Committee
LAC	London Athletic Club
LAT	*Los Angeles Times*
LDL	*Long Distance Log: A Publication for Runners by Runners*
N4A	National Association of Amateur Athletes of America
NCAA	National Collegiate Athletic Association
NDAA	North Dorchester Athletic Association
NFSHSA	National Federation of State High School Associations

NOW	National Organization for Women
NY Trib	*New York Tribune*
NYAC	New York Athletic Club
NYDT	*New York Daily Tribune*
NYEJ	*New York Evening Journal*
NYH	*New York Herald*
NYHT	*New York Herald Tribune*
NYP	*New York Post*
NYRRC	Road Runners Club New York Association
NYT	*New York Times*
PAC	*Petaluma Argus-Courier*
PCDI	*Port Chester Daily Item*
RRC	Road Runners Club [England]
RRCA	Road Runners Club of America
SFC	*San Francisco Chronicle*
SLPD	*St. Louis Post-Dispatch*
ST	*Spirit of the Times*
USIV	Unione Sportiva Italiana Virtus
USTCA	United States Track Coaches Association
USTFF	United States Track and Field Federation
YMCA	Young Men's Christian Association

The American Marathon

1

Introduction

When the marathon footrace first appeared in the late 1890s it was compatible with the image American men had of themselves. Individual competition was a way of life for middle-class men, and competitive athletics expressed this definition of manhood. Because white-collar positions in corporations trapped men in routine and hierarchy and separated them from each other and from physical work, middle-class men asserted their autonomy and physical individuality in sport among their peers.

Before industrialization the harsh working conditions of laborers had at least held the potential for camaraderie and contest. But with industrialization and the decline in the number of skilled workers needed, working-class men had fewer opportunities in the workplace. Instead, they found recreation, identity, and sometimes financial gain in sports. As marathon runners, they not only were seen in a context other than their status as workers but could also expend their energy and initiative for their own satisfaction and profit rather than for the profit of others (Gorn 1986, 142–43, 252–53; Rotundo 1993, 241, 244–455).

Marathon runners participate in both competition and community. Through sport, an affirmational activity, men recognize one another as equals (Gorn 1986, 143). In the anonymity of the nineteenth-century industrial city, middle-class men formed athletic clubs both to pursue their interests in track and field and to ensure the companionship of others of the same social standing. These clubs were "subcommunities based on status" (Rader 1977, 361).

The social organizations of immigrant groups, which were sub-communities based on cultural heritage, encouraged participation in sport as an expression of ethnic cohesion (Rader 1977, 361). Relatively few men from any one community ran in marathons, but they ran as representatives. Marathons were held on city streets, where crowds could watch and make their own appraisals. The success of a single runner was all that was necessary to enhance the honor of an entire group.

The American marathon developed in the Northeast, where several sizable cities within reasonable traveling distances and with their large populations and financial resources could sustain the sport. The city, with its diverse crowds and enterprises, is the traditional American venue for the young man seeking to make his fortune, to prove himself in the community (Brown 1976, 8–9; Halttunen 1982, 27). And the nineteenth-century development of a highly competitive market economy, comprising numerous clerical and managerial positions, created middle-class jobs and the potential for upward mobility. But large-scale enterprises provided individuals little chance to achieve autonomy in business, and increasing urbanization meant fewer opportunities for distinction in community life. Men could rise through the ranks, but they could also fall back drastically. These were liminal men, who assumed their state to be one of transition (Rotundo 1993, 241, 244–45, 248–49; Halttunen 1982, 30).

Competition evokes liminality, a threshold state within, yet exempt from, the restrictions of socialization, status, and even law. Those in a liminal state shed their social positions and class distinctions. Anthropologists regard the liminal state as one stage in the rite of passage: first comes separation from the social structure; then, a liminal state unrelated to the past or future; and, finally, reincorporation of the subject (Turner 1969, 94–95). Although members of an ethnicity, gender, or social class may perceive an individual as representative, competition separates the athlete from the community and rewards only very specific ability.

The uncertainty of competition advances liminality. Anything can happen in the marathon; the runner travels through infinite possibilities between the sound of the starter's pistol and the moment of crossing over the finish line. John MacAloon describes the tunnel under the ancient Greek Olympic stadium as a liminal boundary, through which "athletes had once emerged . . . to the pure moment of decision and, for some, destiny" (1981, 192). But the moment in the tunnel was a private moment. In the American city marathon, the spectators share the participants' experience of liminality.

The large labor pool required by industrialization brought together ethnic and racial groups who acted out their conflicts through sports. Urbanization introduced the same groups to a concentrated residential situation, that not only created new sources of tension but also provided access to information about sport and organizations to encourage the practice of sport. Capitalism and municipal government produced facilities and events in which one could participate in sport as athlete or spectator (Brown 1976, 8–9; Guttmann 1978, 16–26). Stephen Hardy refers to sport's potential to benefit society as the "social function" of sport (1986, 18). Melvin Adelman, in *A Sporting Time: New York City and the Rise of Modern Athletics*, asserts that city residents promoted the ideology of sport because it enhanced economic productivity; sport improved health and character (1986, 8–9). In *City Games: The Evolution of American Urban Society and the Rise of Sports*, Steven Riess discusses the rationale for the sanctioning of team and other "clean" sports that did not involve gambling or violence. "Clean" sports tapped the "pool of potential spectators and athletes" created by the city. Nineteenth-century urban society saw sport as a way to overcome the perceived physical and moral decline caused by sedentary work and city life. This positive sport ideology continued through the twentieth century (1989, 3).

This book on the movement of a twentieth-century sporting event across socioeconomic class lines centers around New York City. The Amateur Athletic Union (AAU), the national governing body for athletics until 1979, began in New York City in 1888 and its headquarters remained there until 1970. The absence of a continuous marathon actually strengthened the New York City marathon culture by opening opportunities for change; as one race declined, another took its place, but with modifications. The demographics of the marathon reflected the social structure of New York City's large and diverse population.

The Boston Athletic Association (BAA) Marathon is the oldest continuous marathon in the United States and has been produced by the
same athletic club since it began in 1897. In the early years the BAA
Marathon had a strong international component, but it was dominated
by New England running clubs that were derived from older Irish
American and Scottish American sport and social clubs. Other
groups—Canadians, Franco Americans, and Italian Americans—participated in the BAA Marathon athletically but not politically; they ran
the 26.2 miles but had no influence on the administration of the race or
the policies of the club. The stability of the Boston Marathon and the
limited social context of the city of Boston often precluded response to
the social changes that were reflected in the richer athletics culture and
more varied society of New York City.

The social and economic forces associated with modernization
shaped the American marathon, determining the direction and extent
to which the event would travel across class lines. Once a sport is sanctioned by society, it is theoretically open to all members of that society.
Equality of opportunity characterizes modern sport, although a close
look often shows inequalities of access and acceptance (Guttmann
1978, 26–36). American marathons were urban events, accessible to a
wide range of ethnic groups and most socioeconomic classes. As an
amateur event, the marathon was suitable for the upper and middle
classes, yet the race was still open to anyone within the urban sport
system that included working-class clubs and athletes. The earliest
marathons held in the United States had no definitive class affiliation.
The first American marathoners were mostly athletic club members
with previous experience as cross-country runners. The marathon
quickly became differentiated from other cross-country races and gradually assumed a standard distance of 26.2 miles (Guttmann 1978,
36–45).

The marathon came under the aegis of the only United States athletics bureaucracy at the time, the AAU, which was oriented toward
club athletics. Multisport clubs, the primary units of the AAU, staged
marathon footraces within the matrix of AAU rules. The AAU determined the conditions of competition and adjudicated the statistics,
thereby establishing the systems of quantification and records that
were integral to the modernization of the event (Guttmann 1978,

47–54). Because information about running was so difficult to come by, marathon activity was limited to a few pockets on the East Coast, particularly around New York City and Boston. Once that private sources, mainly the AAU-affiliated clubs, began to convey information about training for and racing in a marathon, runners gradually spread marathoning throughout the United States. Such public information was another component of the modernization of the event (Adelman 1986, 6).

The marathon developed into a vehicle for urban boosterism. It displayed the city as well as the athletes, and demonstrated municipal support for fitness and amateur sport. For decades community athletic clubs, booster clubs in small cities, and occasionally newspapers produced marathons, and this meant opportunities for working-class athletes to participate in marathon organization. Gradually, at different times and in different places, individuals from the working and middle classes took over marathon administration, gaining experience in the politics of athletics. During the 1950s and 1960s, the working- and middle-class athletes who ran in the marathon fought for representation and control within the athletics hierarchy, which had previously neglected the needs of marathoners.

The Road Runners Club of America, an athletics organization specifically for the promotion of long-distance running, began in the New York metropolitan area amid the political and social changes of the 1950s. New York City changed the marathon in form and function to suit the participant pool. One obvious recent change was the acceptance of women: New York runners and associations were the vanguard; Boston lagged, tradition-bound. New York City also led the way in technological innovation in long-distance running and in establishing the marathon as a business.

Benefits ascribed to the marathon by its participants contributed to the acceptance of the event. The marathon proved manliness, advanced ethnic pride, racial integration, and social interaction, offered protection from heart attacks, and affirmed youth or fitness or self-discipline. The expansion of government support and corporate sponsorship accelerated the progress of the marathon in terms of an increase in competitions and participants. To accommodate a wide range of athletic abilities, the form of the marathon changed. Stephen Hardy de-

scribes the "game form" as an activity embodied in rules that are organized and controlled by the appropriate groups. The bureaucracy of
long-distance running maintained the high number of marathon participants by instituting changes in the event that made it a meaningful
experience for all who entered. According to Hardy, the marathon becomes "a commodity when its producers transfer it, via exchange, to a
separate group of consumers" (Hardy 1986, 17). During the 1970s the
marathon was effectively marketed as a preferred sport of the upper-
middle class. This marketing targeted not only a desirable consumer
group but also companies that would sponsor marathons in order to
reach those consumers. This commercialization contributed to mod-
ernizing the marathon by bringing it to new constituencies, as well as
professionalizing the sport (Adelman 1986, 6, 9–10).

This book is the history of the development of community around
a competitive event, the marathon footrace. As a new event practiced
by very few men, the marathon had to find a niche in the complex
structure of athletic clubs and the expanding sport bureaucracy. Ethnic
heroes popularized the event among minorities, whose enthusiasm for
the event expresssed group cohesion. As immigrants became citizens,
the marathon celebrated the dual heritage of ethnic Americans. In the
prosperity of the 1920s, the marathon became a function of civic pride
and middle-class nationalism.

During the first half of the twentieth century, marathon runners
were mostly working-class men. The marathon had little value for the
collegians who dominated the glamour events of Olympic track and
field. Marathon participation decreased as the Great Depression limited resources for sports and recreation and as resurgent ethnic conflicts limited access to private athletic clubs. In Boston and in New York
City, neighborhood track clubs and industrial teams became the mainstay of the marathon runner.

Competition between the West and the Eastern bloc during the
Cold War increased the importance of the marathon. College runners
gave more attention to the five-thousand and ten-thousand meter
events and began to move up to the marathon, the symbol of endurance and self-discipline. National pride accompanied American
victories in this event. Americans were in competition with other nations not only at the elite athletic meets but also in the overall fitness

level of ordinary citizens. Jogging was first seen as a way to improve cardiovascular health, later as a way to join the community of long-distance runners, and road races changed to accommodate recreational runners.

As sponsoring corporations reached out to desirable consumers, the marathon of the 1970s drew ever-increasing fields of participants. In the context of the feminist movement, women marathoners' struggle for a place in the Olympics gave overtones of gender community to women-only road races. The young, upwardly mobile professional now typified the marathon runner. Marathoning in the 1970s and 1980s developed a population base so strong that marathon fields continued to grow through the 1990s, despite the absence of American marathon victories at the international level. Participation in the marathon as a runner, volunteer helper, or merely spectator has become an American cultural experience.

2

The City and the Sport Bureaucracy

The urban setting and the sport bureaucracy of the late nineteenth century influenced the form and practice of long-distance running and its premier event, the marathon. The dynamics of the city and the sport bureaucracy together determined not only the event's survival or demise but also the style and location of practice and the identity of the practitioners. Boston's support of the event furthered the acceptance of the marathon after its introduction in the 1896 Olympic Games, while the New York City sport clubs and administrative organization determined the place of the marathon, and of marathon runners, in the hierarchy of track and field athletics.

The marathon footrace, like the modern Olympic Games, was originally inspired by the reverence for classical Greece that European educators and intellectuals had held since the Renaissance (Clogg 1992, 1). Nineteenth century archaeological investigation increased the fascination with ancient Greece. The excavation of Olympia late in the nineteenth century led to suggestions for the revival of the ancient Olympic Games (Mandell 1976, 36, 38). The marathon footrace was created for the first modern Olympic Games.

The Olympic setting gave the marathon credence as an athletic event, and every four years renewed the athletic possibilities of long-distance running. But there was no marathon footrace in ancient

Greece, and the 1896 Olympics were not really modeled after the ancient Games. Baron Pierre de Coubertin, a French educator who admired the British system of sport within education, organized the new Games (Mandell 1976, 89–90). The model for the organization and administration of the modern Olympic Games was the nineteenth-century upper-class amateur sports culture that began in England and reached maturity in the United States (Higdon 1979, 54–60; Menke 1977, 35). The marathon was a romantic addition to the program.

Michel Bréal, a classical philologist, proposed the marathon footrace to Coubertin in June 1894 during the preliminary organizational meeting for the 1896 Athens Olympics (Mandell 1976, 89–90). Bréal apparently intended a ritual that would establish a connection to the ancient Greek Olympic Games by commemorating the 490 B.C. Athenian victory at Marathon (Mezo 1956, 21). The story appears in book 6 of *The Histories* of Herodotus:

> At first before they left the city, the generals sent off to Sparta a herald, one Pheidippides, who was by birth an Athenian, and by profession and practice a trained runner. This man, according to the account which he gave to the Athenians on his return, when he was near Mount Parthenium, above Tegea, fell in with the god Pan, who called him by his name and bade him ask the Athenians "wherefore they neglected him so entirely when he was kindly disposed toward them, and had often helped them in times past, and would do so again in time to come?" The Athenians, entirely believing in the truth of this report, as soon as their affairs were once more in good order, set up a temple to Pan under the Acropolis, and, in return for the message which I have recorded, established in his honor yearly sacrifices and a torch-race. (Herodotus 1954, 105–6)

The Roman Lucian presented another version. "Philippides . . . brought the news of victory from Marathon and addressed the magistrates in session when they were anxious how the battle had ended: 'Joy to you, we've won,' he said, and there and then he died." (Lucian 1954, 177). The English poet Robert Browning combined Herodotus's account with the one from Lucian to popularize the story of Pheidippides for nineteenth-century readers. Browning's poem *Pheidippides*

(1879) honors Pan's role in Athens' victory but concentrates on the runner: "So is Pheidippides happy for ever,—the noble strong man / Who could race like a God." (Browning 1981, 585–88, 1067–68).

The race proposed by Bréal referred to ancient Greece only through conveniently erroneous derivation. The marathon footrace is an "invented tradition," what Eric Hobsbawm defines as "a set of practices . . . of a ritual or symbolic nature . . . which automatically implies continuity with the past" (Hobsbawm and Ranger 1983, 1–2). Of course, the 1896 Olympic Games was itself an invented tradition. Claiming ancestry from an intercity Greek rite whose participants would have deplored the excesses of modern sport, the first modern Olympic Games were a group of international sports meets, based around Scottish and Irish track and field events (McNab 1976; Guttmann 1988, 164, 183).

Early in the nineteenth century, formal athletics appeared in the cultural celebrations of various cities' Scottish Highland Societies. Later Caledonian Clubs were organized expressly for athletic competitions. The first was formed in Boston on 19 March 1853; the New York Caledonian Club was organized in 1856. The 1858 New York Caledonian Club Games included track-and-field events such as throwing the hammer, putting the stone, high jumping from a standing position, and running short races. The Caledonian Clubs also initiated international meets; in 1867 the national Caledonian Clubs of Canada and the United States first met for International Games at Jones Wood, New York (Redmond 1971, 36, 40–41, 59; Frank 1935a).

New Yorkers had been intrigued by footraces since the early nineteenth century. John Cumming has written of formal races that were held on a track in Hoboken, New Jersey, in 1824. These races were organized and advertised by the proprietors of the steam ferry that could bring crowds across the Hudson River from nearby New York City (Cumming 1981, 5). An April 1835 race on the Union Race Course in Long Island was sponsored by the wealthy sportsman John C. Stevens, who offered $1,000 to the first man to finish a ten-mile run in an hour or less (Cumming 1981, 8). The event generated so much interest that it is remembered as the "Great Footrace." The winner, a six foot one inch, twenty-four-year-old farmer named Henry Stannard, made a fine American hero; to the spectators, his victory justified the rural American way of life (Adelman 1986, 212; Cumming 1981, 9–10). According to Cumming, Stannard set the first American track record (1981, 10).

A series of races held in 1844 at the Beacon Race Course in Hoboken stimulated national interest in footracing (Cumming 1981, 28). The first race drew a crowd of 30,000, and Stannard won. Among the entrants in the second race were Englishmen, Irishmen, and at least one Native American. Melvin Adelman noted the chauvinistic overtones of these events. John Gildersleeve, a local furniture-maker, won the second event by passing two Englishmen in the last mile of the race (Adelman 1986, 213–14). According to Adelman, "The excitement derived from the fact that the white man beat the red man and the American defeated the Englishman" (1986, 214). Although Englishmen won the next two races, the appeal of the sport was not diminished. Long-distance running remained the most popular track event, and professional runners went on national tours (Adelman 1986, 214–15).

Louis Bennett of the Seneca nation won international fame as the professional runner "Deerfoot." He began competing in local hurdles races of several miles, with about one hundred hurdles per mile. In 1857 he finished a fifteen-mile race in 1:29:50, a feat that brought him to the attention of English promoters (Cumming 1981, 51–52). In Britain, Bennett set records not only in running but also in the size of the crowds he drew. His dramatic appearance probably enhanced his spectator appeal. Bennett has been described as a sturdy, attractive individual, about five feet, ten and one-half inches tall and weighing 162 pounds. He wore an eagle feather in his headband and cloaked himself in a wolfskin. Bennett's ability would have drawn acclaim even without his exotic appearance; his record for the one-hour run was not broken until 1953 (Cumming 1981, 52–62).

Bennett had been born on the Cattaraugus Reservation in Erie County, New York. A strong tradition in distance running had developed among the Six Nations Confederacy, and its athletes competed in Boston and New York as well as in Albany and Buffalo. Most nineteenth-century Native American runners, members of captive nations who were politically and socially denied almost any economic opportunity, concentrated on winning cash prizes at country fairs and other exhibition races (Cumming 1981, 51).

Members of nineteenth-century ethnic sport clubs sometimes accepted prizes of money for competition; the Caledonian Clubs, for example, were considered semiprofessional. Professionalism as a status was defined at that time as competing for money, competing with athletes who had competed for money, or teaching athletics for money. Amateurism was very much a class distinction; it was considered to be unacceptable for amateur athletes to compete against tradespeople or laborers. The first amateur athletic club was Mincing Lane, founded in London in 1863; in 1866 the name was changed to the London Athletic Club (Glader 1978, 103).

The New York Athletic Club (NYAC), organized between 1866 and 1868, was patterned after the London Athletic Club (Glader 1978, 103). The founders of the club were respectably middle-class: Henry Buermeyer had been a captain in the Union Army; William Curtis was a free-lance writer who would eventually become editor of the *Spirit of the Times*, the nineteenth century's most important sports newspaper; and John Babcock was an architect in the construction business (Considine and Jarvis 1969, 6–8, 9–11). The NYAC was determined to adhere to the rules of amateurism, and it dedicated itself to standardizing organized competitions by means of the stopwatch, measuring tape, and scale. The events practiced by the NYAC included gymnastic exercises, boxing, and track and field.

Elite New York City clubs, such as the NYAC, the Manhattan Athletic Club, and the Berkeley Athletic Club, emphasized the social benefits of membership during the 1880s. Club admission became more selective in terms of wealth and position; athletic ability became optional for the majority of the members. Talented athletes still represented the members in meets, but now the clubs competed among themselves to produce the finest facilities and most elaborate clubhouses. The NYAC started this trend, and it remained the standard against which other clubs were compared (Willis and Wettan 1976, 48). On 15 February 1887, a group of two hundred men, most of them already involved in amateur athletics and clubs, met at the Boston Armory to begin a new club. Rather than continue with smaller clubs, these athletes organized the Boston Athletic Association (BAA), in part to combine their resources to build a clubhouse on the grand order of the NYAC. The BAA was a rival of the NYAC almost from the beginning (*BET*, 1887, 2; 17 Feb. 1890, 2; Hardy 1982, 134).

Many sports clubs of the 1870s and 1880s in the New York City area followed the amateur code but replaced its exclusionary class proviso with a preference for athletic excellence. Among these clubs were the Harlem Athletic Club, founded in 1876; the Staten Island Club in 1877; the Jersey City Athletic Club in 1885; and the Crescent Athletic Club in 1886. In 1875 the Scottish-American Athletic Club had broken from its parent New York Caledonian Society for the purpose of competing in amateur meets; the new club did not require that members be of Scottish ethnicity (Willis and Wettan 1976, 46, 55; Frank 1935a, 18; Korsgaard 1952, 28; Meyers 1889, 446). Organized three years later, in 1878, the Irish-American Athletic Club (IAAC) was amateur but modest in the social status of its membership. The IAAC eventually accepted athletes who were not of Irish ethnicity (Frank 1935c, 17). The German American Athletic Club, organized in 1884 mainly for wrestling and weightlifting, however, retained a strong ethnic identity (Frank 1935b, 20).

Club representatives first attempted to uphold the amateur ethic in inter-club activities by creating, on 28 April 1879, an umbrella organization, the National Association of Amateur Athletes of America (N4A). Charter members included the NYAC, the Scottish American Athletic Club, the Manhattan Athletic Club, the Staten Island Athletic Club, and the Union Athletic Club of Boston. But the N4A was provincial, New York–oriented, and lacked authority to control amateur athletics. In May 1886 the NYAC withdrew from the N4A, and on 1 October 1887, representatives of the NYAC formed a new temporary association, with a draft constitution and by-laws (Korsgaard 1952, 47, 55, 62).

The Amateur Athletic Union (AAU) first met on 21 January 1888 at the New York Athletic Club. By 1890 the AAU had reorganized to provide local administrators for each section of the country as well as representatives in the national structure. The AAU remained the governing body of American athletics for over ninety years, closely allied with the NYAC in such issues as the ethics of amateurism and sportsmanship as well as quantification, rationalization, and record keeping (Schroeder 1961, 12; Korsgaard 1952, 64, 109).

By now, the great athletic clubs selected members on such criteria as social status, value of property owned, and university degree. But winning at athletic events was still important to a club's stature, and top athletes were recruited as members "even if their social backgrounds did not measure up," according to Steven Riess. From the latitude that even lower-status clubs allowed their members in paying dues, it could be inferred that many of the high-performing club athletes might be of a lesser socioeconomic status than the rest of the members (Willis and Wettan 1976, 54–55; Riess 1989, 58).

As performances improved and championships became more representative of the entire nation, the New York Athletic Club contemplated an international competition. On 27 November 1894 the NYAC and the London Athletic Club (LAC) began the correspondence that resulted in a championship meet between the two clubs. During the course of the planning the meet was expanded into a contest between nations—Great Britain versus the United States. Each club was permitted to recruit the best amateur athletes from other clubs within its own country (*ST,* 28 Sept. 1895, 360). The two teams met 21 September 1895, on Manhattan Field, New York City. The New York Athletic Club won all eleven events, and international participation became another symbol of prestige among American athletic clubs (Considine and Jarvis 1969, 57).

Long-distance footraces on the track had long been part of American amateur sport; in 1882, J. Saunders set an amateur record at 150 miles (Cumming 1981, 168). James E. Sullivan, later president of the Amateur Athletic Union, competed in three-hour races, sometimes against Saunders (Sullivan 1909a). The event nearest to the marathon, twenty-five miles around a cinder track, was run by John Gassman in 1884—apparently in record time (*New York World,* 1896, 13). But these footraces had fallen out of favor by the 1890s. A long-distance race began in Hamilton, Ontario, Canada, with groups of walkers who circled Burlington Bay as part of a Sunday outing that included a stop for a picnic lunch. In the early 1890s the course was surveyed and a competition developed. R. B. Harris held the walking record, covering the distance in just over three hours. Hoping to improve newspaper circulation, the Hamilton *Herald* sponsored the event in 1894, offering a silver cup to the victor. W. R. Marshall won, running the course in about 2:14. The popular footrace was held again in 1895, and in 1896, when it was moved to Canadian Thanksgiving Day, in early November. The event celebrated Canadian Thankgiving Day for 75 years. Known as the Around the Bay Race, it is still held, but it was moved to March in 1971 (Hemmingway 1909, 24; Blaikie 1984, 12–14).

In the United States, cross-country races covered distances from four to eight miles. The NYAC held individual cross-country championships yearly from 1883 to 1886. The event attracted a mix of top runners from elite clubs as well as competitors from clubs with less stringent socioeconomic requirements for membership, such as the Pastime Athletic Club, St. Bartholomew's Athletic Club, St. George Athletic Club, and the Williamsburg Athletic Club (*ST*, 10 Nov. 1883, 449). In 1887 the National Cross-Country Association was organized and held its first team championship race. Covering this event, the *Spirit of the Times* observed that "eagerness to score a club victory also led to the acceptance of one or more men of most remarkable amateur standing—or, rather, lack of standing" (*ST*, 7 May 1887, 485). The inclusion of athletes of uncertain amateur status indicated that cross-country running was not limited to athletes high on the social scale.

Cross-country racing declined during the 1890s for several reasons. First, there were too few spectators to attract sponsors for the events; the races seemed always to be held in inclement weather because long-distance races are safer and more comfortable for the athletes when scheduled in the cooler months. Second, the geographical requirements of cross-country made it too public an event to appeal to the upper-class runners who regulated athletics. The elite athletic clubs provided private space for their members' activities, but cross-country races covered public terrain that could not be controlled by club members, and from which others could not be excluded (Baynes 1894, 490; Riess 1989, 58–60).

In 1893, Pierre de Coubertin began planning an "International Athletics Congress." In January 1894, Coubertin sent a circular to upper-status athletic clubs in a number of nations, proposing a meet of representative athletes (Coubertin 1896, 39). Having prevailed against the LAC in the 1895 track meet at Manhatten Field, the NYAC considered its position secure and dismissed Coubertin's announcement of an Olympic Games to be held in Athens, Greece. In the 1896 *New York Athletic Club Journal*, only one paragraph refers to the first modern Olympics, suggesting that a runner, E. V. Crum, might participate (Considine and Jarvis 1969, 57).

The AAU similarly showed little interest in the coming Olympic Games. But the Boston Athletic Association (which had resigned from the AAU the year before) raised the funds to send some BAA men and a few Harvard students to Athens (Korsgaard 1952, 184). At Princeton University, William Milligan Sloane, a history professor, had been in correspondence with Coubertin and had attended Coubertin's conferences in 1892 and 1894. Sloane had interested some of his students in the Olympic Games; four were given six weeks off from their studies to travel to Greece. Shot putter Robert Garrett, scion of a Baltimore banking family, financed the Princeton athletes. Amoung the Americans, only Arthur Blake of the BAA planned to enter the marathon (Mandell 1976, 114–15).

The Greeks hosted the new Olympic Games in the hope of accelerating their cultural integration into western Europe. Centuries of Ottoman rule had turned the country to the East, and Greece had been untouched by every major Western upheaval from the Renaissance to the French Revolution. Greece had won independence in the early nineteenth century, but civil unrest racked the new nation, which was dependent on the United Kingdom, France, and Russia. Despite a thriving mercantile class, there was little economic opportunity for the majority (Clogg 1992, 3, 6, 45, 61; Mandell 1976, 98–99).

Western reverence for classical Greek culture assured that Europe and the United States were concerned for the viability of modern Greece. Classical Greece also formed the basis of the new nation's ethnic identity (Clogg 1992, 50). Coubertin's international athletic meet invoked the Olympic Games of ancient Greece and thereby enhanced the prestige of modern Greece. But by the time the marathon was held—on the fifth day of the Olympic Games, 10 April 1896—most of the innovative appeal and splendor of the Games had diminished. The victories in athletic contests up to then had gone mainly to Americans (MacAloon 1981, 225–27; Mandell 1976, 137–38).

The marathon footrace had become a matter of Greek national pride even before the Games began. Greek athletes trained at long distances for about a year, and two trials had been held over the marathon distance to select a team (Mandell 1976, 135; MacAloon 1981, 227). Greek success in the marathon would say that the glory of Greece was not all in the past. A Greek winner would symbolize the continuity of Greek history by connecting the ancient Greek victory at Marathon with the relatively recent Greek triumph over the Ottoman Turks.

The race began in the town of Marathon, about 40 kilometers from

Athens. The French runner Albin Lermusieux took the lead, followed by the Australian Edwin Flack, the American Arthur Blake, and the Hungarian Gyula Kellner. None of the four foreign entrants seemed to have had much experience in such a race. Blake collapsed at 23 kilometers; shortly after, Flack overtook Lermusieux, who had gone out too fast. A bicyclist brought the news of the impending Australian victory to the stadium. But Flack collapsed after 36 kilometers, and Lermusieux fell far behind. The Greek runners pressed on, and now Spiridon Loues began maneuvering to hold the lead (MacAloon 1981, 226–32; Mandell 1976, 136–38). Once again the name of the leader traveled ahead to the crowd waiting at the stadium: "it is doubtful that anything approaching that wave of feeling and meaning that Loues pushed in front of him down Herod Atticus Street has ever occurred again. 'Elleen! Elleen!' A Greek had won the first Marathon" (MacAloon 1981, 232).

As the winner of the first marathon, Spiridon Loues became a hero throughout Greece, and a mythology about him developed almost immediately. His win was variously attributed to faith, prayer, the hardships of his life, his love for his country, and his love for a woman. A peasant, Loues became a symbol of simplicity and virtue. He declined all gifts offered for his accomplishment, and this contributed to his aura of noblesse (Mandell 1976, 137–38; MacAloon 1981, 232). Loues's victory told a story about transcending poverty. Greece was very poor, having declared bankruptcy in 1893. Young men went abroad to find economic opportunity; between 1890 and the start of World War I, about one-sixth of the population emigrated, almost all of them men (Clogg 1992, 71). Loues symbolized the possibilities that still remained in Greece.

The first United States marathon, a 25-mile footrace from Stamford, Connecticut, to Columbia Oval in the Bronx, was held on 19 September 1896 as an event in the Knickerbocker Athletic Club's first open amateur games. John J. McDermott won the first American marathon in 3:25:55 (*ST*, 26 Sept. 1896, 334). McDermott, a lithographer (Derderian 1994, 4), belonged to the Pastime Athletic Club, a club without social class requirements, whose members frequently were cited in the *Spirit of the Times* for their ability at cross-country running. Hamilton Gray of the St. George Athletic Club was second in 3:28:27; Louis Liebgold of the New Jersey Athletic Club was third in 3:36:58. Many of the athletes, including Hamilton Gray and Ernest Baynes of the Knickerbocker Athletic Club, were also established as cross-country runners (*ST*, 26 Sept. 1896, 334).

The Knickerbocker Athletic Club marathon was a result of club and urban rivalry. The American team brought the idea of the marathon footrace home to an athletics club culture so concerned with status that spectators were screened at some competitions. The Knickerbocker Athletic Club, one of the most socially prestigious clubs of that era, appears to have been trying to establish itself as an athletic power, and the marathon was intended to approximate the recent Olympic event (Willis and Wettan 1976, 55–56). Boston had sent athletes to the Olympic Games that New York had ignored. The New York City clubs now defended their position with the presentation of the first American marathon.

Cross-country running provided the pool of athletes capable of running a marathon. Cross-country gave the American marathon a legacy of long-distance training and racing knowledge, nonrestrictive clubs, and mostly middle- to lower-status practitioners. Marathon entrants included members of the Harlem Branch YMCA and St. Bartholomew's Athletic Club. The YMCAs catered to "youthful clerical workers" and middle-class boys (Riess 1989, 157). The 1896 yearbook of St. Bartholomew's, a Manhattan Episcopal church known for its community programs, indicates that membership in its athletic clubs was inexpensive or free to qualified members (p. 298). M. J. McCarthy ran the marathon as a representative of Company B of the Irish Volunteers, a volunteer fire corps. Slow times in the marathon caused the *Spirit of the Times* to dismiss the athletes as "a sorry lot of tenth-class distance runners" (24 Sept. 1896, 334). The poor performances were among the reasons why the event did not appear again in the New York area until 1907.

The Boston Athletic Association Marathon began on 19 April 1897, Patriots' Day in the Commonwealth of Massachusetts. The marathon was one of the events commemorating the rides of Paul Revere and William Dawes through Lexington and Concord to warn of the approaching British troops. The marathon also served as a reminder of the BAA's presence at the 1896 Athens Olympics. The first BAA

Marathon shaped up as an intercity rivalry; Hamilton Gray from New York and Richard Grant of Boston struggled for the lead over the first half of the course. As the race came through Wellesley College, the students cheered for Grant, a Harvard track man. Gray slowed to a walk; Grant dropped out soon after. John J. McDermott was again the winner, this time over a 24.7-mile course that he covered in 2:55:10. J. J. Kiernan of New York's St. Bartholomew's Athletic Club was second; a Massachusetts runner, E. P. Rhell, was third. The next three men were New Yorkers, including Hamilton Gray in fourth place; places seven through ten were taken by Massachusetts men (*BP,* 20 Apr. 1897, 1, 8; Derderian 1994, 3–7).

On 19 April 1898 the Boston Marathon was extended to 25 miles and the winner was Ronald J. McDonald, a Canadian-born Boston College student (*BET,* 20 Apr. 1898, 3). In 1899, Lawrence Brignolia, a blacksmith affiliated with the Cambridgeport (Massachusetts) Gymnasium, won in 2:54:38; Richard Grant was second. McDonald and Grant, both strong competitors, had upper status affiliations, and this factor delayed the marathon's identification as a working-class sport (Derderian 1994, xxv, 8–11). Of the eleven finishers that year, six were from New York, four of them from the Pastime Athletic Club. Marathon runners found club affiliation important for the exchange of information on training and competition. Engaging in activities perceived as unusual, such as long-distance training on public roads, was easier with the support of other marathon runners. Of the five Massachusetts men, J. R. Maguire, like Brignolia, was affiliated with the Cambridgeport Gymnasium, and the other three, two Sullivans and a Harrigan, belonged to the Highland Club of Roxbury, an Irish enclave (*BET,* 20 Apr. 1899, 10; Blodgett 1966, 144, 151).

The presence of many Irish participants anticipated the marathon's potential for the assertion of ethnic solidarity. Irish immigrants had come to Boston throughout the nineteenth century and by the 1880s were quite well established in the city bureaucracy and Boston politics, as evidenced by the election of Hugh O'Brien, an Irish American, as mayor (Miller 1985, 193). In 1900, Irish immigrants accounted for 35.6 percent—by far the largest group—of Boston's foreign-born population (Bureau of the Census 1913, 824).

Irish immigrants had a long track-and-field tradition, and the sport had become part of their cultural celebrations in America. The Gaelic Athletic Association, formed in Ireland in 1884, soon had branches promoting track and field in many American cities (Mandle 1979, 99–101). Irish parishes, Irish neighborhood sport clubs, and Irish volunteer fire departments all encouraged athletic competition (Riess 1989, 36, 94; Rader 1977, 361). In the mid-nineteenth century, the working classes had found entertainment in watching professional long-distance running and walking contests among members of their own socioeconomic group. In the Boston area these "pedestrians" were mostly Irish, and a long-distance running culture developed among Irish Americans (Cumming 1981, 37–38, 47, 51).

Sports participation by the Irish celebrated their ethnic identification but did not further their social acceptance. Rather than becoming integrated into Boston's cultural or economic institutions, the Boston Irish of necessity constructed parallel institutions of their own within a system of churches, parochial schools, fraternal societies, and neighborhood saloons (Ryan 1989, 14, 113; Stack 1979, 7). Irish immigrants and Irish Americans ran in the Boston Marathon, which they sometimes won, but they rarely belonged to the Boston Athletic Association. The Irish entered the marathon, but the Yankees were elected to the BAA board of governors, and they controlled the Boston Marathon.

When the Irish ran in the Boston Marathon, they told their own story of a journey by foot to America. Early in the nineteenth century, Britain attempted to limit Irish immigration to the United States by setting much less expensive fares for passage to Canada. Much of the Irish American population had emigrated first to Canada, to the Maritimes, Quebec, or Upper Canada (Ontario), then to the United States. Irish immigrants could travel south most cheaply by walking (Daniels 1990, 127–29). The Irish, who settled throughout New England, became the predominant immigrant group in Boston. Boston's large Irish population was tied to Canada by friends and relatives left behind or along the journey in the processes of migration (Handlin 1973, 54–55). Economic interactions bonded the Maritimes, Quebec, and Ontario to Boston; for example, Boston served as a trading center for the Maritime Provinces (Warner 1976, 5). Thus, for an athletic exchange between Canada and the United States, Boston was a logical venue.

Five veterans of the Hamilton, Ontario, Around the Bay Race came

to Boston in April 1900 (*BP,* 20 Apr. 1900, 3). The Hamilton race had always inspired intensive bookmaking, and the Canadian runners' way
to the Boston Marathon had been paid by backers who bet heavily and
openly on the outcome (Blaikie 1984, 1, 3, 20). John Caffrey, son of Irish
immigrants and a teamster by trade, won in 2:39:44. He ran for St.
Patrick's Athletic Asociation, wearing the team's shamrock emblem on
his chest. Two runners from the Hamilton YMCA followed: William
Sherring, a railway brakeman, in second place, and Frank Hughson in
third place. Caffrey won Boston again in 1901; William Davis, a Canadian of the Mohawk nation, came in second (*BP,* 20 Apr. 1900, 3; *BP,* 20
Apr. 1901, 1; Blaikie 1984, 1, 3, 20; Derderian 1994, 13).

The 1901 Boston third-place finisher, Samuel A. Mellor, Jr., of
Yonkers, New York, went on to become the unofficial national champion in July 1901 by winning the race in Buffalo at the Pan American
Exposition. Mellor came back to Boston to win in 1902, accompanied
by other New York talent: W. H. Schlobohm, like Mellor a member of
the Hollywood Inn Athletic Club, and Arthur Ziegler of the Pastime
Athletic Club (*BET,* 21 Apr. 1902, 1; Martin and Gynn 1979, 18). Mellor
returned again in 1903 with Frederick Lorz and J. J. Donovan, both
members of Mellor's new club, the Mohawk Athletic Club of Yonkers.
With Arthur Ziegler and Michael Spring of Pastime, New Yorkers took
second through sixth places in the Boston Marathon (*BET,* 21 Apr. 1903,
8). In 1903, when a local man, John C. Lorden, won the Boston Marathon, the *Boston Daily Globe* ran a front page headline, "Marathon Run
a Race of Marvels"; the *Boston Evening Transcript* called the 1903 race
the "Greatest of Marathon Runs." Lorden was an Irish immigrant who
worked long hours at the Pump Manufacturing Company of East Cambridge during the day and trained at night (Derderian 1994, 24, 26).

Marathon runners were more and more working class men and so
the marathon declined in prestige as it gained in adherents. The many
runners from outside the Boston area contributed to the distinction between marathon participants and marathon producers even when the
former did not fit the emerging stereotype. In 1904, twenty-one-year-
old Michael Spring of New York, employed by the Edison Company to
design powerhouses, won the Boston Marathon. Spring, a technical
school graduate, was Jewish; like his teammates Arthur Ziegler and
Louis Marks, Spring ran wearing the blue Maltese cross of the Pastime

Athletic Club (*BET,* 20 Apr. 1904, 8; *BET,* 20 Apr. 1905, 4; *BDG,* 19 Apr. 1904, 1; Derderian 1994, 26, 28). The continued New York presence contributed to the prestige of the Boston Marathon and to the BAA's dominance of the event; the New York City area abounded in cross-country and road races around five to ten miles, but Boston was where one went to run a marathon.

The second Olympic marathon was run through the streets of Paris on 19 July 1900 in heat up to 102 degrees. Eight athletes finished, in this order: two French runners, one Swedish, another French, then the four American runners, Arthur Newton, John Cregan, Richard Grant, and Ronald McDonald (Martin and Gynn 1979, 17). The United States Olympic team was very much an upper-status group. The NYAC sent several runners; most of the team were university men from Chicago, Georgetown, Michigan, Pennsylvania, Princeton, and Syracuse (Lucas 1980, 52).

The second Olympics depreciated both the Games and the marathon. The Paris Olympics were held in conjunction with the Paris Exposition of 1900, but the Games took a subordinate role. There was no proper stadium, funding, or leadership; Coubertin had been pushed aside as games organizer by Daniel Merillon (Mezo 1956, 22). Allegations of course-cutting compromised the marathon. Michel Theato, the Olympic marathon winner, was a baker's deliveryman whose familiarity with Paris byways may have disadvantaged the other runners (Martin and Gynn 1979, 17, 24; Lucas 1980, 52–53).

James E. Sullivan was then secretary-treasurer of the AAU, the national governing body of track and field headquartered in New York City. And Sullivan did not think highly of the marathon. His objection to the marathon became clear at the 1904 Olympics, held in conjunction with the World's Fair in St. Louis, Missouri. On 31 August 1904, the day after the marathon, the *St. Louis Republic* ran a front-page article on "Chief Sullivan's Opinion of the Marathon Race":

> The marathon race was a decided success from an athletic point of view, but I think they should be dropped from the list of events.
> I saw the finish of the Paris and yesterday's races, and I think they are man-killing in effect.
> Although there were plenty of machines on the road to render as-

sistance to the runners, they are so fixed on winning that they do not stop until they drop from sheer exhaustion.

The Marathon race has been run, but give me the track and field events.

Sullivan's dislike of the marathon caused, by default, the Boston Athletic Association's continued dominance of the event in its formative years in America.

Sullivan was determined that track-and-field events would remain the center of Olympic competition. As secretary-treasurer of the AAU (he was president from 1906 to 1909, and secretary-treasurer again from 1909 to 1914), Sullivan was concerned with maintaining standards of amateurism and consistency that were quite difficult to enforce in the early marathon. Sullivan had included a marathon in his 1901 Pan American Exposition games at Buffalo, but he was not ready to accept the event as part of track and field. In addition, the marathon was essentially the creation of his rival, Coubertin, a romantic (Lucas 1980, 67–69). Sullivan, an American nationalist, took a business-like approach to advancing American athletics (65, 70).

The national governing body of track and field, based in New York City, rejected the marathon, but the event found a home in Boston. Boston's authority was further strengthened when John J. Hicks of Cambridge, Massachusetts, won the 1904 Olympic marathon. This race, run in ninety degree heat, was marred by Fred Lorz's early run into the stadium as a "joke"; he had ridden part of the way in an automobile. Banned from amateur competition by the AAU, Lorz was reinstated in time to win the 1905 Boston Marathon (Martin and Gynn 1979, 20–23). The *Boston Evening Transcript* reported that Lorz, a member of the Mohawk Athletic Club, "was born in New York, is twenty-one years old, a bricklayer by trade, and by reason of his business must do all his practice running at night" (20 Apr. 1905, 4).

In 1905 an annual marathon began in St. Louis under the auspices of the Missouri Athletic Club. Among the fifteen runners who entered the 1905 St. Louis Marathon six were men of apparently Greek origins: Bel Valones, James Valones, Theodore Karboulas, Louis Caporal, and Louis Lambrakis (*SLDP*, 5 May 1905, 16; 6 May 1905, 1). Greek-born inhabitants of St. Louis comprised only one percent of the population

(Bureau of the Census 1913, 824); Lambrakis had come from Keokuk, Iowa. The Greeks who came to the United States had a strong sense of their unique nationality and pride in the cultural achievements of ancient Greece (Daniels 1990, 201). Karboulas, Lambrakis, Caporal, and James Valones finished the marathon, but none of them was under four hours (*SLPD*, 1905 sec. 4, p. 6). Greek American participation was likely a result of the publicity surrounding Loues's win at Athens. The marathon emphasized their Greek identity in America.

When a runner from the Old Country won an important marathon, the event would be very popular among members of that nationality in America. Sport participation was part of the transition from immigrant to ethnic American. Individuals of the same language group or nationality might be quite different in education, economic status, politics, or region of origin. To unite their constituencies, immigrant groups invented their own ethnicities by creating traditions, symbols, and slogans (Conzen et al. 1992, 3–5). Sports enhanced group solidarity. Traditional ethnic sports were obviously useful, but ethnic communities encouraged both traditional and American sports for their potential to efface political and class distinctions within the group (Rader 1977, 361).

The ethnically identified marathon runner personified the agenda of invented ethnicity. He was a symbol that unified the group, defined the group culture, presented its claims to power and status, and demonstrated the compatibility of the ethnic group with American ideals. The successful marathoner embodied the characteristics valued by the dominant culture in America. He was an energetic, active individual who showed assertiveness and self-confidence by running in the marathon, and willpower and self-control by staying the course. The marathon suited the purposes of ethnic Americans because it had no valid associations with any nationality. The marathon was invented for an international sporting meet. Like Greek philosophy and drama, the marathon ostensibly belonged to all of Europe and Euro-America (Conzen et al. 1992, 5–6; Mrozek 1983, 167–69, 191, 226–29).

The increasingly working-class face of the marathon also encouraged ethnic participation. Immigrants have traditionally entered at the lower level of the occupational scale (Thernstrom 1973, 34), beginning the process of Americanization in the workplace by learning from established groups and earlier immigrants. The Irish were particularly significant in the acculturation of later groups to the labor movement, the political machine, and the Irish bachelor sports culture (Barrett 1992, 1001–3; Riess 1989, 17). The many working-class and Irish marathoners opened the way for other immigrants to learn what they had to do to finish a marathon.

Working-class links between Ontario, the Maritimes, and Boston—networks of friends and places to stay—may have encouraged Canadian runners to participate in the Boston Marathon. English-speaking Canadians accounted for 24 percent of the foreign-born population of Boston in 1900 and were the second largest ethnic group after the Irish (Bureau of the Census 1913, 824). Their numbers were augmented by migrants from the Maritimes searching for temporary work, competing for jobs in Irish-dominated trades such as construction (Blodgett 1966, 149).

After the various blunders in presentation of the 1900 and 1904 Games, the Olympics were not held in high regard and neither was the Olympic marathon. In 1906, Athens hosted an interim Athenian Games. The schedule of events was limited but well organized and, unlike Paris or St. Louis, was not overshadowed by concurrent fairs or expositions. The Athenian Games restored a measure of dignity to the Olympics (Lucas 1980, 56; Guttmann 1992, 37). Running on a macadam course, William Sherring of St. Patrick's Athletic Club, Hamilton, Ontario, won the 1906 Athens marathon (Martin and Gynn 1979, 24–25; Blaikie 1984, 29).

A Chicago marathon under the auspices of the Illinois Athletic Club began, like the St. Louis Marathon, in 1905. The two cities developed a rivalry. Sydney Hatch of the Chicago Athletic Club was second in the 1905 St. Louis Marathon, losing to a local man, twenty-four-year-old Joseph Forshaw, who finished in 3:16:57 (*SLPD*, 7 May 1905, sec. 4, p. 6). Hatch frequently won the St. Louis Marathon; in 1907, he placed seventh at Boston. Forshaw took the bronze in the 1908 Olympic marathon (Martin and Gynn 1979, 22–23, 26–27, 31).

Born of urban boosterism and Olympic fervor, the St. Louis and Chicago marathons lasted little over a decade. The Boston Marathon, however, continued because the race celebrated Boston's unique history. Each year the Boston Athletic Association presented the marathon as a gift to Boston on Patriots' Day in honor of Paul Revere's ride and American autonomy. The marathon also commemorated the BAA's presence at the 1896 Olympic Games and its refusal to submit to the sport hegemony of New York City and the AAU. Irish Americans running in the marathon symbolically reenacted a difficult overland journey to find opportunity and freedom. The marathon had patriotic memories and significance for both Yankees and Irish Americans because it told their stories. The Boston Marathon would persist.

3

The New York City
Marathon Culture

The marathon footrace returned to the New York City area in 1907 to be claimed by a new sport constituency. After ten years the race had evolved into a sport with mostly working-class participants. It was public, boisterous, and earthy. Runners passed close by the spectators, streaming with sweat, their labored breathing clearly audible as they kicked through the dust of the roads. The marathon gave ethnic groups a way to participate in patriotic celebrations by watching representative sports as the middle class did, but on working-class terms (Guttmann 1986, 182–83). John Bodnar explains, that "immigrants sought to enter capitalist society on their own terms and formulate their own definition of their status and condition" (1985, 185).

The Amateur Athletic Union represented official culture in the marathons held in and around New York City starting in 1907. Marathons run throughout the United States would be held under AAU sanction and within the parameters established in New York. The opportunity to invest the challenge of the marathon with community, ethnic, and personal meaning assured the integrity and continuation of the New York City marathon culture.

In New York City, the marathon would convey the ethnic consciousness of working-class groups. There would be no equivalent to the Boston Athletic Association Marathon, which represented Boston;

the BAA was part of the Boston power network. Unlike the Boston Brahmins who had perpetuated their control by joining the new entrepreneurial upper class, the Knickerbockers and other Old Guard elites had relinquished political and economic power, and their withdrawal from the scene amounted to an abnegation of cultural responsibility (Jaher 1982, 62–63, 250–52, 259, 271). New cultural organizations reached out to a broader community and emerged beyond the aegis of the old upper class (Hargreaves 1986, 2, 7). The large, upper-status clubs that had dominated New York City athletics in the late nineteenth century had been diminished in number by their tendency to overexpand and acquire expensive property and buildings. The 1893–97 depression contributed to this demise through both the depreciation of the clubs' real assets and the inability of members to pay high dues. The New York Athletic Club and the Crescent Athletic Club, however, weathered the hard times, maintaining both financial and athletic standing (Willis and Wettan 1976, 58–60).

The AAU retained its strong influence in New York City in part because it granted full membership to all clubs regardless of their size or social sphere. By 1914 James Sullivan would openly support small, non-restrictive clubs as the mainstay of the AAU (*NYT*, 5 Apr., sec. 5, p. 2). New York City had produced a number of excellent long-distance runners through company teams and politics, through the imposed good works of settlement houses, and through immigrants' own desire to participate in sport as a rite of Americanization. New York City athletics, especially middle- and working-class clubs, shaped the marathon and determined the direction the event would take throughout the United States.

Middle-class clubs thrived during the prewar period in response to changes in the parameters of middle-class masculinity. Interest in personal improvement led to increased concern for the care of the body; exercise offset the negative effects of the office work or "brain work" that engaged the expanding managerial class. As family togetherness gained ideological importance, new clubs accepted women, and the family-oriented tennis club appeared (Marsh 1988, 170). The Hawthorne Athletic Club, a typical middle-class club, began in 1902 as a group of young people interested in lawn tennis in the middle-class suburb of Flatbush, Brooklyn. Baseball and running were most popular when the club was incorporated in 1906; within three years the club had a playing field with a track and a clubhouse (*BDE*, 22 Apr. 1909, 5). The Mercury Athletic Club of Yonkers was a similar club; in 1906, Thomas Morrissey, one of its members, had placed third in the Boston Marathon.

During the 1890s, Luther Gulick contributed a philosophy of physical education as an enhancement to the mission of the Young Men's Christian Association (YMCA). At his urging, the YMCA began an organization-wide Athletic League in 1896. Gulick stressed the importance of participation in group games for those who daily "went to business": "When they come to the gymnasium their primary need is recreation. They are exhausted mentally, perhaps they are tired physically. They need to be stirred up, made to laugh and throw off their business" (quoted in Hopkins 1951, 265).

A proliferation of working-class clubs characterized athletics in New York City during the first decade of the twentieth century. Many such clubs represented ethnic communities or neighborhoods (Rader 1977, 361). Mostly small in membership and with few athletic facilities, these clubs found the footracing events their best possibilities for competition. The marathon was quite compatible with their athletic potential and limited resources (Riess 1989, 109). A number of working-class clubs were based in settlement houses, which endorsed sports as a catalyst for Americanization and as a way of bringing together people of diverse backgrounds (Cole 1910, 18–22). The Union Settlement began in 1895 in the largely Irish, German Catholic, and Jewish neighborhood of East Harlem. Members of the Union Settlement Athletic Club favored track and boxing (Union Settlement 1970, n.p.). The University Settlement at 26 Delancey Street on the Lower East Side had a gymnasium open from 7:30 to 10:30 P.M. on Mondays and Wednesdays (University Settlement Society 1893). After an initiation fee of twenty-five cents, members paid dues of five cents a week. The mostly Jewish constituency practiced basketball as well as boxing and wrestling (Riess 1989, 166). Hudson Guild on West Twenty-Eighth Street favored track and field. The area served by the Hudson Guild, while strongly Irish, included Italian, Jewish, German, and Greek residents (Hudson Guild 1933, 6, 10).

Early twentieth-century corporate culture perceived sport as a vehicle for the development of individual restraint and as a form of social control; American sports were credited with imparting uniquely American values (Mrozek 1983, xviii, 38, 74, 229, 233). Recreation could provide a desirable work force by introducing immigrant workers to the values of the managerial class and by accommodating the working class to the new social order. A competitive company team also was supposed to be a source of pride to the employees and a focus of loyalty to the corporation. Employers frequently included recreational facilities among other employee benefits meant to encourage workers in bettering themselves (Brandes 1976, 12, 78, 82). The New York athletics bureaucracy accepted company teams on an equal standing with the independent teams.

In 1908 employees of John Wanamaker New York formed an athletic club at the behest of their employer (Schmertz [1967?], 8). The club joined the AAU even before it adopted the name of Millrose, in honor of Rodman Wanamaker's summer home. John Wanamaker's department stores in Philadelphia and New York extended employees benefits such as in-service education ("John Wanamaker Commercial Institute," the store school) and various "supervised pleasures." Many of Wanamaker's ideas were inspired by the YMCA. John Wanamaker had worked from 1857 to 1860 as the first paid secretary of the YMCA; from 1868 to 1887 he was president of the Philadelphia YMCA. He remained active in the organization and a YMCA financial supporter for the rest of his life (Appell 1930, 31, 429). John Wanamaker donated a clubhouse at Bath Beach in Brooklyn with facilities that included substantial grounds and a running track (Schmertz [1967?], 8). The Millrose Athletic Association and its organized track meets advertised Wanamaker's department store and promoted the advantages of employment at Wanamaker's to potential workers and athletes (Nelson 1975, 101–2).

The Millrose Games would rank among the most important indoor track meets in the world. Fred Schmertz, then working in Wanamaker's delivery department, helped present the first Millrose indoor track meet. As a high school student, Schmertz had managed the track team of Clark House Settlement in the Bronx. He continued with the Millrose Athletic Association, becoming meet director of the Millrose Games in 1934 and retaining this position until shortly before his death

Fred Schmertz (right), meet director of the Millrose Games from 1934 to 1974. Howard Schmertz (left), Fred's son, meet director since 1975. Photograph courtesy of Howard Schmertz.

in 1976. Schmertz also stayed on with John Wanamaker New York, studying law through evening classes at New York University and finally retiring as store attorney after fifty years of employment (Schmertz [1967?], 11–12, 19). His son, Howard Schmertz, continues his work with the Millrose Games.

Millrose was a major power among New York athletic clubs because of its endowment as well as its membership. It was composed mainly of working-class athletes, but governed by upper-status individuals, including members of the Wanamaker family. High-performing working-class athletes sometimes received employment at Wanamaker's in the expectation that they would join the Millrose Athletic Association. Abel Kiviat was already known as a runner when he got a job in Wanamaker's sporting goods department through the efforts of some track friends. Kiviat began setting records as a competitor in New York City's Public Schools Athletic League. His Russian-Jewish parents expected their son to work after school, but they still supported his athletic career as best they could (Simons 1986, 242, 252). Kiviat was the world record holder in the 1500 meters when he went to the 1912 Olympics, where he won the silver medal in the event. He died in 1991 at age 99.

The Irish-American Athletic Club (IAAC) had started as a vehicle for the assimilation of Irish immigrants. Now it reached out to the later immigrant groups, and ability took precedence over ethnicity as well as social class in the recruitment of new members. As Millrose served the Wanamakers, the victories of the IAAC answered the needs of its officers, New York City politicians faced with shifting boundaries in traditional ethnic communities and the continuous influx of new immigrants (Riess 1989, 82; Miller 1985, 536). Stanley Frank ascribed the IAAC's success to egalitarianism:

> There was a time, however, when boys and men who worked all day for a living were picked up off the city streets, coached in the finer points of their specialities and presently became champions of the world. That was when the old Irish-American AC was at the peak of its power . . .
> The Irish-Americans really started to come into prominence in 1903, when the scions of such aristocratic Hibernian families as Abel Kiviat, Jim Rosenberger, Alvah Meyer, Charley Cassazza, and Meyer Prinstein joined the club (Frank 1935c, 17).

Like Millrose, the IAAC had assets enough to provide a clubhouse, a three-story brownstone at Sixtieth Street between Lexington and Third Avenues. The more talented athletes were probably subsidized, at least to the extent of training and competition expenses (Simons 1986, 249, 254). But they had little say in the running of the club, according to Abel Kiviat: "Athletes weren't officers. Athletes didn't go to meetings. The only time the athletes went to the clubhouse was when there was a social event or trophies were awarded" (Simons 1986, 250).

The IAAC functioned as part of New York City politics to unite different ethnic groups for the appropriate candidates as well as behind an athletic team (Riess 1989, 72–86). Abel Kiviat recalled wearing the uniform of the Irish-American Athletic Club and marching in the St. Patrick's Day parade (Simons 1986, 250). A Jewish athlete holding a respected place in the celebration of an established group was a strong symbol of Jewish acceptance by American society—in this case, acceptance by the Tammany politicians who supported the IAAC and courted the Jewish vote (Riess 1989, 109). Jewish sports participation filled a specific need to efface the stereotype of the slope-shouldered yeshiva scholar; twentieth-century Zionism extolled "muscular Judaism" (Postal, Silver, and Silver 1965, 11, 14–15).

Sport, whether practiced or watched, provided a sense of community to the heterogenous populations of municipalities and corporations (Guttmann 1986, 182–83). Ethnic groups participated in patriotic American holidays, but each in its own way, acknowledging American working-class identity while affirming the uniqueness of their specific ethnicities. Among the new cultural expressions acquired in America were these "countless parades and celebrations" as well as "exaggerated displays of patriotism" (Bodnar 1977, 152). The Thanksgiving Day football game had been entrenched among upper-status athletes and spectators since the 1880s. By the 1890s, the Thanksgiving Day game had spread throughout America, to high school and athletic clubs, but as an emulation of upper-status, nativist behavior. Football, as "the college game," was part of a milieu not possible for most immigrants (Smith 1989, 79–80).

The Yonkers Marathon, first held on Thanksgiving Day 1907, reflected national trends in sports and patriotism. Though a New York suburb, Yonkers was still out in the country and thus a good venue for cross-country races. The Harlem and Hudson lines of the New York Central brought Westchester County within easy reach of members of New York City athletic clubs. Yonkers was growing rapidly; its population increased by over 50 percent between 1900 and 1910. Immigrants comprised one-third of that population, and Irish and Italians were the two largest ethnic groups (Bureau of the Census 1913, 242). They were drawn to the city of Yonkers by opportunities for work on public construction projects, private real estate developments, and unskilled jobs in industry. Skilled British immigrants also formed a significant group, having established themselves in supervisory positions in Westchester's carpet and textile mills by the turn of the century (Weigold 1983, 62, 66–67, 104).

The Mercury and Mohawk athletic clubs of Yonkers had developed a number of competitive distance runners (*NYT*, 10 Feb. 1907, sec. 2, p. 11). On 22 February 1907 the biggest cross-country field ever seen in America assembled for a six-mile race held by the Mohawk Athletic Club. Participants represented the Pastime Athletic Club, Irish-American Athletic Club, Xavier Athletic Club, Star Athletic Club, Mott Haven Athletic Club, Trinity Athletic Club, National Athletic Club, and St. Bartholomew's Athletic Club of New York City, as well as the Mercury and Mohawk clubs of Yonkers. The race attracted crowds so thick that at times the spectators left little room for the runners to pass (*NYT*, 23 Feb. 1907, 7). Perhaps the popularity of this cross-country race encouraged the staging of the first Yonkers marathon.

The many New York City runners who did well at Boston were another factor in the staging of a local marathon. Of the first thirteen finishers in the 1906 Boston Marathon, six were from the New York City area: Thomas Morrissey of the Mercury Athletic Club, Ben Mann of the Mott Haven Athletic Club, James McCherry of the Xavier Athletic Club, and P. Laffargue, John Hayes, and Harry Goldberg of St. Bartholomew's Athletic Club (*BET*, 20 Apr. 1906, 14). In 1907 top finishers in the Boston Marathon included John Hayes of St. Bartholomew's, John Lindquist of the Swedish Athletic and Gun Club, and Carl Schlobohm, Michael Ryan, and Thomas Morrissey of the Mercury Athletic Club (*BET*, 20 Apr. 1907, 6). Now established as an Olympic event, the marathon compelled American runners to strive for excellence at the long distances rather than dismiss those races as athletic eccentricities. The continuity of the Boston Athletic Association Marathon, and to a much lesser extent the marathons in Chicago and St. Louis, had given the event a sense of tradition.

On 28 November 1907 the *Yonkers Daily News* sponsored a marathon that began and ended at the Hollywood Inn in Yonkers; the Mercury Athletic Club provided the race administrators. The 1907 Yonkers marathon was run through the streets of Yonkers, over Westchester roads, through the nearby towns of Hastings, Dobbs Ferry, and Ardsley. The *New York Times* noted that "The course was laid out in such a manner that the athletes could be seen from any stage of the journey" (29 Nov. 1907, 10). Led by th mayor of Yonkers, John H. Coyne, and expediently won by the Irish-American John Hayes, the marathon displayed elements of the parades that were already part of immigrant working-class culture; it was also a sporting event, after the established manner of celebrating Thanksgiving Day. The race results, which showed a cross section of the finest marathon runners outside the Boston and Ontario clubs, indicated New York City's potential to become the center of marathon organization and competition.

The next Boston Marathon confirmed New York City ascendancy as well as Irish American distance-running ability. "New Yorker Wins Boston Marathon," the *New York Times* exulted on 21 April 1908, when Thomas Morrissey, running for the Mercury Athletic Club of Yonkers, came in first; John Hayes, now of New York's Irish-American Athletic Club, finished second (1908a, 7). Morrissey and Hayes, as well as the fourth place Michael J. Ryan, also of the IAAC, and the ninth place Alton Welton, of Lawrence, Masssachusetts, were chosen for the 1908 Olympic marathon team. Sydney Hatch and Joseph Forshaw, first and second at the Missouri Athletic Club marathon in May, were added later, along with Louis Tewanina, a Native American (Martin and Gynn 1979, 27, 31).

British Olympic officials left the management of the marathon to the Polytechnic Harriers, the club that had recently presented a 22.5 mile race over much of the proposed Olympic marathon course. According to the rules of the marathon, the distance was to be 40 kilometers (AAU Minutes 1908, 21–22). But British officials decided that the Princess of Wales should start the race in the presence of the royal grandchildren. To accommodate them, the starting line was pushed back to the lawn at Windsor Castle. The marathoners would have to run 26.2 miles to finish in White City Stadium at Shepherd's Bush (Kieran and Daley 1961, 70).

The 1908 Olympic Games were charged with tension between the United States and Great Britain, particularly over track-and-field events. Only a few Irish athletes participated for "Great Britain and Ireland," but many Irish American athletes competed very effectively for the United States. The problem of Irish nationalism and home rule colored these athletes' reactions to the British and may also have affected the British officials' responses to contested results (Lucas 1980, 58–60).

The first runner to finish the Olympic marathon, Dorando Pietri of Italy, was disqualified for having received assistance; he collapsed twice after entering the stadium and each time was helped to his feet. John Hayes, the Irish American, came into the stadium immediately after Pietri and crossed the finish line unaided. The United States protest of the 1908 Olympic marathon called attention to the rules surrounding the marathon footrace. Most of the violations listed by the AAU had to do with the conduct of the British Olympic officials toward Dorando Pietri: "When he was literally carried into the arena he was so dazed he did not know which way to go, and from that point to the finish of the race he was constantly attended by the British Olympic officials, who assisted him and thereby broke the laws they were supposed to enforce" (AAU 1908, 20).

Rules six, seven, and eight governing the marathon race specifically forbade such assistance by attendants. Although Hayes was declared the winner of the marathon, the English had such sympathy for Pietri that special prizes were awarded him for his effort, and he became world-famous for his courage (Lucas 1980, 58–60). American marathoners in addition to Hayes did well at the 1908 London Games: Joseph Forshaw was third, Alton Welton was fourth, Louis Tewanina was ninth, and Sydney Hatch was fourteenth.

The intense dispute over the 1908 Olympic marathon finish became part of Irish-Italian rivalry in the United States. Both were major ethnic groups, although the Irish had been in America longer and were far better established. New York City had elected its first Irish Catholic mayor, William R. Grace, in 1880 (Shannon 1966, 73, 182). But by the early twentieth century the Irish were not as economically and socially advanced or as secure as German Americans, the other major mid–nineteenth-century immigrant group. The Irish position was still threatened by newer groups, and the Irish and Italians had a number of points of conflict. There were frequent fights between Irish and Italians over jobs in construction and in the garment industry, and over the eth-

nic identity of neighborhoods (Bayor 1978, 3–5). The Irish, who dominated the Catholic Church in America, disparaged Italian Catholicism.
Italians, in turn, were uncomfortable in Irish Catholic churches,
schools, and lay organizations (Orsi 1985, 16).

The ruddy, boyish John J. Hayes made an appealing hero who ad-
vocated a healthy life-style (Hayes 1908). Hayes was employed by
Bloomingdale Brothers, a major New York City department store that
made arrangements for him to train on a cinder track laid out on the
building's roof (Martin and Gynn 1979, 32). After winning the 1908
Olympic Marathon, he was promoted from assistant in the superinten-
dent's office to manager of the sporting goods department (Hayes
1908). He retired from a successful career as a professional runner to
become a running coach at the university level.

A professional race between Hayes and Pietri was held on the
Madison Square Garden track on 25 November 1908. Many viewed this
event as a manifestation of Irish-Italian competition as well as an opportunity to resolve the 1908 London Olympic marathon dispute. Pietri
won in 2:44:20.4, with Hayes close behind, finishing in 2:45:05.2. On the
front page of the *New York Times* the next day was a story documenting
the ethnic rivalry:

> the excitement grew until the thousands packed from the roof down
> to the ground were in a state approaching hysteria. The Italian specta-
> tors led the way to this point, but the Irish-Americans representing
> every patriotic and athletic organization in the city, accepted the lead
> eagerly, and the partisanship of the countrymen of the rivals in the
> end swayed the entire assemblage. (26 Nov. 1908b)

Ethnic pride shaped many of the professional marathons held in
the New York City area from November 1908 through May 1909. In
Madison Square Garden on 15 December 1908, Pietri raced a Native
American, Thomas Longboat, the 1907 BAA marathon winner, who
had dropped out of the 1908 Olympic marathon. This was Longboat's
chance to redeem himself, and he won in 2:45:05.4 (*NYT*, 16 Dec. 1908,
1–2). While later marathon "derbies" had several runners in competition, the early professional marathons were man-against-man races,
featuring former amateur marathon champions. They ran a 26.2-mile

course, duplicating the 1908 Olympic marathon distance. Such races were occasions of heavy betting. In 1909, Pietri went on to similar matches in Buffalo, St. Louis, and Chicago, returning to Madison Square Garden to race against Hayes once more on 15 March 1909.

These man-to-man competitions over the marathon distance demonstrated what Allen Guttmann has called "representational sport": "individual identification with the athletes and collective membership in the community combine. . . . The athletes are proclaimed representatives of a school, town, nation, race, religion, or ideology. There is, in short, an apparently irresistible impulse to allegorize the sport contest" (Guttmann 1986, 182).

By May 1909 professional marathons in which small numbers of athletes competed for money prizes were less representational sport than contests among top-level athletes and their popularity fell as the contest lost meaning for the ethnic following. Nevertheless, these races were significant in establishing the marathon distance at 26.2 miles. In a professional marathon held at New York City's Polo Grounds on 8 May 1909, Henri St. Yves won out of a field of thirteen starters (NYH, 1 May 1909, sec. 1, p. 13); St. Yves had previously won the Marathon Derby at the Polo Grounds on 3 April 1909 (NYT, 4 Apr. 1909, 1). "Not half the crowd that saw the 'Marathon Derby' witnessed this 'International $10,000 Marathon,'" noted the New York Herald (1 May 1909, sec. 1, p. 13).

Amateur marathons, reflecting a strong sense of ethnic identification, were more effective as representational sport. Four thousand spectators watched over 145 runners start the second annual Yonkers Marathon on 26 November 1908. More than half the competitors dropped out before reaching the Empire City track in Yonkers, where a crowd of 20,000 waited to cheer the winner, James J. Crowley of the Irish-American Athletic Club, and the other finishers. But Crowley was probably referring to his club when he said, "Boys, I did my best. I started out to win, and—well, you see I've done it. I did it for the Irish-Americans" (NYT, 27 Nov. 1908, 7).

The spectators of any sport identify to some extent with its athletes, and there is a tendency for representational sport to become participant sport (Guttmann 1986, 150–53). Even though ability level circumvents this tendency, psychological identification is limited by what Allen Guttmann calls "the boundaries of the self," (1986, 181), and physical identification is curtailed by the boundaries of the "sacred space" (Guttmann 1978, 22) in which the athletes perform, but the marathon was held on public roads, and many spectators shared bonds of ethnicity and class with the runners. Only their access to races with cash prizes and offers of payment for performance distinguished professional marathon runners from amateurs. In discussing the similarities between professionalization and specialization, Guttmann acknowledges the continued use of the term *professional* to describe athletes paid for their effort, but he points out that "the crucial factor in professionalization is not money but time—how much of a person's life is dedicated to the achievement of athletic excellence?" (Guttmann 1978, 39). Although most maintained their amateur standing, marathoners in 1908–9 who finished in less than three hours surely were dedicating far more time to race preparation than those who finished in over four hours.

On 26 December 1908, a marathon sponsored by the *New York Journal* and managed by the AAU attracted more than 700 applicants; two thirds of them were rejected because they were not even members of the AAU (*New York American*, 25 Dec. 1908, 13). Only 106 actually started the race; 53 finished, and Irish-born Matthew Maloney of the Trinity Athletic Club won in the record time of 2:36:26.2. The list of finishers shows mostly Irish surnames; several Italians appeared toward the back of the pack. Those runners affiliated with athletic clubs belonged to nonrestrictive organizations. That 19 runners were not even sport club members indicates they might not have had much experience at competitive long-distance running (*NYT*, 27 Dec. 1908, sec. 4, p. 1). The slow times of the back-of-the-pack runners confirm inexperience. Yet some of the quite average runners in this race would eventually become among the top marathoners of the prewar era. A Brooklyn–Sea Gate Marathon was held on Abraham Lincoln's birthday, 12 February 1909. A field of 164 runners began the race: James Clark of the Xavier Athletic Club finished first in 2:46:52.6; James J. Crowley of the Irish-American Athletic Club second in 2:49:16.6; and Harry Jensen of the Pastime Athletic Club third in 2:54:09. At the finish, according to the *New York Times*, "the judges took the times of twenty-nine, no others being in sight" (13 Feb 1909, 7).

The Brooklyn Marathon was held on George Washington's birthday, 22 February 1909, under the auspices of the Fourteenth Regiment Athletic Association. The *New York Times* commented on the participants:

> Of the 104 athletes entered in the Great Brooklyn Marathon race to be held on the afternoon of Washington's Birthday in Brooklyn, the majority are stalwart Irish-Americans. It may not be that many of them were born on the "ould sod," but they are certainly of Irish extraction.
>
> Among the entrants in the big race tomorrow may be found such good old Irish names as Devlin, Doherty, Slater, Moriarty, Moran, Reilly, O'Rourke, Kelly, McMann, Ireland, Dugan, McFadden, and a score of others. Many of them will race in the colors of the Irish-American Athletic Club, but the majority of them are scattered among various smaller athletic clubs and associations.
>
> There is another nationality that is well-represented in the list of entrants for Monday's race, and that is the Italian. *Il Progresso*, the Italian daily newspaper, has offered a prize to the first Italian to finish. (21 Feb. 1909, sec. 4, p. 2).

The marathon reproduced in ritual form the shared experiences of many immigrant groups in America. The common experience for all recent immigrants was the journey to America—an uncomfortable, intimidating trip, but one that ended in new potential for the traveler. The marathon footrace, with its physical demands, uncertainties, and emphasis on individual accomplishment, symbolized coming to the United States; as a journey, the marathon also acknowledged ties to a distant homeland. Participation in the marathon footrace may be seen as an expression of certain elements of immigrant culture in America. For example the Irish, with a tradition of athletics in Ireland and of long-distance running in America, competed very successfully in the marathon. The event presented challenge and uncertainty, offsetting the occupational preference for security that often thwarted upward mobility among Irish Americans (Ryan 1989, 105–6).

In the amateur marathons of 1908 and 1909, runners with Italian surnames did not do nearly as well as those with Irish surnames. Italian Americans likely did not have the same access to training as

Irish Americans. Most recreational activities for Italian Americans were sponsored by neighborhood organizations that also served as political associations and social clubs. Boxing matches and bocce, a type of lawn bowling, might be contested in the streets, but Italian immigrants often thought sports were a waste of time. Their children, however, participated in American sports, in part as a demonstration of Americanization (Orsi 1985, 34–35, 110–11; Riess 1989, 105–6).

Italian participation in the marathon had precedents in the religious *feste*, celebrations with roots in the old world. In *The Madonna of 115th Street*, Robert Orsi compares the festival of the Virgin of Mount Carmel of 115th Street (who had immigrated to America with her followers) to a reenactment of the journey from Italy to America (1985, 165–67). Such a *festa* was a public celebration, "a working-class redemption of time" (197) and "an occasion for the display of energy and enthusiasm not appropriate or possible in the work place" (200).

In the marathon, the symbolic journey was translated into sport and blended into the celebration of an American patriotic holiday. Early Italian participation in the marathon was an affirmation of community, a demonstration of pride in Italian American culture, and a form of resistance to the hegemony of dominant groups (Orsi 1985, 199–200). The runner, who was free, was the antithesis of the worker. The marathoner flaunted control of his own time and energy, in defiance of the world of work and the factory system. And there was the ethnic conflict. In the workplace, Italians were often subject to Irish foremen; at the marathon starting line, they were equals. Italian American marathon participation eventually produced some fine runners, among them Gaston Strobino, from Paterson, New Jersey, who won the bronze medal for the United States in the 1912 Stockholm Olympic Games.

In America the marathon celebrated public memories that combined official and vernacular cultures. The first five amateur marathons in New York City after the 1908 Olympics were held on Thanksgiving Day, the day after Christmas, New Year's Day, Washington's Birthday, and Lincoln's Birthday—days that also held special meaning for ethnic communities, according to John Bodnar: "Memories of the ethnic past were grounded ultimately in the social reality of the present" (1992, 77). The reality of the present was America, and ethnic celebrations particularly honored the pioneers, the first members of the group to emigrate (75). The journey of the marathon was a fitting commemoration.

While often held on days of national significance, the marathon became important as an autonomous component of working-class culture. In New York City, the marathon footrace became part of smaller, more local structures, such as working-class athletic clubs, armory associations, and ethnic communities. Marathon running in New York City answered the needs of these constituencies. The New York City marathon boom increased the possibilities of presentation and explication of the marathon.

The AAU was for the most part an extension of the New York City athletics bureaucracy, and New York City became the guiding force in American working-class amateur athletics. The AAU had to respect the needs of working-class clubs and athletes in order to maintain its authority as a national governing body for athletics. The broad representation of ethnic groups in New York City combined with a relatively egalitarian sport bureaucracy to create a vital working-class sport culture. The National Collegiate Athletic Association was beginning to claim increasing control over university sports, leaving private, ethnic, and neighborhood clubs as the mainstay of the AAU.

Henri Renard, a Nashua, New Hampshire, millhand of French Canadian descent, won the 19 April 1909 Boston Marathon in 2:53:36.8 and the four men who followed him were products of New York City athletic clubs (*BET*, 20 Apr. 1909, 8). The second place finisher, New York City runner Harry Jensen, might have won the 1909 BAA Marathon if he had not raced at home less than three weeks before Boston. On 1 April 1909, the *Irish-American Advocate* Athletic Union had sponsored a marathon at the Celtic Park track on Long Island; Jensen, of the Pastime Athletic Club, won in 2:48:17 (*NYEJ*, 12 Apr. 1909, 7). The New York City marathons continued after the 1909 Boston Marathon. On 22 April 1909, thousands turned out along the streets of Brooklyn to watch the Columbia Athletic Club Marathon, won by W. J. Wilson of the Xavier Athletic Club in 2:46:00.4 (*NYEJ*, 22 Apr. 1909, 13). Two amateur marathons were held on 8 May 1909: George Obermeyer of the National Athletic Club won the marathon held at Saratoga Park by the Acorn Athletic Club in 3:01:58 (*NYT*, 9 May 1909 sec. 4, p. 1); Al Raines, a former member of the Xavier Athletic Club, won the Bronx Marathon in 2:46:04.6 (*NYT*, 9 May 1909, sec. 1, p. 13). On 15 May 1909, James Crowley of the Irish-American Athletic Club won an amateur event, the New Jersey Marathon, held in Jersey City, New Jersey, out of a field of 180 starters. Because this was an amateur event, Crowley was awarded an elaborate bronze trophy; the Mercury Athletic Club won the team award (*BDE*, 16 May 1909, 10). Crowley also won the Flatbush Marathon on 29 May 1909 (*BDE*, 30 May 1909, 7).

Although the "marathon boom" declined in intensity after 1909, marathon footraces continued in New York City as established athletic events. The Yonkers Marathon, intended as an annual Thanksgiving Day event, was plagued by difficult weather and occasionally delayed for weeks or months but nonetheless continued until 29 November 1917 under the administration of the Mercury Athletic Club (*NYT*, 27 Nov. 1917, 15). The Brooklyn–Sea Gate Marathon continued after World War I but was not an annual event (Martin and Gynn 1979, 68).

The 1908–1909 marathon boom derived from New York City ethnic conflict. In Boston such formal confrontation was averted by the geographic and cultural isolation of the Italian community in the North End, West End, and East Boston. Italian Americans in Boston were further isolated from the power structure by Yankee social and economic prejudices and by Irish political discrimination. Boston Irish Americans outnumbered Boston Italian Americans by over three to one. There was sporadic gang violence between Irish and Italians, but no institutionalized athletic rivalry (Stack 36–37, 149). The combination of strong municipal sanction and popular support assured the continuation of the BAA Marathon. A second annual marathon, the Brockton Fair Marathon, began on 2 October 1908. Like the Patriots' Day event, the fall marathon was held under the auspices of the Boston Athletic Association (*BET*, 2 Oct. 1908, 14) but never achieved the importance or longevity of the BAA Marathon because it lacked official significance.

Sport administrators were beginning to recognize the commercial potential of even the amateur marathons. Race sanction and assistance were easily available from the AAU, which recognized many varieties of marathons. The Yonkers Amusement Company staged a 1 January 1909 marathon that ended on the Empire City Racetrack in Yonkers. James E. Sullivan was the referee and Bartow S. Weeks was chief scorer.

(AAU president in 1898 and 1899, Weeks would be AAU secretary in 1914.) The Yonkers Amusement Company charged admission to spectators who wished to see the finish at the track (*NYDT,* 2 Jan. 1909, 5). Under the name Madison Square Athletic Club, the same company planned another marathon on 9 January 1909. Questioned about the acceptability of the venture, Sullivan told the *Brooklyn Daily Eagle* that any reliable organization could get a sanction from the AAU to conduct a race, even if it was held only for financial reasons (1909a, 6).

The popularity of the marathon led Sullivan to publish a small manual on the sport. *Marathon Running* contained extensive advice on training, a history of marathon races in the United States, and the rules of marathoning. The booklet also suggests that by 1909 the AAU had acknowledged the validity of the marathon footrace. As Sullivan put it: "In the past we have neglected long-distance running and have specialized in sprinting and middle-distance running. Numerous Marathons will have a tendency to strengthen the claim that America has and will produce the greatest long-distance runners in the world" (1909b, 3).

The interest shown in professional marathons during 1908, 1909, and 1910 continued as professional long-distance running at increasingly greater distances. Professional running was intended as a spectator sport; because there was no real artistry or technique to admire, audience satisfaction depended upon the observation of excesses of effort or of fatigue (Raitz 1995, 23). Very long distances, including six-day races, had been professionally contested during the nineteenth century, but this pedestrianism had declined about 1884 (Cumming 1981, 94). Both the rise of amateur track and field and the strength of the large amateur clubs accelerated pedestrianism's demise, as did the other spectator sports competing for audiences. Melvin Adelman, however, regards the economic context of pedestrianism as the more detrimental factor; entrepreneurs did not adequately promote professional running in the late nineteenth century (1986, 219).

The emergence of a substantial twentieth-century working-class leisure market produced recreational entrepreneurs who had the resources to commercialize professional footracing effectively (Rosenzweig 1983, 171–73). On 1 January 1911, Eugene Estoppey set a world endurance record by finishing a 1,000–mile run on a twelve-laps-to-the-mile track in Los Angeles; he had started on 20 November 1910 (*NYT*, 2 Jan. 1911, 10). Estoppey had been an amateur marathoner competing in the 1896 New York City marathon and in a number of the early Boston Marathons, finishing in sixth place with a 2:58:49 in 1898 (Derderian 1994, 10). Now he was a professional earning $1,000 and his expenses for, quite probably, answering a personal challenge (Shapiro 1980, 127). And intense wagering just as probably held the interest of the spectators. For running ultra–long-distances, a professional circuit developed: Boston, New York, Philadelphia, Los Angeles, and Chicago (Shapiro 1980, 127). The post-World War I appearance of the tabloid newspaper in shaping national tastes encouraged running entrepreneurs. Tabloids specialized in sports, entertainment, and fads and fashions as well as natural disasters, high-profile divorces, and columns of advice on personal matters (Cashman 1989, 60–61). The deleterious effects of industrial society on individual health, fitness, and success concerned tabloid readers (Ewen 1976, 44–47). The long-distance runner personified triumph over such problems.

Professional long-distance running reached its apogee with the Transcontinental Races arranged by Charles C. Pyle in 1928 and 1929. The 1928 race began in Los Angeles, with over 100 runners attempting to run across the United States; the winner was to receive $25,000. Pyle expected to finance the venture with an accompanying variety show that would be presented at the end of of each day's run (Shapiro 1980, 117–19). One entrant, Arthur Newton, who set the world record for 100 miles in 1928, remembered the Maxwell House Coffee Pot, "a splendidly equipped car shaped like a great jug . . . to disgorge hot nourishment gratis to each runner as he came along" (quoted in Shapiro 1980, 119). Pyle envisioned marketing opportunities that would make for a golden age of chiropody; "The human foot is going to come into its own" (*NYT*, 28 May 1928, 15). Andy Payne, a twenty-year-old Oklahoma farm boy, won (Shapiro 1980, 120). Despite many financial embarrassments associated with the first race, Pyle conducted a similar event in 1929, when runners ran the opposite direction, from New York City to California. Finnish Amercan John Salo of Passaic, New Jersey, won the second race (Shapiro 1980, 125).

Pyle's Transcontinental Races provided a continuing drama of physical challenge and personal hygiene in an industrialized world;

they were a wonderful source for the tabloids. The races also publicized ultramarathon running. On 17 March 1928 Clarence DeMar broke the record for forty-four miles in the Providence-to-Boston race (*SFC*, 19 Mar. 1928, 4H). On 21 May 1934, Hugo Kauppinen broke the fifty-one-year-old American record for fifty miles in a Metropolitan AAU race (*NYT*, 21 May 1934, 24). Ultradistances survived professionalism and emerged with the AAU sanction necessary to their future in international competition.

John Hayes went to the 1912 Stockholm Olympic Games as the trainer of the United States marathon team. Gaston Strobino of the South Paterson (New Jersey) Athletic Club, was an alternate on the American team; he placed third in the Olympic marathon, after the South Africans Kenneth McArthur and Christopher Gitsam. Despite the Games' excellent organization, a Portuguese runner, Lazaro, collapsed during the race, probably of heatstroke or a heart ailment, and died the next day. Overall, the United States did quite well in the 1912 Olympic marathon. Andrew Sockalexis of the Penobscot nation, Old Town, Maine, who was affiliated with the North Dorchester Athletic Association, was fourth; John Gallagher of Yale was seventh; Joseph Erxleben of St. Louis was eighth; Richard Piggott of Medford, Massachusetts, was ninth; Joseph Forshaw of St. Louis was tenth; Clarence DeMar of the North Dorchester Athletic Association, Boston, was twelfth; Louis Tewanina, representing the Carlisle Indian School, was sixteenth; Harry Smith of the Pastime Athletic Club, New York, was seventeenth; and Thomas Lilley, of the North Dorchester Athletic Association, Boston, was eighteenth (Martin and Gynn 1979, 55–57).

David E. Martin and Roger W. H. Gynn regard the 1912 Olympic marathon as a turning point, "a gem of organizational perfection" (1977, 831) resulting from increased knowledge about marathoners' needs as well as about race administration. Martin and Gynn state that the large field and fast times in this race were also due to the spread of rational information about marathoning (1977, 831). The distance of 26.2 miles was popularly accepted as the marathon distance by the spectators and participants of the 1908–1909 marathon boom, but it would be years before that distance was accepted officially. Race organizers did not seriously attempt to standardize the distance until the 1920s. Athens 1896 was 40 kilometers, Paris 1900 was 40.26 kilometers,

St. Louis 1904 was 40 kilometers, Athens 1906 was 41.86 kilometers, and Boston was about 39.75 kilometers throughout this period (Lucas 1980, 65). Even over identical distances, courses could differ in loss or gain of altitude. Changes in the road surface and variations in terrain also affected performance.

The 1912 Stockholm Olympics contributed a higher level of organization to the Games in general and to athletics in particular. Sigfrid Edstrom, a Swedish engineer and businessman, directed the planning of the Stockholm Games (Guttmann 1984, 22). In the wake of this track-and-field triumph, Edstrom founded the International Amateur Athletic Federation (IAAF), the transnational organization that is the highest level of athletics administration. In matters concerning track and field, race walking, and cross-country and long-distance running, the International Olympic Committee defers to the IAAF. There were no universally accepted boundaries for the preservation of amateurism at the 1912 Games. At an August 1913 meeting in Berlin, the IAAF attempted to draft a definition of *amateur*. James Sullivan, chief IAAF member from the United States, greatly influenced the ensuing proposal, although there were a variety of opinions. Despite this convocation, no significant improvement in defining amateurism came about until after World War I (Glader 1978, 136–37).

The 1913 IAAF meeting proposed a standard athletics program for all future Olympics. Track and field was now so committed to standardization at the international level that events the IAAF omitted, such as standing jumps and aggregate throws, disappeared from competition. The IAAF also set up a list of events eligible for world record competition. The two lists were not identical; the Olympic program included only 100, 200, 400, 800 meters for the sprints, while world records could be set at 100, 200, 400, 500, and 800 meters, and at 100, 220, 440, 600, and 880 yards. The IAAF set the Olympic marathon at 40.2 kilometers, the distance of the Stockholm race, while world records in the marathon would only be considered at 26 miles 385 yards, the distance contested not only in the 1908 Olympic Games, but also in the 1908–1909 marathon boom (*NYT*, 11 Jan. 1914, sec. 4, p. 3). The Olympic measurement may have been meant to ensure the integrity as well as the unique nature of the only officially international amateur marathon.

The International Amateur Athletic Federation's decisions changed the marathon during the second decade of the twentieth century. The New York City athletics bureaucracy responded positively to the IAAF decisions and, with its leadership position in the Amateur Athletic Union, imposed those decisions upon AAU associations throughout the United States. The IAAF legitimated the marathon as a serious international athletic event, while New York City marathon activity and the AAU assured accessibility of the marathon to a wide ethnic and geographical range of Americans.

4

Middle-Class Nationalism

City road races became the most popular opportunities for long-distance running after the decline of the 1908-1909 marathon boom. New York City's *Evening Mail* Modified Marathon attracted working-class men and boys to healthy, outdoor, amateur sport (Riess 1989, 3). Patriotism became the overriding theme of many road races. On 13 May 1917, 1,200 runners were assembled at the starting line in New York City "when President Wilson, in the White House at Washington, pressed the button that unfurled the huge American flag and sent the runners on their way at 1:45 P.M." (*NYT*, 13 May 1917, sec. 3, p. 1).

The *Evening Mail* Modified Marathon began in 1911 with a twelve-mile road race from the Bronx to lower Manhattan. Starting on Jerome Avenue near Fordham Road, the course went to Central Bridge, then down Seventh Avenue to 110th Street, to Fifth Avenue, Washington Place, and Broadway, ending at City Hall. Because the course utilized major thoroughfares, the race drew about one million spectators. The event was equally noteworthy for the number of competitors; nearly 1,000 runners entered and over half finished. Louis Tewanina won, representing the Carlisle Indian School, and the Irish-American Athletic Club took the team prize (Copland 1911).

The *Evening Mail* Modified Marathon, which took place annually from 1911 through 1919, was a festival in which middle- and working-class citizens celebrated New York City as spectators, elite athletes, or somewhere in between—runners who dropped out after a few miles. In 1912 this race had 1,300 starters (*NYT,* 5 May 1912, sec. 4, p. 2), and in 1913, 1,400 (*NYT,* 11 May 1913, sec. 4, p. 1). The 1914 race had even more participants: 1,786 men starting at Jerome Avenue (*NYT,* 3 May 1914, sec. 5, p. 1). The course itself, a modified marathon, brought out the athletes and hopefuls. Training for a 26.2-mile race meant a daunting investment of time and energy. A shorter distance was more accessible to working-class individuals in an era when men and women often walked miles to save carfare. Another important factor was that the race was held wholly within the city. The many who dropped out along the way were not far from home and at least had had the exhilaration of participating. Friends and relatives lined the course (*NYT,* 7 May 1911, sec. 2, p. 1). Working-class boisterousness and public sociability characterized the crowd behavior (Rosenzweig 1983, 199), but middle-class order dominated.

> The spectacle of upward of 1000 youngsters racing along the city's principal thoroughfares, all under the espionage of the most perfect police arrangements, under the personal direction of Deputy Commissioner Driscoll, who caused an absolute cessation of traffic during the race, was a novelty in New York's athletics, and this feature, in conjunction with the conduct of the actual race on the part of the officials, will undoubtedly go down in athletic history. (Copland 1911)

That usually the same group of men appeared among the top runners on the finishers' lists of the *Evening Mail* Modified Marathon showed the development of a marathon community in the Northeast. Louis Tewanina, Harry Smith of the Pastime Athletic Club, and Gaston Strobino of the South Paterson Athletic Club all ran the Modified Marathon and did well in the 1912 Olympic Marathon (Copland 1911). John J. Reynolds of the Irish-American Athletic Club, Edward H. White of Holy Cross Lyceum, and Harry Jensen of Pastime Athletic Club had all won local marathons in 1909. Charles Pores and Nick Giannakopulos of the Millrose Athletic Association, Fred Travelena of the Mohawk Athletic Club, and Frank Zuna of the Irish-American Athletic Club would be among the great runners of the 1910s and 1920s (Martin and

Gynn 1979, 57). Arthur Roth won the Boston Marathon in 1916 and William Kennedy in 1917; James Henigan of the Dorchester Club, who placed fourth in the 1917 Modified Marathon, would finally triumph in Boston in 1931 (*NYT*, 13 May 1917, sec. 3, p. 1). A number of the top African-American runners participated; Aaron Morris of St. Christopher's Club would place sixth in the 1919 Boston Marathon (Derderian 1994, 80–81).

The *Evening Mail* dropped the event in 1920 and the race was not held for five years, but in 1925 the *Graphic* revived the Modified Marathon to the same enthusiasm it had previously enjoyed; "hundreds of thousands" of spectators cheered the 411 entrants (*NYT*, 24 May 1925, sec. x, p. 1). In 1926 and 1927 over five hundred runners started the race, a following that should have ensured continuity except for the logistical problems of a city race (*NYT*, 2 May 1926 sec. x, p. 5). Albert Michelson won in 1927 by "threading his way through automobiles, trolley cars, buses and scores of thousands of people" (Field 1927). In 1928 the Italian newspaper *Il Progresso* held a modified marathon that met with substantial disapproval from the Metropolitan Association of the AAU; the threat that automobile traffic presented to the runners led the AAU to consider denying sanction to long-distance races conducted within the city (Field 1928).

The presence and strength of the full marathons in the New York City area undercut the importance of the Modified Marathon. From 1909 to 1914 the Brooklyn–Sea Gate Marathon celebrated Lincoln's Birthday with a race over the distance of 26 miles, 385 yards (*BDE*, 12 Feb. 1909, 1). In 1915 bad weather convinced the officials to postpone the race to Washington's Birthday and shorten the course to twenty miles. Charles Pores won the race and the prize of a trip to San Francisco for the Panama Pacific Exposition Marathon on 28 August 1915 (*BDE*, 23 Feb. 1915, 12). John J. Reynolds of the Irish-American Athletic Club won the 24 November 1910 Yonkers Marathon over a field in which Irish American athletes were prominent. The Yonkers Marathon, which generally celebrated Thanksgiving Day, was held under the auspices of the Mercury Athletic Club from 1907 through 1917 (*NYDT*, 25 Nov. 1910, 9).

Cross-country races and the Olympic Club dominated San Francisco long-distance running (Spitz 1993, 1). The Olympic Club began in

San Francisco in 1860 as a social and athletic club; it supported a number of cultural events and fielded teams in almost every sport (Altrocchi 1949, 206). The stature of the Olympic Club was such that all the major San Francisco newspapers covered a race put together by club members in 1905. This event became the Dipsea Race, a cross-country race from Mill Valley, "over the poison oak covered hills of Tamalpais" (Spitz 1993, 2) to Stimson Beach. The Olympic Club responded to the 1909 marathon boom by staging a marathon on 22 February 1909. Otto Boeddiker of the Olympic Club finished in 2:40:31.6; of the twenty-seven starters, six finished under 2:50, the next five in under three hours, and the last runner finished twenty-fifth in 3:26:13. These excellent finishing times attest to the success of the venture and the potential for a marathon culture in San Francisco. The *San Francisco Chronicle* confirmed the marathon's promotion of societal values: "It is to be hoped that the love of clean manly sport thus awakened by the club will not be allowed to die out. There should be more Marathon races, more field days" (McGeehan 1909, 10).

The marathon, however, did not flourish in San Francisco. The marathon footrace next appeared in the area at the Panama Pacific Exposition in 1915. Edouard Fabre, a French Canadian runner from Montreal, the 1915 Boston Marathon winner, won the 1915 San Francisco Marathon in 2:56:41.8. Hugh Honohan of the New York Athletic Club was second in 3:01:22.4. Oliver Millard of the host Olympic Club of San Francisco was third, and Manuel Cooper of the Chicago Hebrew Institute was fourth, followed by Pat Coyne of New York, H. C. Dobler of Chicago, W. O. Johnson of San Francisco, and A. L. Monteverde of New York (*NYT*, 29 Aug. 1915, sec. 3, p. 5). The *San Francisco Chronicle* was unimpressed with the race: "Yesterday's winner got a bronze plaque or something and the rest of the field got something or other and now all hands must return to the workbench or the office" (30 Aug. 1915, 1). This newspaper's remarks indicate that the marathon was not an important event on the West Coast, perhaps because it was so far from Olympic venues and the center of American marathon running in the East.

San Francisco expressed municipal pride with the Cross City Race, an event much like New York City's *Evening Mail* Modified Marathon. Sponsored by the *San Francisco Bulletin*, the Cross City Race began on

New Year's Day 1912 at the Ferry building. The participants ran over asphalt streets until they were in Golden Gate Park. The winner for 1912 and 1913 was Robert Vlught of the Christian Brothers' St. Mary's College (*SFC*, 2 Jan. 1913, 13). Oliver Millard of the Olympic Club won in 1914 and 1915 (*SFC*, 1914, 11). The number of entrants stayed around one or two hundred at first, and most were local runners. The Cross City Race persisted year after year, evolving into San Francisco's famous Bay-to-Breakers (Wallach 1978, 29–32, 44–45). After having no local marathons for decades, the city and its long-distance runners, heartened by the increasing numbers of both participants and spectators, found a sense of community around this race.

Changes in the American working class during the period after World War I effected changes in the marathon footrace. Immigration had declined with the beginning of European hostilities in 1914; after the war, legislation restricted entry for southern and eastern Europeans as well as all Asians (Bogen 1987, 18–19). As a result, the workforce remained fairly stable in ethnic composition (Bernstein 1960, 47–48). Without continued immigration to reaffirm their origins, the Old Country became increasingly distant to ethnic Americans (Conzen et al, 1992, 24–25). Business and economic influences on athletics strengthened class consciousness over ethnicity.

Interest in marathon running spread across different ethnic groups whose members either worked together or had some residential proximity. Interclub meets gave athletes of various ethnicities a chance to interact as well as to assess one another's potential (*NYT*, 4 Dec. 1910, sec. 4, p. 7). The *New York Daily Tribune* chronicled cross-country races involving clubs in New York City during the prewar era (13 Feb. 1911, 8; 20 Feb. 1911, 8). Michael Ryan and John J. Reynolds, both of the Irish-American Athletic Club, entered these runs; so did William Meyers and H. Jacobson of the Unione Sportiva Italiana, a sports club founded for Italian waiters (Federal Writers' Project 1938, 67). Long-distance and cross-country running clubs found that having members from a wide variety of ethnic groups improved team performance. In 1912 the IAAC brought Hannes Kolehmainen to the AAU Track and Field Championships. As a member of the Pastime Fellows of Helsinki, Finland, he competed unattached (AAU 1912, 30; 1915, 43); he would later become an official member of the IAAC.

Clubs provided coaching, fellowship, and training tables. In addition, they received disbursements from the AAU to enable athletes to travel to meets. In 1911 the AAU Championship Committee received $4,000 from the *Pittsburgh Press* to bring athletes to the track and field championships in Pittsburgh on 30 June and 1 July 1911. The New York Athletic Club, the Irish-American Athletic Club, the Chicago Athletic Association, and the Seattle Athletic Club each received $350; the Olympic Club of San Francisco received $600. The New England Association of the AAU received $300, and the Middle Atlantic Association $150. The largest disbursement, $650.25, was for the officials' expenses. Clubs such as the Pastime and Mohawk Athletic Clubs of New York received small amounts (AAU 1911, 21).

• • •

From 1911 to 1917 a substantial number of the top finishers in the Boston Marathon had Irish last names, for example, the winners Michael Ryan (1912), James Duffy (1914), and William Kennedy (1917). Many marathon runners of the Boston area belonged to the North Dorchester Athletic Association (NDAA), located in an Irish enclave. Sport had provided new Irish immigrants with some social mobility as well as serving as an expression of Irish nationalism, traditions, and manliness (McCaffrey 1976, 137). Although still mostly blue-collar in occupation during the first two decades of the twentieth century, Irish Americans had experienced enough upward mobility to identify increasingly with the middle class (Miller 1985, 523). Recent immigrants from Italy and Eastern Europe made the comparatively Americanized Irish more acceptable to the Anglo-Saxon establishment, and Irish Americans in turn sought respectability from that establishment (Eisinger 1980, 42). The Irish American middle class promoted American patriotism, and celebrations of Irish American pride blended ethnic and religious expressions with distinctly American symbols (Bodnar 1992, 68–69).

In Boston the history of Irish working-class immigrants colored Yankee perceptions of Irish Americans. According to John Stack, the Boston Irish were "locked into a rigid socioeconomic caste unlike the Irish who immigrated to Chicago or St. Louis. . . . In Boston, their working-class status was defined by the 'weight' of the past" (1979, 43). The Irish in Boston created a complete society that paralleled the dominant society but left the Irish Americans apart. The most successful Irish Americans formed a separate upper class (Kennedy 1974, 50–52), while Boston Irish control of the city's political process, as well as the police and fire departments, often alienated Italian and Jewish minorities (Stack 1979, 33). Irish institutional completeness separated the Irish from the Brahmin/Yankee hegemony as well as from other ethnic groups. There was Irish-Jewish contact through shared residence in Roxbury, Dorchester, and Mattapan, but Boston's Jews, through upward mobility, cultural values, and education, became integrated into Boston's Yankee community (Stack 1979, 8, 35). The Italian and African American communities in Boston remained relatively isolated (Stack 1979, 151–55).

There was ethnic conflict in New York City, but there was also extensive contact. Italians in the New York City garment industry joined unions begun by Jewish workers; these unions consciously integrated their membership in order to maintain their strength. Irish politicians needed the votes of the new immigrant groups to remain in power (Bayor 1978, 4–5). And New York City did not show the residential isolation of Boston's minorities. Ethnic neighborhoods often housed several groups or were so small in area that residents could not avoid interacting with other ethnic groups (Lagerquist 1910, 1).

African Americans in turn-of-the-century New York City lived in a number of very small ghettos surrounded by white neighborhoods, generally on the West Side betwen Twentieth and Sixty-Third Streets. Migration of southern blacks to the north had begun after the Civil War, intensifying between 1890 and 1910. By 1910, New York City had the second largest black urban population after Washington, D.C. An institutionally complete African American community existed in New York City by the time of World War I. With increasing numbers, New York City's black community expanded, and the center of the community moved north on Manhattan. By 1920, New York City had the largest urban African American population in the United States, and two-thirds of that population lived in Harlem (Osofsky 1963, 12–34).

Practically every major Negro institution moved from its downtown quarters to Harlem by the early 1920s: the United Order of True Reformers; Odd Fellows, Masons, Elks, Pythians, and other fraternal orders; the Music School Settlement; the Coachmen's Union League; the African Society of Mutual Relief; the *New York Age;* West Fifty-third Street YMCA and YWCA; almost all the Negro social service agencies, including local offices of the Urban League and NAACP; the AME Home and Foreign Missionary Society; all the major churches. (Osofsky 1963, 120)

The *New York Age* reported two African American marathon victories in March 1909: Howard Hale won a Pittsburgh marathon, and Charles Burden won a marathon in New Orleans. In 1909 information on the specific training and racing techniques for long-distance running had yet to reach much of the United States; Hale won in the rather slow time of 3:29:54 (18 Mar. 1909, 9). The *Brooklyn Daily Eagle* reported "a gentleman of color named Walker and another bearing the name of Henry Irving were among the entries" in the 22 April 1909 Columbia Athletic Club Marathon in Brooklyn. Walker finished fifth. Irving finished third, but he was disqualified (22 Apr. 1909, 7). Walker was unattached; Irving was affiliated with the Trinity Athletic Club, the club of Matthew Maloney, winner of the 26 December 1908 *New York Journal* Marathon (*NYEJ,* 22Apr. 1909, 13).

Such club acceptance was unusual. Black and white individuals, even when they worked together, generally engaged in segregated recreation (Edwards 1973, 37). African American track men learned to run in public schools but organized their own athletic clubs: the Salem-Crescent Athletic Club and St. Christopher's Club of New York, and the Smart Set Athletic Club of Brooklyn. In 1914, the *New York Times* assessed the potential of African American athletes in the New York Metropolitan District of the AAU:

Up to the present the colored athlete has devoted his attention to track events, especially in the sprints and middle distances, but with the growth of colored athletic clubs capable trainers will be secured and with systematic development in long-distance events will be certain to bring out long- distance runners and candidates for field honors. The Negro's proficiency in athletics has become a source of much speculation and discussion in athletic clubs. (18 Oct. 1914, sec. 4, p. 4)

Earlier that year Aaron Morris of the Smart Set Athletic Club tied for first place with Jake Maier of the Bronx Church House in the Morningside Athletic Club eight-mile cross-country run (*NYT,* 27 Apr. 1914, 13). In 1915, Morris competed in a fifteen-mile race that included such runners as Hannes Kolehmainen, considered the foremost distance runner in the world, and Charles Pores of the Millrose Athletic Association (*NYT,* 3 May 1915, 9).

During the 1910s the Millrose Athletic Association expanded its athletic influence by recruiting the best athletes, regardless of ethnicity. The Millrose team for the Panama Pacific Exposition included Willie Kyronen, of Finnish birth; Nick Giannakopulos, known as Nick the Greek; Charles Pores, a Jewish runner; and John Cahill—all accompanied by coach Mel Sheppard (Schmertz, [1967?], 23). Washington's Birthday marathons persisted in the New York City area. Arthur Roth of the Mohawk Athletic Club won the first annual Bronx County Marathon, about twenty-five miles, contested on 22 February 1916 (*NYT,* 23 Feb. 1916, 14); Hans Schuster won the second event on 22 February 1917 (*NYT,* 23 Feb. 1917, 13). World War I ended the Yonkers, St. Louis, and Brockton Fair marathons in 1917. The 1918 Boston Marathon was run as a relay among fourteen military teams; victory went to the divisional team at Camp Devens. Sergeant John Sullivan, the first athlete to cross the finish line, had been a member of the Irish-American Athletic Club of New York (*NYT,* 20 Apr. 1918, 10).

On 11 April 1917, nine days after President Wilson asked Congress to declare war on Germany, the Board of Governors of the Irish-American Athletic Club suspended all activities of the club, assuming competitive members would leave for military service. A spokesperson for IAAC said, "Sports is a minor consideration, even to an athletic club, in a time like this" (*NYT,* 12 Apr. 1917, 12). This patriotic act may have been an attempt to compensate for prewar Irish American opinion; during the years of American neutrality, Irish Americans had openly opposed the United States' entering the war on the side of England (Bayor 1978, 5).

Marathoning resumed after the Armistice. The Boston Marathon was run over twenty-five miles on 19 April 1919. Carl Linder of the Hurja Athletic Club of Quincy, Massachusetts, won, but the field included a number of New York men, including Otto Laakso of the Kaleva Athletic Club and Aaron Morris running for St. Christopher's Club (*NYT*, 20 Apr. 1919, 21). In New York City, the Fifth Company, Thirteenth Regiment, revived the Brooklyn–Sea Gate Marathon on 23 February 1920 as a twenty-five mile race (*NYT*, 24 Feb. 1920, 15). Frank Zuna, born in Bohemia but now representing the Frank B. Whitney Post of the American Legion, won; he had previously won the Trenton to Camp Dix race. On 3 April 1920, Charles Mellor of Chicago, the American Expeditionary Forces' marathon champion, won the Auto City Marathon from Pontiac to Detroit (*NYT*, 4 Apr. 1920, 19).

Sixty runners entered the 1920 BAA event; the field comprised mainly experienced athletes who trained seriously and specifically for long distance. Many were immigrants, but they entered the race for the athletic opportunity, not to represent a subcommunity. Twenty-three-year-old Peter Trivoulidas, born in Greece but now a New York resident, won the Boston Marathon on 19 April 1920; Arthur Roth was second, Carl Linder was third, and Frank Zuna was seventh (*NYT*, 20 Apr. 1920, 11).

The Olympic Trials marathon, held over the distance of 26 miles, 385 yards, under the auspices of the New York Athletic Club on 5 June 1920, comprised representatives of many ethnic groups and states east of the Mississippi (*NYT*, 6 June 1920, sec. 8, p. 2). Hannes Kolehmainen won and went on to win the 1920 Antwerp Olympic Marathon, competing for Finland. Although Finns were a small group in America, there were many Finnish runners in American long-distance races. They began coming to the United States in the late nineteenth century, with the greatest wave of Finnish immigration from 1908 to 1914. Over ten thousand Finns lived in New York City (C. Ross 1972, 140). The Finnish runners, many former or potential Olympians, were readily accepted by American clubs and long-distance runners.

A wide range of clubs supported by the athletics bureaucracy fostered long-distance running from 1910 to 1920. The social forces deriving from industrialization in twentieth-century America turned marathon practitioners toward increasing cohesion among themselves and toward conformity to nativist culture. During the second decade of the century, ethnic identifications within the marathon diminished. Urbanization contributed to anonymity and upheaval. Sport clubs provided a sense of community as well as a milieu in which men could receive recognition for their individual accomplishments (Rader 1977, 356).

Commemorative events such as the marathon attracted additional support during the postwar wave of American nativism. Although increased immigration met manpower needs, it also fed the growing hostility toward new immigrants. The Red Scare of 1919–1920 emerged from the fears brought on by European revolutions, a business depression, and a profusion of radical literature. Schools, churches, and public institutions responded with encomiums on American history and traditions (Coben 1964, 59, 68–69).

In the prosperity of the 1920s, cities in the United States staged diversions and recreations for their inhabitants (Brandes 1976, 141). Celebrations such as the nation's approaching sesquicentennial manifested an overarching patriotism involving many ethnic groups. These patriotic occasions often included marathons. Always associated with civic pride, the marathon became an even stronger patriotic symbol. The number of continuing marathons increased nationwide, and the marathon solidified its position in the sport bureaucracy when the Amateur Athletic Union began a national marathon championship in 1925.

Corporate interests such as John Wanamaker in New York and Pennsylvania; United Shoe Machinery in Beverly, Massachusetts; and the Edgar Thomson Steel Works in Pittsburgh encouraged and supported cross-country and long-distance running teams. Running for the Edgar Thomson Steel Athletic Association, R. Earl Johnson, an African American, won the AAU Senior Cross-Country Championship on 19 November 1921 (AAU 1921, 89, 98). (Johnson later competed in the 1924 Olympic Games 10,000 meter cross-country race, finishing third after Paavo Nurmi and Willie Ritola.) Company teams were part of "welfare capitalism," a paternalistic system of services that employers provided for workers (Brandes 1976, 4–5). Company sports and recreations, like company gardens and canteens and even company doctors, were intended to alleviate dissatisfaction with jobs that required little skill or mental effort and with work situations in which workers were powerless (Meyer 1981, 38, 96). Welfare capitalism by its nature and its source was an extension of the power relationships of the workplace (Brody 1980, 57).

Long-distance running, whether company-sponsored or not, was a denial of powerlessness; the marathon runner had mastered a specialized skill over which he had control. In industrialized society the conditions of work circumscribed manliness (Gorn 1986, 141). Success as a breadwinner affirmed masculinity for the middle class, but wealth was very unevenly distributed in 1920s American society (Cashman 1989, 44). Long-distance running was one way a working-class man could assert his worth.

Positive aspects of the working-class culture that developed around the factory system carried over to long-distance running. Work was a shared experience that drew workers together to help each other; getting and holding a job depended on friends, relatives, and connections in the field (Montgomery 1987, 88). In order to run in the few marathons that were held in the early 1920s, an athlete had to find transportation and a place to stay. The marathon runner needed assistance to pursue his sport, and that assistance generally came from a team. Increasingly, working-class teams included members of several minority groups who were united by their working-class status as well as by their interest in long-distance running. The Irish-American Athletic Club was such a team, but it never returned as an athletic power after World War I.

The two most important athletic clubs in the New York City area in the 1920s were the New York Athletic Club and the Millrose Athletic Association, but NYAC members ran marathons infrequently. The Millrose Athletic Association took the place of the IAAC as the leading multiethnic club. When he won the 1920 Boston Marathon, Peter Trivoulidas was employed in John Wanamaker's department store restaurant (*NY Trib*, 20 Apr. 1920, 15). After representing Greece in the 1920 Olympic Marathon, Trivoulidas joined Millrose (*NYT*, 20 Apr. 1921, 14).

A number of ethnic groups were represented in the Boston marathon fields of this period. In 1921, Frank Zuna of the Paulist Athletic Club set a new record for the BAA Marathon, 2:18:57.6, breaking

Michael Ryan's 1912 record of 2:21:18.2. Zuna worked as a plumber in Newark, New Jersey (*NYT*, 20 Apr. 1921, 14), and had previously won the Brockton Fair Marathon in 1915. In 1922, Clarence DeMar won the Boston Marathon in 2:18:10. The list of finishers in the 1922 BAA Marathon indicates the breadth of the marathon, both geographically and in terms of ethnic groups (*NYT*, 20 Apr. 1922, 18). In 1923, DeMar won again, in 2:23:47.6. Newspapers identified Clarence DeMar as a printer—a highly skilled worker—but not as a member of a specific ethnicity (*NYT*, 20 Apr. 1922, 18).

Clarence DeMar of Melrose, Massachusetts, became the foremost marathon runner of the 1920s. Born in Madeiro, Ohio, on 7 June 1888, DeMar moved east with his family at age eleven. He received his training as a printer at a residential vocational school, the Farm and Trades School on Thompson's Island in Boston Harbor; he had been placed there after his widowed mother found it impossible to provide for her six children. DeMar went on to study agriculture at the University of Vermont for two years, during which time he took up running (DeMar 1981, 11–15). He entered his first marathon, the 1910 Boston Marathon, and finished second in a field otherwise dominated by Canadians and New Yorkers (*BET*, 20 Apr. 1910, 14). On 7 October 1910 he finished third in the Brockton Fair Marathon (*BET*, 7 Oct. 1910, 16).

On 19 April 1911, DeMar won the Boston Marathon for the first time (*BET*, 20 Apr. 1911, 12). Accepted to the United States Olympic Team, DeMar stayed out of competition during the spring of 1912 in preparation for the Olympic Marathon. After the 1912 Stockholm Olympics, in which he placed twelfth, DeMar returned to work nights at the printing plant of the Rand Avery Company. He skipped the Brockton Fair Marathon in October 1912: "I didn't feel that I should waste a day's pay to run" (DeMar 1981, 58). Marathon runners such as Clarence DeMar tended to have skilled trades that could be practiced independently or in small, fairly autonomous shops. Such workplace structures provided enough flexibility and free time to allow marathon training and racing. Clarence DeMar would have lost a day's pay if he had run in the 1912 Brockton Fair Marathon, but he did not fear losing his job. He had some control over his workplace situation because he had a valuable skill.

DeMar did not run marathons for several years after the 1912

Olympic Games, although he did participate in shorter races. He gave physicians' warnings about the dangers of marathon running as one reason for his hiatus and his religious convictions as another: "As a member of the Baptist church I had a suspicion that the whole game of running was a selfish vain-glorious search for praise and honor" (De-Mar 1981, 58). DeMar taught Sunday School during this period and had other obligations; he worked at a fairly demanding job as a compositor and was taking extension courses at Boston University and at Harvard (DeMar 1981, 61).

In June 1915, DeMar received an associate's degree from Harvard. Within a year the war in Europe showed signs of involving the United States. "I disliked the whole business of war, but what could I do about it? If I dissented from the mad majority and went to jail my mother would miss what I did to help the family. So I decided to string along with the patriots. But if I went to war I might get killed. Why not have a little fun at marathoning first?" (DeMar 1981, 67). In this statement about the approaching war, DeMar shared the sense of powerlessness that marked the working class in the semiskilled primary labor force (Jacoby 1985, 5, 8). DeMar responded by turning to the skill and situation he could control—the marathon. He finished third in the 1917 Boston Marathon.

For the working classes the 1920s began what David M. Gordon, Richard Edwards, and Michael Reich call the "segmentation period." The labor market was not a mass of semiskilled operatives directly controlled by a managerial class; rather, a structure of rules and rewards drove productivity, while personal advancement could be achieved through the educational system. As a result, the labor market was divided according to type of job, organization of work, and degree of worker independence. Large corporations employed a primary labor force that used very specific skills under close supervision, bounded by rules and restrictions—the subordinate primary segment. Within the same large firms, technical and professional jobs requiring formal education and cognitive skills made up the independent primary sector. Industries that serviced the large corporations, such as machine tool shops, employed the secondary labor force. Because the demand for their products was cyclical, workers in the secondary labor force were particularly susceptible to seasonal unemployment (Gordon, Edwards, and Reich 1982, 162–65, 200–202). Marathon runners belonged to either the independent primary sector or the secondary labor force. Flexible work schedules, or even periodic unemployment, gave them time to train.

An important skill or trade gave the runner mobility as well as some control over his time. William "Bricklayer Bill" Kennedy first appeared among the Boston Marathon finishers in 1912 in twenty-third place (*BET*, 20 Apr. 1912, 7). Affiliated with the Missouri Athletic Club of St. Louis, Kennedy had had access to marathon training and racing in his hometown. He won the St. Louis Marathon in 1913 after he had moved to Chicago and become a member of the Illinois Athletic Club (*NYT*, 20 Apr. 1913, sec. 3, p. 8). Later he was affiliated with the Bricklayers' Athletic Club, under whose colors he ran to sixth place in the 1916 Boston Marathon (*NYT*, 20 Apr. 1916, 15). When he won in 1917, Kennedy belonged to the Morningside Athletic Club of New York and worked in Pawtucket, Rhode Island, as a bricklayer (*NYT*, 20 Apr. 1917, 13). He settled in Port Chester, New York; by 1922 he was running for the Cygnet Athletic Club. Kennedy actively encouraged both talented long-distance runners and the sport of marathon running. In 1939, the *Port Chester Daily Item* referred to Kennedy as the " 'Daddy' of marathon stars" (1939, 8A).

The sports team provided the social benefits of a steady job to men who depended on short-term employment. The friendship of longtime co-workers often determined success or even survival in the industrial workplace (Montgomery 1977, 107); for men like Kennedy, teammates were the source of support and assistance. Just before the 1923 Boston Marathon, Kennedy wrote to Larry Sweeney of the *Boston Globe* about his fellow marathoners, "they are absolutely square. I never knew one yet I would not loan every nickel I had to, for I know they will pay back" (*BG*, 18 Apr. 1923, 13).

Runners who had once expressed pride in their ethnic communities now subordinated ethnicity to Americanization. In addition to his "Bricklayer" handle, Kennedy was best known for the red, white, and blue kerchief he wore on his head during races (Semple 1981, 32). The experience of community came increasingly from communities of consumption—i.e., individuals who organized to share interests or activities (Rotundo 1993, 284). With its sport clubs and annual competitions, long-distance running came to serve as a community for its practitioners by the mid-1920s. Kennedy's letters to the *Boston Globe*, about the great runners of the past and the glories and hardships of marathon running, affirm this sense of community.

Kennedy eventually started his own business, becoming a contractor "for All Branches of Mason Work," according to his advertisement in the *Port Chester Daily Item* (15 Aug. 1925, 4). Skilled blue-collar workers could earn as much as or more than lower-level professionals in the 1920s (Dubofsky 1975, 25). In 1922, New York City's West Side YMCA began offering courses in the building trades—tile setting, bricklaying, and plastering—"to prepare men for potential $12 a day jobs in the open instead of $25 a week positions in offices" (*NY Trib*, 4 Mar. 1923, 13).

Abraham Lincoln Monteverde, born in New York City of French Canadian ancestry, was self-employed as a bookbinder. He traveled around the country doing contract work, an arrangement that allowed him to run marathons in San Francisco, Boston, St. Louis, Chicago, and a number of other large cities. In 1916, Monteverde worked several months on a bookbinding job for a large glove manufacturer in Johnstown, New York. In his spare time he helped stage the 1916 Johnstown Marathon, won by Sidney Hatch. Monteverde was still running marathons when he was past the age of sixty; he had become quite wealthy at the bookbinding trade and could afford travel to many races (Leonard 1928, 17).

Marathon runners now were as highly skilled at their sport as they were at their trades. Runners in the early years of the marathon had to improvise training and racing methods. Marathon fields had expanded during the boom of 1908–1909 because of the participation of many inexperienced runners. After the 1912 Olympic Games, the fields shrank but now comprised mainly trained marathon runners, specialists at the event. Generally the same top runners appeared in all the major marathons. Specialization of the athletes strengthened the marathon, rather as the International Amateur Athletic Federation's imposition of standards would again strengthen it in 1924. The 1924 Olympic Marathon course measured 42.195 kilometers (26.2 miles); by International Olympic Committee decision, all Olympic Marathons now would be held at the 1908 London distance. Marathons all over the world conformed to this distance (Martin and Gynn 1979, 77).

Marathon runners began to understand their importance in Olympic years. Clarence DeMar protested the team selection and coaching procedures for the 1924 Olympic Games on behalf of the American marathoners. DeMar, who had been allowed to determine his own training program, captured third in the marathon. Burdened with inappropriate coaching, the others fared poorly in the competition. "We all agreed never to submit to a coach and trainer in any future Olympic marathon runs" (DeMar, quoted in *NYT*, 5 Aug. 1924, 12). This statement expressed defiance of the sport bureaucracy; runners demanded the same respect and independence in their training as they had earned through their skills on their jobs.

Changes in the sport bureaucracy reinforced the working-class identity of the marathon. Organized in 1905 to regulate university and college sports, the National Collegiate Athletic Association (NCAA) originally addressed problems in collegiate football, baseball, and basketball. By 1920 the NCAA's jurisdiction over college track and field caused friction between the NCAA and the AAU. Representatives of both organizations, along with others, served on the Team Selection Committee of the American Olympic Committee (Flath 1964, 26, 42, 55). Olympic track-and-field athletes increasingly came from the colleges, but colleges and universities did not stage marathons. Marathon runners were developed by the AAU clubs. The conflict between the NCAA and the AAU over jurisdiction and the sanctioning of athletes deprived the marathon of university support and talent.

There were only a few marathons in the United States during the early 1920s, and most were in the East. The Auto City Marathon, also known as the Pontiac-to-Detroit Marathon, began in 1920 as one of the official trials for the Olympic Games. It continued under the auspices of the local Irish-American Athletic Club. Charles "Chuck" Mellor of Chicago won the Auto City Marathon in 1920, and Willie Kyronen of New York finished second in 1920 (*NYT*, 4 Apr. 1920, 19). In 1921 the field comprised mainly Chicagoans, New Yorkers, and Canadians. Mellor won; Frank Zuna of Newark, New Jersey, finished second; and Edouard Fabre of Montreal finished third. The first Detroiter to cross the finish line, Arne Suominen of Cass Technical High School, was ninth (*DN*, 3 Apr. 1921, 6). Fifteen Detroiters numbered among the 39 entrants in the 1922 Pontiac-to-Detroit Marathon; most of the rest were from Toronto, Chicago, or Buffalo (*DN*, 1 Apr. 1922, 12). Mellor won for the third time in 1922, while Toronto's Gladstone Athletic Club took the team prize (*DN*, 2 Apr. 1922, sec. 4, p. 1).

Zuna won the Pontiac-to-Detroit Marathon in 1923 and 1924, when he was affiliated with the Millrose Athletic Association (*NYT*, 30 Mar. 1924, sec. 10, p. 2). Schou Christensen of the Illinois Athletic Club won in 1925 (*DN*, 5 Apr. 1925, sec. 4, p. 1), and forty-year-old Percy Wyer of the Monarch Athletic Club of Toronto, Ontario, won in 1926 (*DN*, 4 Apr. 1926, sec. 4, p. 1). An annual Laurel-to-Baltimore Marathon began in 1923, when Albert "Whitey" Michelson of the Cygnet Athletic Club, East Port Chester, New York, won in 2:48:23.8. Frank Zuna won the Laurel-to-Baltimore Marathon in 1924, Albert Michelson won again in 1925, and Clarence DeMar won in 1926 (*Baltimore Sun*, 10 May 1926, sports sec., p. 3).

On 20 April 1925 the BAA Marathon became the first National AAU Marathon Championships, an acknowledgment of the increasing prestige of the marathon (AAU 1925, 61). The San Francisco *Bulletin*'s Cross City Race was arguably the best known long-distance event on the West Coast. William Churchill of the Olympic Club won the Cross City Race in 1920, 1922, 1923, and 1924 (Wallach 1978, 61, 67, 71, 74). DeMar invited Churchill to visit over the 1924 Boston Marathon weekend, and Churchill finished the BAA race in fourth place, qualifying for the 1924 United States Olympic marathon team (Derderian 1994, 98, 100).

Italian Americans strongly influenced the long-distance running scene, particularly in San Francisco. By mid-1920s only New York City had a greater proportion of Italians among its foreign-born population (Cinel 1982, 19). San Francisco elected an Italian American, Angelo Rossi, as mayor in 1931, two years before Fiorello La Guardia became mayor of New York City (Nelli 1983, 167). The most prominent Italian American sport clubs in San Francisco were Unione Sportiva Italiana, Sporting Italiana, and the Virtus Club. In 1926 the Unione Sportiva Italiana and the Virtus Club combined to form the Unione Sportiva Italiana Virtus (USIV), taking second, third, and fourth places in that year's Cross City Race. The USIV's Pietro Giordanengo won the race in 1928 and 1929 (Wallach 1978, 85, 87).

Immigrants want to be recognized for what they accomplish in America. Italian immigrants at first identified themselves by their region of origin and sought recognition by their regional groups. Italian nationalism superseded such regionalism with the rise of Mussolini in the 1920s (Cinel 1982, 239). Mainstream American respect for Mussolini grew as he confronted domestic problems and heightened Italy's international presence. Italian Americans hoped this would win admiration for their culture. American acceptance was most important for Italian Americans moving from cities to middle-income suburbs after World War I (Nelli 1983, 156, 159).

In 1920, Italian Americans were the largest group of foreign-born inhabitants of affluent and mostly residential Westchester County. A substantial working-class population lived in Port Chester, one of Westchester's few industrial centers; over half of the foreign-born population of Port Chester was Italian American (Bureau of the Census 1922, 689, 695, 702, 704). By 1925, Port Chester was New York State's largest village, with a population over 25,000 and about 140 manufacturing plants. The village was proud of its industrial base and held an annual Merchants and Manufacturers Exposition (*PCDI*, 9 Oct. 1925, special sec., p. 1).

The Cygnet Athletic Club had been formed in East Port Chester in 1916, raising money for its first activities with a public dance. In 1917 the club staged a ten-mile road race. Ninety-five percent of Cygnet members served in World War I, almost ending the club, but the Cygnets regrouped after the war and continued their road race, shortened to eight miles, as an annual event. In addition to running, club members participated in bowling; only in 1925 did the club begin swimming and baseball teams. The road race remained the club's signature event. While the Millrose Athletic Association in nearby New York City was primarily a track-and-field club, Cygnet concentrated on cross-country and long-distance runners (*PCDI*, 9 Oct. 1925, special sec., 8–9).

The bricklayer Bill Kennedy of the Cygnet Athletic Club and the free-lance sportswriter Tommy McNamara, both Port Chester residents, presented the idea of a local marathon footrace to the Port Chester Chamber of Commerce, which agreed to sponsor the race and hold it on Columbus Day, 12 October 1925, as part of the Merchants and Manufacturers Exposition (Lewin 1938). The Chamber of Commerce planned the race as an advertisement of Port Chester's desirability as a residential community as well as its suitability for business and industry (*PCDI*, 6 Oct. 1939, 1).

Much of the 1925 Port Chester Marathon followed, in reverse, the route of the first American marathon in 1896. The Port Chester Marathon started from the Maine Monument at Columbus Circle in Manhattan, ran up Central Park West, through the Bronx (where the 1896 marathon finished), then through a number of the towns such as Rye, New York, that had been along the route of the first American marathon. The *Port Chester Daily Item* of 9 October 1925 remarked on its front page that "Runners Will Follow Route Now Historic." The newspaper also recalled another marathon that used part of the course, the 26 December 1908 *New York Journal* Marathon from Rye to Columbus Circle (9). The marathon was developing a history and tradition that would further enhance the New York City marathon culture. The Port Chester marathon came into special prominence of its own in having Sigfrid Edstrom, president of the International Amateur Athletic Federation, as honorary referee (8). The race was officially called the Port Chester National Marathon, and almost every important United States runner entered, as well as runners from Canada, Germany, and Finland. About 250,000 spectators cheered the runners from Columbus Circle to Liberty Square in Port Chester. Albert Michelson of Stamford Connecticut, the Cygnet Athletic Club's star runner, won in 2:29:01.8. Michelson, Bill Kennedy's protégé, was, like his mentor, employed as a bricklayer. Michelson, who was of Finnish birth, was nicknamed "Whitey" because of his light blond hair (*NYHT*, 13 Oct. 1925, 22).

The running of a marathon from New York City to Port Chester on Columbus Day acknowledged the Italian American contribution to Port Chester and to Westchester County in general. According to historian John Bodnar, "When ethnic groups were highly influential, so too was the attempt to accommodate their interests in commemoration" (1992, 246). But Columbus Day was not an ethnic Italian holiday; it was an expression of Italian American pride and, even more, a patriotic American celebration of the European discovery of America. Columbus Day is a "mixture of cultural threads" that can be interpreted in different ways to appeal to many "new" immigrant groups (Bodnar 1992, 249). Because World War I interfered with immigration and immigration was restricted after the war, most recent immigrant groups had been in the United States for over ten years by 1925. During the period from the mid-1920s to the eve of World War II, identification of new immigrant groups with the Old World gradually weakened as their commitment to America grew. Both American and Old Country flags graced immigrant events, affirming the double identity. Eventually immigrant culture began to combine both American and Old Country elements (Conzen et al. 1992, 25–27).

By reenacting the trip to America as ritual, the marathon footrace committed the immigration journey to a consensual past. The decision to be part of America was now irrevocable. For the older groups from Great Britain, Germany, or Ireland, the journey to America was generations past, and mostly forgotten. But southern and eastern European Americans had made the trip themselves or had two parents who told of the journey. African Americans did not share the recollection of European emigration; the horrifying "middle passage," their own ancestral Atlantic crossing, was well over a century before and not comparable to the European American experience. But the Great Migration had quite recently brought many African Americans from the South to northern cities. Columbus Day, which had received increasing recognition during the period of new immigration, also celebrated the journey that is part of many Americans' pasts. Both the marathon footrace and Columbus Day celebrated public memories (Bodnar 1992, 108–9).

Marathon activity increased throughout the United States in the sesquicentennial year of 1926. The year started out disappointingly for American marathoners, with Canadian runners taking marathon honors in the United States. John Miles of Nova Scotia won the Boston Marathon. But then Clarence DeMar came through to win the AAU National Championship in Baltimore in May. DeMar's own sense of municipal pride had led him to transfer his affiliation from the Dorchester Club to the Melrose (Massachusetts) Post of the American Legion. "It seemed much better to represent something in Melrose. The post always honored me for marathon victories far more than I deserved" (DeMar 1981, 89).

The Sesquicentennial Marathon honored Philadelphia'a role in the American struggle for independence. The official course ran from Valley Forge to the Municipal Stadium in Philadelphia, over terrain that was part of Revolutionary War history. In the blazing June sun, a crowd of 100,000 watched the event. DeMar won in 2:38:30.6. One entrant, Arthur Gavrin, had come to the United States from Poland in 1921. Now a dark-haired, handsome New York University freshman who dreamed of becoming a dentist, he entered the event against the advice of his coach and finished fifth in 2:53:53 (*NYHT*, 3 June 1926, 25). John Semple had also emigrated in 1921, coming to Philadelphia from Scotland, where he had run for the Clydesdale Harriers and trained as a joiner. Semple, who finished fifteenth, found out about the marathon while laying floors in the Japanese pavilion in the Sesquicentennial Exposition (Semple 1981, 29). DeMar won the 1926 Port Chester Marathon (*PCDI*, 13 Oct. 1926, 1), while Harvey Frick of the Millrose Athletic Association won the Lakewood (New Jersey) Marathon, held on the Saturday after Thanksgiving Day (*NYHT*, 28 Nov. 1926, sec. 2, p. 4.).

Clarence DeMar won the Baltimore Marathon on 19 March 1927 and the Boston Marathon on 19 April 1927. He discussed his success with the *Boston Evening Transcript:* "The printing business has been somewhat slack in recent months, and I did part-time work in five different shops. I trained for the marathon by running between jobs in Cambridge, Jamaica Plain, and Boston. Yesterday's race was not particularly exacting" (20 Apr. 1927, 12).

On 15 May 1927, a marathon began in front of the New York Athletic Club building, at Sixth Avenue and Central Park South in Manhattan, and finished at City Hall in Long Beach, New York. Four Native Americans from a New Mexico reservation were among the 135 starters who included Albert Michelson, Harvey Frick, and Percy Wyer. These better known marathoners finished in that order: second, third, and fourth. The winner was Chief Quanowahu, a sheepherder representing the Hopi nation (Abramson 1927, 1). Later that month, Frank Zuna, running for Millrose, won the Detroit Marathon (*NYHT*, 20 May 1927, 14), and Cliff Bricker of Galt, Ontario, won the Buffalo Marathon (*NYHT*, 31 May 1927, 24).

The 8 October 1927 Port Chester Marathon entry list showed 189 hopefuls from many ethnic groups, including ten entrants from the African American Salem-Crescent Athletic Club and two entrants from the New York Institute for the Deaf (*Official Program, Third Annual Port Chester National Marathon,* 1927). Ranked by the AAU as a potential Olympian, Horatio Stanton, who competed for the Italian Athletic Club of Westerly, Rhode Island, was actually a Native American. Overall, 119 runners started the Port Chester Marathon, and 53 finished; Albert Michelson won in 2:31:11 (*PCDI,* 10 Oct. 1927, 5).

Marathon activity increased in early 1928 as runners prepared for the coming Olympics. The AAU listed nine United States marathons held in 1928 during the four-month period of March through June, including one in Pittsburgh, Pennsylvania; one in Phoenix, Arizona; and one in San Francisco, sponsored by the *Examiner* (AAU 1928, 58, 60). Andy Myrra of the Olympic Club won the San Francisco marathon in 2:58:16. Myrra, of Finnish descent, was a frequent competitor in the Cross City Race. Harry Chauca of the Hopi nation, a member of the Los Angeles Athletic Club, was second in 3:10:41.4. Harry Hooker of the Unione Sportiva Italiana Virtus was third in 3:18:40.8 (*San Francisco Chronicle Sporting Green,* 19 Mar. 1928, 1). The marathon was now truly a national event. Boston, New York City to Long Beach, and Baltimore served as trials, producing the Olympic Marathon Team of Clarence DeMar, winner at Boston; Joie Ray, winner at Long Beach; and William Agee, winner at Baltimore; as well as Harvey Frick, Albert Michelson, and James Henigan.

The United States team performed poorly in the 1928 Olympic Marathon; Joie Ray, the highest finisher, earned fifth place. Ray earned a living as a taxi driver in Chicago, where he ran for the Illinois Athletic Club. One of the great track men of the 1920s, he set records at 1,000 meters, 1 mile, 1 1/2 miles, and 2 miles before coming to the marathon (Donovan 1976, 44–45). Like Kolehmainen and Ritola, Ray brought a track man's speed to long distance.

Held in October after the disappointment of the 1928 Olympic Marathon, the Port Chester race was billed as "the leading event of its kind of the year" (*PCDI,* 11 Oct. 1928, 1). This is an indication of the strength of the New York City marathon culture, now centered around the Port Chester event. Arthur Gavrin, twenty-four, won in 2:57:37; De-

Mar, age forty, was second in 3:01:40.4. The terrible heat of the day was probably responsible for the slow times (*PCDI*, 12 Oct. 1928, 1).

Arthur Gavrin graduated from New York University in 1930. In the depression economy, he found work as a printing jobber. In 1934 he started Gavrin Press, eventually specializing in business products such as carbon-interleaved forms (Gavrin 1948, 1). The firm was doing $5 million a year in business by 1960. According to his obituary (*New Rochelle Standard Star*, 13 Oct. 1967, 1), Arthur J. Gavrin Press, Inc., was acquired In 1961 by Allied Paper Corp., Chicago, with Gavrin becoming one of Allied's directors. He had substantially moved up in socio-economic class. In addition to his business history, Arthur Gavrin's obituary presented his many activities in Jewish and civic affairs, and his membership in the Rochelle Heights Tennis Club. No mention at all was made of his career as a marathon runner.

During the 1920s there were fewer immigrants to maintain working-class ethnic consciousness, and the working class began to share certain characteristics with the middle class. Although income inequality persisted, highly skilled blue-collar workers were well paid, and the overall standard of living was comparatively high (Bernstein 1960, 47–49, 65). The opportunity to be one's own boss was available, and men like Abraham Monteverde, William Kennedy, and Arthur Gavrin took advantage of it.

In emulation of middle-class goals, marathon runners controlled their own skills, such as bricklaying or printing. Marathoners also controlled their own running, mainly by default. The National Collegiate Athletic Association had no marathons within its jurisdiction, while the Amateur Athletic Union had acceded to the 1924 request that Olympic marathoners be allowed to determine their own training by eliminating the position of marathon coach for the 1928 Olympics (De-Mar 1937, 96).

The marathon became accessible and acceptable to the middle class as it became useful to civic society. The Port Chester Marathon was probably the first continuing marathon event to be sponsored by a municipal Chamber of Commerce. As Chamber of Commerce members were middle class, the Port Chester event was their marathon, serving their city. The middle class could watch the marathon as a demonstration of civic responsibility, and, under the same cloak of respectability, they could even enter it. As an amateur sport beyond the jurisdiction of universities, long-distance running was mainly a form of recreation. And recreation—leisure—could now be shared by the middle and working classes in public places such as parks, movie theaters, and all along the marathon route (Rosenzweig 1983, 226).

5

Max Silver's Boys

Marathons such as Boston, Port Chester, and the AAU Championship thrived during the early 1930s; but, as the Depression progressed, marathons felt the straitening of local and regional resources and had to rely on private support. Still, the major events continued, and athletic and civic clubs established new marathons. The marathon returned a sense of pride to cities that now required federal help to fulfill municipal responsibilities to the destitute and dependent. Minority conflicts arising from the economic crisis limited runners' access to club affiliation, coaching, and other athletic opportunities and undermined the strength of the New York City marathon culture. The 1933 election of Fiorello La Guardia as mayor of New York City threatened Irish dominance of politics and of the civil service in that city, as La Guardia opened more appointments to Jews and Italians. Of the resultant ethnic conflicts, the Irish-Jewish was the most severe. In the long history of Irish American anti-Semitism in New York City, street violence and vandalism were frequent manifestations (Bayor 1978, 24–27, 156, 165–67).

Irish American anti-Semitism and nativist anti-Semitism converged in the sports world, most noticeably in the New York Athletic Club, the single most powerful club in the AAU. Although Irish Americans had first entered the NYAC as active athletes, they rose to administrative posts and social acceptance as their group became established in American society. The president of the NYAC from 1926 to 1932, Major William Kennelly, led New York City's St. Patrick's Day Parade on Fifth Avenue; it was "one of his favorite public appearances" (Considine and Jarvis 1969, 79). Irish Americans were openly accepted, while the NYAC did not even permit Jews to become members (*NYT*, 26 Aug. 1937, 11). The Millrose Athletic Association was probably second to the NYAC in influence and importance. Millrose accepted only high-performing athletes, like the NYAC, but Millrose did not have a concurrent social function for upper-status, noncompetitive members. And Millrose was not anti-Semitic; Fred Schmertz, Millrose's meet director and later vice-president, was Jewish.

German-Jewish relations in New York City were traditionally amicable, and Jews of German background were accepted by German American organizations (Bayor 1978, 4–6), including the German-American Athletic Club (GAAC). The GAAC became a major power in the marathon during the early 1930s. Among its members were William Steiner, winner of the Jewish marathon championship held in Tel Aviv in 1935 (*NYT*, 7 Oct. 1946, 28), and Max Silver, the great track coach who had guided the GAAC marathon team to victory in the AAU National Marathon Championship the same year (*NYT*, 2 June 1935, sec. 5, p. 3).

In the early years of the Depression, President Hoover remained confident in American economic vitality and encouraged corporate and personal spending to keep the economy buoyant. He endorsed voluntary cooperative action in business, industry, and agriculture to continue investment and maintain wage rates. Hoover increased funding for public works, but he disapproved of large, comprehensive work relief programs and left public assistance to state and local agencies (McElvaine 1984, 66, 73, 77, 79). Boston was better able to care for its destitute citizens than other cities of comparable size; Boston was wealthier, and it had a well-developed, well-financed assistance system. Yet on 6 March 1930, 4,000 men and women demonstrated on Boston Common, demanding work and decent wages (Trout 1977, 33, 55, 305). In early 1932 most local funding for assistance, at best inadequate, had been exhausted; the summer encampment of the Bonus Expeditionary Force in Washington, D. C., clearly showed the desperation of many families. By 1933, federal relief was necessary. With the national bank crisis of 1932–33, established businessmen as well as the working class feared the whole economic system might collapse (McEl-vaine 1984, 90–93).

Sport affirmed conventional rules at a time when the traditional values of hard work and saving had failed (Cooney 1995, 6). Clarence DeMar won the 1930 Boston Marathon (*BET*, 21 Apr. 1930, 9). He also won the Pawtucket, Rhode Island, marathon on 17 May and the 8 June marathon in Los Angeles (AAU 1930, 117). And on 13 October 1930, he won the Port Chester Marathon, coming in five minutes, fifteen seconds before the next runner. DeMar was then forty-two years old. At the dinner after the race, speakers substantiated President Hoover's emphasis on optimism, celebrating the Port Chester Marathon as a significant advertising vehicle for the village and its business and industrial base (*PCDI*, 14 Oct. 1930, 1). Karl Koski of the Finnish-American Athletic Club won the AAU National Marathon Championship on 23 March 1930 at Silver Lake Park on Staten Island, New York. The Millrose Athletic Association won the team championship; the Cygnet Athletic Club was second. John Semple placed fourth, running for the Meadowbrook Club of Philadelphia (Daley 1930, 18). The Meadowbrook Club was the athletic association of the Philadelphia department store John Wanamaker, founded under the same circumstances as the Millrose Athletic Association (Schmertz [1967?], 15). Semple hitchhiked to Boston four weeks later and finished seventh in the 1930 Boston Marathon. Jobless after the marathon, Semple moved into his brother's home in Boston and found employment with the YMCA in Lynn, Massachusetts, as a locker-room attendant. The job paid eleven dollars a week (Semple 1981, 44).

Semple augmented his meager salary by participating in the ten-mile handicap races that were the central events of summertime New England social club picnics: "These clubs pulled the best runners in America because they offered merchandise prizes. . . wrist watches and toasters, things we needed. It was the Depression, and often we sold or traded the merchandise to get money for food" (Semple 1981, 40).

John Semple finished sixth in the 1930 Port Chester marathon as a member of the running team he had put together at the Lynn YMCA. Paul de Bruyn, twenty-two years old, finished in fifteenth place in his first marathon (Abramson 1930, 25). Born in Oldenburg, Germany, de Bruyn was a German national, running for the Deutscher Sports Club.

He moved up to seventh place in the 1931 AAU Metropolitan Marathon Championship. Millrose men—Albert Michelson, Fred Ward, Harvey Frick, and Arthur Gavrin—took the first four places. The AAU Metropolitan Marathon Championship was held on 5 April, exhausting runners before the 20 April 1931 Boston Athletic Association Marathon (Daley 1931b, 30), a sign of the continuing marathon rivalry between New York City and Boston.

James P. Henigan of Medford, Massachusetts, a thirty-eight-year-old shipping-room foreman, won the 1931 Boston Marathon. Semple finished well back in the field, in twenty-eighth place (Carens 1931, pt. 2, p. 4), but the Lynn YMCA team he coached took first place in the 16 May 1931 AAU National Marathon Championship (AAU 1931, 178). In October, Semple himself won the New England Marathon Championship held that year in New Hampshire, from Boscawen to Manchester. The New England race, held on Columbus Day, was a clear challenge to New York's Port Chester Marathon, held on the same day. In 1931 that race was won by Dave Komonen, a Finn living in Canada (*NYT*, 13 Oct. 1932, 27; Daley 1931a, 31).

The 1931 Port Chester Marathon had 116 entrants, the largest number ever. According to the *Port Chester Daily Item*, runners came to the Port Chester Marathon because it had gained national prestige as a well-organized event. They also expected it would be considered an Olympic trials race, but the American Olympic Committee chose other events (10 Oct. 1931, 1). The 1932 United States Olympic marathon team was selected from the runners at Boston on 19 April 1932; at a marathon on 28 May 1932 in Maryland, from Cambridge to Salisbury, won by Hans Oldag of Buffalo, New York; and at a marathon held shortly thereafter, in Los Angeles, won by Albert Michelson. The final team comprised Michelson, Oldag, and James Henigan, who was second at Boston (AAU 1932, 60). William Steiner, winner of the 8 May 1932 AAU Metropolitan Marathon Championship, was considered a strong contender but was not chosen for the team (Daley 1932, 22). The winner of the Boston Marathon, Paul de Bruyn, now a member of New York City's German-American Athletic Club (*BET*, 19 Apr. 1932, 1), went to the 1932 Games as a member of the German Olympic team. In the Olympic Marathon, Michelson finished eighth, Oldag finished eleventh, Henigan dropped out, and de Bruyn finished fifteenth. The disappointing level of performance of the United States in the 1932 Olympic marathon continued in the 1932 AAU National Marathon Championship; the team prize was taken by the Monarch Athletic Club of Toronto, Ontario (*NYT,* 21 Aug. 1932, sec. 3, p. 2). The usual sponsors of the Port Chester Marathon abandoned the race in 1932, and Bill Kennedy, one of the founders of the event, found private support in the Port Chester area. He presented the marathon as a handicap race on 16 October 1932 and organized the Interstate Sports Club to assist in maintaining the event (Abramson 1932, 16).

Major races such as Boston, Port Chester, and the AAU National Championship still brought runners from Canada and Europe as well as most of the best American runners (*PCDI,* 10 Aug. 1931, 1). The regional championships and the smaller local marathons, such as the Irish Day Marathon held in August in Cleveland (*NYT,* 18 Aug. 1933, 10) or the marathon from Amsterdam to Schenectady, New York, held on 14 July 1935, generally attracted only a few national class competitors (*NYT,* 15 July 1935, 15).

In New York City members of the German-American Athletic Club started entering long-distance competitions in the early 1930s. Founded in 1884, the club disbanded in 1917 in reaction to anti-German sentiment accompanying World War I, and the nativism of the 1920s delayed its reorganization. Dietrich Wortmann, a member of the German-American Athletic Club since 1901 and its president since 1910, revived the club in 1927. It merged with the German Athletic Club in 1928 and bought a clubhouse, the "Scheffelhalle," a German American landmark. This purchase indicates that the club had substantial discretionary funds, important in attracting top athletes who might need subsidies for travel and other competition and training expenses. Many of the German-American Athletic Club's active members, such as Paul de Bruyn, were born in Germany. And, especially in the track and field events, many members were Jewish, among them the coach Max Silver (Frank 1935b, 20).

With Paul de Bruyn's win at Boston in 1932, the German-American Athletic Club became a local and national force in the marathon footrace. De Bruyn won the 1933 Port Chester Marathon; together, de Bruyn, William Steiner, and Harvey Lichtenstein won the team trophy for the German-American Athletic Club (Abramson 1933, 23). In the 25

March 1934 AAU Metropolitan Marathon Championship, Steiner, de Bruyn, and Russel Jekel finished in first, second, and third places, respectively, securing the ascendancy of their team. "When Russell Jekel came home in third place it gave the German-American Athletic Club a perfect score and enabled Max Silver's boys to capture the team trophy easily" (Effrat 1934, 25).

Boston runners challenged the dominance of the German-American Athletic Club in the marathon. The declining economy caused John Semple to lose his job with the Lynn YMCA, but the United Shoe Machinery Company, planning to present a footrace as part of a spring festival, hired Semple for his running expertise and gave him a job cutting dies and washing the floor. Semple assembled a team of United Shoe employees and ex-YMCA runners (Semple 1981, 65–66). In the 1934 AAU National Marathon Championship, the United Shoe Machinery team took first place and the German-American Athletic Club second (AAU 1934, 66). The 1934 Boston Marathon team prize went to the North Medford [Massachusetts] Club; one of their runners, John A. Kelley, who had placed thirty-seventh in 1933, was second in 1934 and still improving (Derderian 1994, 144–45). Formerly of the Irish-American Athletic Club of Newark, now running for the German-American Athletic Club of New York, Melvin (Mel) Porter won the 1934 Irish Day Marathon in Cleveland, Ohio (*NYT*, 24 Aug. 1934, 18), and the 1934 AAU Middle Atlantic States Marathon Championship in Newark, Delaware (*NYT*, 4 Nov. 1934, 8). On 12 October 1934, the German-American Athletic Club again won the Port Chester Marathon team trophy, although the first place finisher was Frank (Pat) Dengis, a thirty-one year old toolmaker running for the Stonewall Democratic Club of Baltimore, Maryland (*NYT*, 13 Oct. 1934, 21).

Running without club affiliation, John A. Kelley won the 1935 Boston Marathon (Carens 1935, 1). Otherwise, 1935 belonged to the German-American Athletic Club. On 17 March 1935, de Bruyn won the AAU Metropolitan Marathon Championship; German-American Athletic Club runners finished first, second, third, fourth, and sixth. On 1 June, Pat Dengis won the AAU National Marathon Championship, but Hugo Kauppinen, Mel Porter, and Edward Wesolowski took the team trophy for the German-American Athletic Club (*NYT*, 2 June 1935, sec. 5, p. 3). Leslie Pawson, a gardener from Pawtucket, Rhode Island, won the 12 October Port Chester Marathon; Dengis was second, and the German-American Athletic Club, coached by Max Silver, won the team prize for the third consecutive year (*NYT*, 13 Oct 1935, sec. 5, p. 9).

Ethnic tensions had once determined the course of the marathon. Dormant in times of prosperity, these tensions revivified as the Great Depression wore on. The European political situation expanded the American ethnic rivalries that were played out in the world of sport. In the 1930s the United States as a whole experienced a resurgence of anti-Semitism, exacerbated by Nazi propaganda. The Nazi movement in America centered in New York City, home of the nation's largest Jewish community. Deterioration in German-Jewish relations started with the 1933 Jewish boycott of German goods. Often, even merchants who did not sell German goods were affected, and Nazi organizations took advantage of the resultant problems. In July 1933 a number of small Nazi groups in New York City united to form Friends of the New Germany, later known as the German-American Bund. The Bund extended its influence to German-American cultural and sporting societies with offers of funding (Bayor 1978, 59–60, 68–69, 71, 165–67).

Organized anti-Semitism among German Americans had previously been insignificant; now, the rise of Naziism along with the Depression led to ethnic antagonism between the two groups (Bayor 1978, 5, 24–29). The sportswriter Stanley Frank of the *New York Post* denied that the German-American Athletic Club had such prejudices in a 3 January 1935 article emphasizing that the club's policy was not to make any religious or political commitments (1935b, 20). On 10 January 1935, officials of the German-American Athletic Club replied to Frank's article in the *Deutscher Weckruf und Beobachter*, the American Nazi German-language newspaper; Dietrich Wortmann was one of the signers of this reply. In December 1935 a translation, from which the following excerpts are taken, appeared in the *Columbia Daily Spectator*, with the headline "Leaders of German-American AC, Key Men in Olympics Committee, Are Termed Pro-Nazi.""[The *Post* article] was published without our agreement and was aimed at the creation of dissentions in the ranks of German-American sports. . . . our sympathies belong to 'New Germany.' All our performances took place under the sign of sovereignty of Nazi Germany "(3 Dec. 1935, 4).

The Nazi swastika was prominently displayed at the German-

American Athletic Club championship games on 8 September 1935. Jewish members of the German-American Athletic Club threatened to resign; Wortmann asked them to stay. Max Silver, the track athlete Sol Furth, and the shot putter Danny Taylor, among others, stayed. Silver, who volunteered his services as coach, did not want to desert his long-distance runners before the important Port Chester Marathon and the Thanksgiving Day cross-country meet (Frank 1936, 158-59). The club's Jewish members gradually left over the next few months. After the club won both the Port Chester Marathon and the Thanksgiving cross-country meet, Max Silver stated that Wortmann was a Nazi sympathizer and resigned (*Columbia Daily Spectator*, 3 Dec. 1935, 1).

The conflict within the German-American Athletic Club took place within the context of the larger conflict over the AAU's certification of American athletes for the 1936 Berlin Olympic Games. In 1931, before Hitler came to power, the International Olympic Committee had granted Garmisch-Partenkirchen, Germany, the 1936 winter games and Berlin the 1936 summer games. By 1934, Jews in Germany experienced increasing discrimination, and American Jewish groups demanded a boycott of the 1936 Olympics. Concern about Jewish athletes in Germany reached the December 1934 AAU convention, delaying AAU acceptance of Germany's invitation to the Games (Guttmann 1984, 62, 70–71). The boycott campaign increased in momentum throughout 1935, and a number of AAU associations instructed their delegates to vote against American participation at the next AAU meeting (Abramson 1935d, 26).

At the 8 October 1935 meeting of the Metropolitan Association of the AAU, Charles L. Ornstein presented a resolution condemning the Nazi government and requesting that the national AAU refuse certification for the Berlin Olympic Games to American athletes. The resolution was favored by the national AAU president, Jeremiah T. Mahoney, a member of the Metropolitan AAU and a former New York State Supreme Court justice, but the Metropolitan Association voted, seventy-seven to thirty-two by secret ballot, to table it. The choice of a secret ballot was unusual for the Metropolitan Association, and Mahoney accused the Metropolitan Association president, Patrick J. Walsh, "with attempting to railroad the resolution out of the meeting," in the words of the noted track writer Jesse P. Abramson (1935d).

The meeting ended with the selection of Metropolitan Association delegates to the national AAU convention in December 1935. Both Jeremiah Mahoney and Patrick Walsh were selected, along with Dietrich Wortmann of the German-American Athletic Club and Charles L. Diehm, vice-president of the Metropolitan AAU (Abramson 1935d). The 10 January 1935 letter to the *Beobachter* had stated, "Men like [Avery] Brundage [chairman of the American Olympic Committee], Major Walsh, and Charles Diehm are friends or members of our clubs" (*Columbia Daily Spectator* 3 Dec. 1935, 4). Other Metropolitan AAU delegates included Charlotte Epstein, Charles A. Elbert, Frederick W. Rubien, John J. Flaherty, Jr., Roy E. Moore, Arthur M. Wehrmann, Melvin W. Sheppard, and Thomas T. Reilley. Reilley, a City Court judge and chairman of athletics at the New York Athletic Club, strongly favored American participation in the 1936 Olympics (Abramson 1935d).

On 7 December 1935, responding to a motion by Patrick Walsh, the national AAU convention voted to table a resolution to boycott the 1936 Olympic Games (Abramson 1935b). On 8 December, the AAU associations and the allied organizations voted for American participation in the Berlin Olympics; the vote of the Metropolitan AAU was overwhelmingly in favor of Olympic participation. On 9 December, Mahoney resigned from all AAU committees (Abramson 1935a); Avery Brundage was elected national president of the AAU, and Patrick Walsh was elected first vice-president (Abramson 1935c).

Because it involved the German-American Athletic Club, one of the most important marathon teams in the United States, the conflict subtly undermined long-distance running in the New York metropolitan area for years afterward. Athletic activities in New York City felt obvious repercussions quite soon; in February 1936, Abel Kiviat and Max Silver, Jews who had been against participation, were summarily dropped as AAU officials. Kiviat was the press steward for most of the major metropolitan track meets; Silver had been an official at every local meet since World War I. According to Charles A. Elbert, secretary of the Metropolitan AAU, "They were accidentally overlooked, yes, accidentally overlooked, that is all" (Abramson 1936).

After five years the Great Depression had become a constraint on the American marathon. Public subscription funded the 1935 Port Chester Marathon, and the small group that organized the race suggested creating a Port Chester National Marathon Association to ensure continuity of the event. Philadelphia's Meadowbrook Club had been disbanded, although many of its marathon runners got together to form the Philco Athletic Association. There were even rumors that the Boston Marathon might not be held in 1936 (*PCDI*, 12 Oct. 1935, 1; 13 Oct. 1935, 11).

Mel Porter, New York City's hope for the Olympic marathon team, maintained his affiliation with the German-American Athletic Club through the two Olympic trials marathons, Boston and the AAU National Marathon Championship in Washington, D.C. At Boston, Ellison (Tarzan) Brown, finished first (Carens 1936, 1, 4). A Native American, Brown came from Rhode Island's Narragansett people. He was coached by Thomas (Tippy) Salimeno, who had also coached the Native American Horatio Stanton. William McMahon of Worcester, Massachusetts, running for the local Ancient Order of Hibernians, finished second; Porter came in third (Derderian 1994, 152). At the AAU National Marathon Championship, McMahon was first; John A. Kelley of Arlington, Massachusetts, running unattached, was second; and Porter was again third (*NYT*, 31 May 1936, 4). The team championship went to the first three runners of the Millrose Athletic Association: Fred Ward, Joseph Mundy, and William Steiner, the former German-American Athletic Club champion. Brown, McMahon, and Kelley made up the Olympic team. They were all New Englanders; that year the AAU specifically commended its New England Association for presenting the most extensive long-distance running program (AAU 1936, 50).

The Great Depression and the local New England road races combined to become an ideal environment for one optimistic man who accepted life as it presented itself to him. John Adelbert Kelley, born in 1907 the first of ten children, grew up in Boston's Irish American community. He was a cheerful, scrappy, black-haired boy who first saw the BAA Marathon when he was thirteen. He ran track and cross-country in high school, graduated in 1927, and began entering some of the road races that abounded in New England. The Great Depression limited his opportunities to find work: "I worked here and I worked there. . . . there was nothing permanent, nothing steady. Running was fun. It helped kill time" (Kelley, quoted in Lewis 1992, 19). When he got a good job with the Boston Edison Electric Company in 1937, he held onto it until he retired. As a mechanical maintenance man, Kelley worked at "hard physical labor. In the boiler room, out on the dock, up on the roof, everywhere. But it was forty hours a week and I was very fortunate" (Kelley, quoted in Lewis 1992, 51). He ran his first marathon in 1928, in Pawtucket, Rhode Island, finishing seventeenth. Later that year he entered the BAA Marathon but did not finish. But he continued to run. His wins at Boston in 1935 and 1945 and his places on the United States Olympic Marathon team in 1936 and in 1948 testify to the depth of his love of the marathon. He still appears at Boston every year, no longer running the full course but still a most admirable figure.

The United States did not do well in the 1936 Olympic Marathon: Kelley finished eighteenth; Brown and McMahon dropped out. Tarzan Brown redeemed himself in the autumn marathons starting on 10 September 1936, when he won the Bridgeport Centennial Marathon (*NYT,* 11 Sept. 1936, 33). Then, in October, Brown won two marathons in two days. First he won the Port Chester Marathon on 11 October 1936; Pat Dengis was second; Mel Porter, now running unattached, was third (*PCDI,* 12 Oct. 1936, 1, 6). On the following day, Brown won the annual Columbus Day marathon from Boscawen to Manchester, New Hampshire. Porter's redemption came when he won the 8 November 1936 Yonkers Marathon (Worner 1936).

Although the economy seemed to be improving in 1937, the indicators did not match the reality (McElvaine 1984, 297–98). Walter Young won the 1937 Boston Marathon in the hope that the resulting fame might get him a job, and get his family off public assistance (Carens 1937, 1). His bid paid off. By the time Young won the 30 May marathon from Lawrence, to Salisbury Beach, Massachusetts, he had been given a position as policeman in his hometown of Verdun, Quebec (*NYT,* 1 June 1937, 33). After transferring to the Millrose Athletic Association, Mel Porter, thirty-four years old and a tunnel engineer, won the 12 June 1937 AAU National Marathon Championship in Washington, D.C. Welsh-born Pat Dengis, now thirty-seven years old and an airplane mechanic but still running for the Stonewall Democratic Club of Baltimore, placed second. In the fall Dengis won the Port Chester and the Yonkers Marathon, while John Semple's United Shoe Machinery Athletic Association of Cambridge, Massachusetts, took the team first place in both races (AAU 1937, 57).

Max Silver returned as a race official for the thirteenth annual Port Chester National Marathon in 1937. At the awards dinner after the race, Silver thanked the organizing committee for avoiding the usual cups and medals. "I know [the winner] Pat Dengis will be happy that he has won a radio—he can take that home and make good use of it" (*PCDI*, 13 Oct. 1937, 5). Exactly how Dengis used the radio is not known; as was noted before, during the Depression runners often sold prizes to get money for food and rent.

Because of ethnic conflict and economic pressures, the athletic clubs were in flux during the late 1930s. The German-American Athletic Club had lost its marathon coach and best long-distance runners; the United Shoe runners performed below expectations in 1938 and 1939, and Canadian teams were all too frequently winning American races. When the company administrators of United Shoe Machinery expressed their disappointment in the team, John Semple turned to the Boston Athletic Association, which had never had a formal long-distance team. "I disbanded the United Shoe team and shortly thereafter regrouped the team under the banner of the BAA Unicorn" (Semple 1981, 70). The fortunes of the BAA had declined almost steadily since the turn of the century (Derderian 1994, 83). Now the activities of BAA long-distance runners oriented the club around the Boston Marathon. Autotelic, with its own marathon team, the BAA Marathon drew further away from the New York City marathon culture.

In New York City the Millrose Athletic Association, already an established track-and-field force on a par with the New York Athletic Club, increased its power as a marathon team. When Pat Dengis and Mel Porter finished first and second, respectively, in the 30 May 1938 Lawrence-to–Salisbury Beach marathon, both were Millrose members, and Millrose was the winning team (*NYT*, 31 May 1938, 24). Millrose also won the team prize at the 12 October 1938 Port Chester Marathon, with a team comprised of Dengis, Porter, Willie Wiklund, Hugo Kauppinen, and Albert J. Bradh (*PCDI*, 13 Oct. 1938, 1). Pat Dengis also won the 6 November 1938 Yonkers Marathon, although Millrose took second team place to the Marathon Athletic Association of Montreal (Worner 1938, 17).

Long-distance running on the West Coast continued in such city races as San Francisco's Cross City Race. A wide range of ethnic running clubs appeared there, including the Chinese Club, the Russian Club, the Japanese Athletic Club, and the Catholic Filipino Club. Ethnic rivalry was present in San Francisco athletics, but, with the exception of the Italian Athletic Club (formerly the Unione Sportiva Italiana Virtus), none of the ethnic teams ever achieved enough importance in long-distance running to be a political influence. None of them even entered enough runners for a team score in the Cross City Race. The event was dominated by the Olympic Club, the Italian Athletic Club, and the Petaluma Spartans (Wallach 1978, 99, 110).

In 14 April 1935 the Petaluma Spartans began an annual marathon at the official distance of 26.2 miles. Formed in 1925, the Spartan Club organized most sports activity in Petaluma, including baseball, football, wrestling, and track (Ross 1959, 4). The first Petaluma Marathon was part of a major track-and-field day (*PAC*, 12 Apr. 1935, 4). The second, on 17 April 1936, was "billed as the only marathon race in which Pacific Association of the AAU members may qualify to secure a recommendation from that body to the Olympic try-outs" (*PAC*, 18 Apr. 1936, 4). The Petaluma Marathon was not part of the national marathon circuit. Held in mid-April, the race conflicted with the venerable Boston Marathon; regional in design and purpose, it had no need to attract the great runners of the East. The race seldom had more than ten to fifteen starters in its early years. The competitors were often members of the Petaluma Spartans or the Olympic Club who competed in the Cross City Race: Andy Myrra, Leland Smith, Paul Chirone, and Jack Kirk. Leland Smith won the 1935 event in 3:23:20 (*SFC*, 15 Apr. 1935, 12H).

Petaluma, a suburb of San Francisco, prospered since the invention of the incubator and the protective egg box enhanced the local poultry business in the nineteenth century. By the twentieth century Petaluma dominated the California poultry industry. After inspiring the establishment of National Egg Day in 1918, Petaluma held annual Egg Day celebrations from 1918 through 1926 and took great pride in its designation as the "World's Egg Basket" (*PAC*, 23 Apr. 1996, supplement, 2, 13). Yet the Petaluma Spartans Marathon never officially celebrated Petaluma's major source of income and identity. The race kept going year after year primarily through the efforts of Ed Fratini of the Spartan

Club. In 1944 there were only two entrants, but the race went on (Torliatt 1952, 25).

Depression-era marathons returned a sense of self-esteem to cities that had difficulty fulfilling municipal responsibilities. The Chippewa Club of Yonkers revived the Yonkers Marathon, last run in 1917, just after a November 1934 municipal crisis; New York City had attempted to annex Yonkers as a sixth borough, citing Westchester's inefficient and expensive system of government as a reason. Yonkers strongly resisted annexation (Crider 1934, 7). Whether or not the race was a reaction to the threat of annexation, the Yonkers Marathon definitely was urban boosterism. William H. Schlobohm of Yonkers worked tirelessly to promote the race. He had been a competitor in pre–World War I marathons, placing fifth at Boston in 1902 and fourth in 1904, and was also a member of the AAU Long-Distance Committee. In 1936 the AAU commended Schlobohm for his ability at race organizing (AAU 1936, 49). The Yonkers Marathon drew prestige from the AAU and from the New York City marathon culture. It would remain one of the nation's most important marathons in the decades after World War II. A shorter race in Berwick, Pennsylvania, had begun in 1908 and would continue through the Depression, World War II, and the running boom. Local merchants and the Chamber of Commerce still support the "Run for the Diamonds," the pride of Berwick (Berwick Marathon 1994, 18).

The Petaluma Marathon was not an essential part of Petaluma; it did not celebrate a local holiday, as did the Boston Marathon, nor did it serve a civic purpose. Its most famous winner, Jesse Van Zant, left California to join the Boston Athletic Association. In 1948 and 1951, Wan Chang Ling of China won the event (*PAC*, 18 Aug. 1955, 4). The Petaluma Marathon had to compete with San Francisco's Cross City Race for status within the local association of the AAU, and AAU officials threw their weight behind the established and much larger Cross City Race (Wallach 1978, 102). Tangential to its city and to the athletics bureaucracy, the Petaluma Marathon did not survive into the years of the running boom.

Although Ellison Brown won the Boston Marathon again in 1939, the year belonged to Pat Dengis of the Millrose Athletic Association. Dengis won the Salisbury, Massachusetts, marathon on 30 May, Waterbury on 3 September, and, on 7 October 1939, he once again won Port Chester (*NYHT,* 8 Oct. 1939, sec. 3, p. 9). On 12 November 1939, Dengis won the Yonkers Marathon for the third year in a row (Worner 1939). But tragedy struck on 17 December 1939, when Dengis was killed in the crash of a small airplane. At the 1940 Yonkers Marathon, to honor Dengis, the number 1 was not issued (*NYHT,* 11 Nov. 1940, 21).

Marathon activity ebbed during World War II. The Lawrence-to–Salisbury Beach marathon, a local race that brought in the best runners, was suspended after the 1941 race and was not run again until 1948. The premier American marathons, Yonkers and Boston, continued with greatly diminished participation throughout the war, and so did the Petaluma Spartans Marathon. The same top runners competed, often as members of the military. An infantry sergeant in the Canadian Army, Gerard Cote, won the Boston Marathon in 1943 and 1944 (Martin and Gynn 1979, 143–46). Charles Robbins, a Navy pharmacist's mate, moved from his former status as a University of Connecticut track star to win the Yonkers Marathon in 1944 and 1945. The Millrose Athletic Association took both the National and Metropolitan AAU Championships in 1945, remaining the most influential long-distance club in the New York City area (*NYT,* 13 Nov. 1944, 22; 12 Nov. 1945, 25).

The discrimination against minority groups connected with the German-American Athletic Club and the New York Athletic Club ended the direct involvement of traditional multisport clubs with long-distance running. Marathon runners preferred either clubs that specialized in track and field or even more specialized cross-country and road racing clubs. The Yonkers Marathon became the AAU National Marathon Championship in 1938, an honor it retained until 1967. The naming of the Yonkers event as the National Marathon Championship and the growing strength of the Millrose Athletic Association marathon team contributed to the eventual political and athletic rejuvenation of the New York City marathon culture despite all the problems arising during the Depression.

6

Joe Yancey and the New York Pioneers

The difficulties that many long-distance runners faced in pursuing their sport were related to the greater societal problems of racism and anti-Semitism. The New York City marathon culture found an activist vanguard in the New York Pioneer Club, which started as a black track team in 1936 and emerged as a force not only in the marathon but also in civil rights during the 1940s and 1950s. The Pioneers became an integrated group in 1942 and used team unity to challenge discriminatory AAU policies. The Pioneers' experiences and achievements taught long-distance runners that they could change the sports bureaucracy.

Organized in the economic and social unrest of late 1930s Harlem, the New York Pioneer Club had a political as well as an athletic agenda; the club was founded to promote higher education for Harlem youth and to advance racial understanding (Booker 1951, 7–8, 16–17). While New York City's leaders searched for answers to African American problems, the Pioneer Club initiated changes by protesting segregated track meets and sponsoring integrated competitions. The resulting confrontations with the AAU fit into the greater plan of the civil rights movement as a nonviolent assault on discrimination in employment, in housing, and particularly in the educational system (Brooks 1974, 50–51).

The Depression had hit Harlem more severely than any other section of New York City. Most African Americans were already poor and had been denied access to skills and education; they would be the first to take wage cuts or lose their jobs. Racial discrimination jeopardized the jobs of all African Americans, including those in the professions (Capeci 1977, 38). African American unemployment soared as even the lowest-paying positions were now sought by whites. Decades of residential segregation resulted in overcrowding as well as high rents and food prices in Harlem. Despite the implementation of New Deal programs, services and public assistance available to African Americans remained inadequate (Greenberg 1992, 398–99).

The strength of African American institutions ensured the stability of Harlem through the early 1930s. African American churches, political organizations, and social societies set up programs to distribute food and clothing—even small amounts of money—and to locate jobs (Greenberg 1992, 399–400). The ability of the Harlem community to help its jobless was limited because most black-owned businesses supplied personal services, thus requiring few employees (Capeci 1977, 37).

The major retail food and clothing operations in Harlem were white-owned and hired only white workers (Greenberg 1991, 127). Leaders of the "Don't Buy Where You Can't Work" campaign of 1934 insisted that white-owned businesses in Harlem hire black employees. This employment campaign, as with other African American economic programs, became part of the increasing politicization of Harlem; blacks began demanding that whites join them in acting against racism and discrimination. But the protests failed and, in the end, resulted only in harassment and police action. The institutional core of Harlem, the organizations and community actions, seemed almost powerless by 1935 (Greenberg 1991, 121–31).

On 19 March 1935, the apprehension of a young shoplifter on 125th Street was quickly followed by a series of misunderstandings that ended in rumors of the shoplifter's death. The incident assumed racial overtones. Soon, with no organized way to express themselves, thousands of Harlemites were rioting. While issues of race and class, as well as the connection between frustration and violence, were contributory factors, there was also a relationship between the 1935 riot and the collapse of Harlem's political efforts, such as the "Don't Buy" cam-

paign. African American anger toward white-owned Harlem businesses that would not hire blacks was a major component of the riot
(Greenberg 1992, 398–419).

Harlem came through the 1935 riot with a new unity. Harlemites
revitalized their existing institutions and created ancillary associations
to supplement them (Capeci 1977, 43), while new African American political vehicles engaged many people who had not previously been active (Greenberg 1991, 138). Harlem especially needed organizations to
provide its children with benefits and basic services of every kind. Af-
ter-school supervision and recreation were among the priorities when
both parents worked long hours at menial jobs far from the home
(Greenberg 1991, 190–91).

In 1936 three Harlem businessmen started an AAU-registered athletic club, the New York Olympic Club; the name was soon after
changed to the New York Pioneer Club. Robert Douglas owned the Renaissance Ballroom, where fundraising events for the club would be
held. William Culbreath was a trainer at New York University. Joseph J.
Yancey, a college-educated member of Harlem's middle class, had gone
into his father's undertaking business. Yancey had had an athletics
background in high school and college and later ran for and coached
the Mercury Athletic Club of Harlem. These three men began the New
York Pioneer Club "on the sidewalks of New York" as a track club for
Harlemites who had neither the funds nor expertise to join one of the
city's competitive teams (Booker 1951, 7).

The Pioneers had no clubhouse. Yancey got them into the 369th
Regiment Armory at 142d Street and Fifth Avenue in winter; in nice
weather they ran at McCombs Dam Park in the Bronx, a popular training venue for cross-country and long-distance runners. White runners
saw the group and began training with them (Booker 1951, 7), fostering
Yancey's plans for racial cooperation. In 1942 the members changed the
club's constitution so that white athletes could became official members (Abramson 1945, 11, 15). A hand-written copy of the 1942 constitution stated:

> The objects of this organization are to support, encourage, and
> advance athletics among the youth of the Metropolitan District, re-
> gardless of Race, Color, or Creed.

Joseph J. Yancey, a founder of the New York Pioneer Club.
Photograph by Eli Attar Photo Studio, courtesy of Edward Levy.

To encourage and further the ambition of our youth for higher
education that they might become intelligent, civic-minded citizens,
and to work toward a better racial understanding through the
medium of education and sports.

Edward Levy joined the Pioneer Club when he was sixteen. He
later earned bachelor's and master's degrees from New York University, and rose through the ranks of the administration of the New York
City school system. Levy retired in 1990 after twenty years as principal
of Public School 157 in the Bronx, but he remains manager of the Pioneer Club. He was assistant manager of the men's track team for the
1996 Olympics and head manager for the 1997 United States team for

the World Championships in Greece. In a 1992 interview Levy emphasized the club's acceptance of any athlete who wanted membership.

> The message was that we were open to this. Others' message
> was that they were not open to this. You know the organizations I
> could refer to that were very restricted at that time. And some other
> organizations only wanted the top five athletes. They weren't inter-
> ested in development, they wanted ready-made people. But [Yancey]
> was always a grass-roots person, the club was always grass-roots. The
> newspapers referred to us as the "Sidewalks of New York Club." So
> that's where we were. That was the focus of the organization, not in
> the elite, but it was everyman's club. (Levy 1992)

The Pioneer Club became a vehicle for integration by bringing
white athletes into a black club, and by bringing both black and white
youths the middle-class values with which Yancey had grown up. By
creating the New York Pioneer Club as "everyman's club," Yancey was
able to reach many young men who previously had been uninvolved
in minority politics and mainstream expectations.

> And many, many people began to come down and join. We would
> have nights when in the Armory here you might have 150 kids, train-
> ing and learning. Outside during the summer months it swelled to
> even greater numbers. A lot of this was due to the fact we had a very
> large and integrated team. We never turned anyone away because of
> any racial or ethnic consideration. At that time, the country was
> largely segregated right down to the social aspects. (Levy 1992)

The Pioneer Club's liberal admission policy did not constrain the
more talented members; Yancey produced national-class athletes. By
1945 the Pioneers had won a substantial number of national and metropolitan individual AAU championships as well as team awards, including two metropolitan junior championships, one national junior
championship, and a national 400 and 1600 relay (Abramson 1945, 11).
But Yancey continued to offer training to any athlete who wanted to
run. His open membership policy was a precursor of the wide participant base that made possible the marathon boom of the 1970s and

1980s. Murray Melnick remembered Yancey's impact on local high school athletes.

> I first heard of the club when I was a student at the Bronx High School of Science. That must have been about 1946. . . . It was my understanding that the club was largely Black but that was not particularly significant for me at the time. What was important was that it was possible for us high-schoolers to have access to a kind of organized running outside of the high school. . . . The thought that regardless of how we did on the school team we would be welcome at the Pioneers was a great, great infinitely pleasant and intriguing opening for me. It represented the possibility that I was not stuck, that I was not mediocre, that I too could move beyond. (Melnick 1994)

Yancey used competition to expand his message. Sanctioned track-and-field meets call for proper deportment on the part of the athletes; a track meet is a carefully structured occasion, and a milieu of propriety and formality surrounds the displays of bursting speed and strength. Athletics competition demonstrates the compatibility of manliness and restraint.

> [Yancey] did a lot of talking about being a gentleman first, and the values of sportsmanship and growing up to become good citizens. And much of the talking and teaching that we had every night was a lecture of some kind. And these are the topics that we covered in addition to how to run, how to strategize your races and so on. But a great amount of time was spent in personal development and subjects to that nature. (Levy 1992)

The Pioneers' field trips became opportunities to learn the finer points of social interaction. Yancey particularly emphasized polite, modulated speech and correct table manners and dress. Competing members were not permitted to enter the meet venue without shirts, ties, and jackets. The club helped the needier members, buying them clothes and paying for haircuts. Community responsibility was Harlem's way, part of its activism; the club even assisted some members' families with rent and utility bills. And the Pioneers' founders had the contacts with higher education that would enable them to suggest candidates for university scholarships (Levy 1992).

The long history of civil rights activism in Harlem determined the course of the Pioneer Club. Yancey was a captain in the reserves of the 369th Regiment, formed in 1916 as New York State's first African American military unit. In December 1917 the 369th had arrived in France to serve with the French army. While most African American soldiers in the American army in World War I were assigned to work as stevedores, the 369th fought on the front lines. Their status and fine performance in the military (many of the 369th received the Croix de Guerre) were a source of pride to Harlem (Anderson 1981, 101–2, 107). As a member of the 369th, Yancey was part of a long Harlem tradition of protest against all forms of racial inequality. Yancey transmitted these values to the next generation, both black and white, through the New York Pioneer Club (Morris 1984, x).

During World War II, African Americans challenged segregation with nonviolent civil disobedience. As the nation prepared for war in 1941, new jobs in defense industries opened, but not for African Americans. A program led by A. Philip Randolph of the Brotherhood of Sleeping Car Porters brought enough pressure on the federal government to end this discrimination. On 25 June 1941, President Roosevelt took official action to ensure equal opportunities in government employment. African American employment rose significantly as jobs were generated by World War II. In 1943, James Farmer and others in the Chicago area formed the Congress of Racial Equality (CORE) after participating in a 1942 sit-in to integrate a local restaurant (Brooks 1974, 27–50).

Mayor La Guardia of New York City was sympathetic to the problems of African Americans; though racial discrimination persisted, their overall situation in New York was better than in many other places. The verbal abuse of African American soldiers, most common in the South, was particularly incendiary. On 1 August 1943 such an incident in a Harlem hotel led to the shooting of a black soldier by a white policeman. Although the soldier was only superficially wounded, rumor spread that he had been killed. Rioting, looting, and vandalism swept Harlem before midnight. Continued contumelies precipitated the Harlem riot of 1943, although both white and black communities attributed the actions to hoodlums. Quickly contained by the New York City Police Department, the 1943 riot led New York City and

Harlem leaders to address the intertwined issues of discrimination, juvenile delinquency, and racial pride (Capeci 1977, 100–101, 121, 145, 173–75, 183).

The New York Pioneer Club would probably have been just another great track team had not its mission to encourage higher education and racial understanding fit the model of black assertiveness that resulted from the wartime disturbances. Joe Yancey was a civil rights activist whose reach across levels of economic status was part of the African American tradition of protest (Morris 1984, 3). Ed Levy explained Yancey's approach:

> it was all practiced through the club, you see. As we presented ourselves, as an integrated group, as a group of gentlemen, well-spoken, well-behaved . . . People had other expectations, but when they saw you in action that dispelled what myths they had in their minds about people. . . . that was the main thrust of the thing, you know, not to mirror society, but to change it. (Levy 1992)

Yancey did not permit women to belong to the New York Pioneer Club; this decision was more strategic than sexist. Shortly before the August 1943 riot, the Savoy Ballroom, a jazz dance club in Harlem, was closed by the police department on charges of vice (*NYT*, 25 Apr. 1943, 14). According to Dominic Capeci, author of *The Harlem Riot of 1943*, "Closing the Savoy seemed to have been prompted by race-mixing on the dance floor" (1977, 138). Joe Yancey was a civil rights activist and a track man who chose his battles; the possible presence of interracial couples on the team might have complicated the Pioneer Club's struggle for fully integrated conditions surrounding track meets.

Yancey prepared to fight for civil rights by building the New York Pioneer Club into a top competitive club, probably one of the first to support full outdoor and indoor track-and-field teams (Corbitt 1975). Because the AAU tacitly condoned racial inequities in track meets, sanctioning meets that covertly or openly practiced discrimination, the club had a ready arena for action (Senate 1965, 537). Many of the white athletes coming into the Pioneer Club were Jewish, and they shared the African American members' concern with the AAU's prejudices. During the 1940s, Jews and African Americans forged an alliance based on their similar concerns about discrimination in employment, education, and housing (Glazer 1984, 105–7). New York City became the most important center of this alliance, which extended into athletics; both groups faced blatant discrimination by the powerful New York Athletic Club (*NYT*, 5 Mar. 1951, 26).

In 1944 and 1946 the Pioneers became team champions in the Metropolitan AAU junior track-and-field games. Months before the 1946 championship, the Pioneer Club stated its refusal to attend the upcoming 28–29 June 1946 AAU national track-and-field championships in San Antonio, Texas, the first major open meet to be held in the South. This boycott meant that Pioneers such as Tom Carey, the 60-yard indoor champion, and Reggie Pearman, a 1:54.8 half-miler, would not compete. On 19 June 1946 the Grand Street Boys Association, an integrated team that included the black quarter-miler James Herbert as well as the field athletes Bernard Mayer, Irving Kintisch, and Irving Mondschein, joined the Pioneers' protest (*NYT*, 20 June 1946, 29). The Grand Street Boys Club did not forbid its members to go to the AAU Nationals; the club just refused to supplement the expense money allotted them by the Metropolitan AAU. Mayer and Herbert received enough AAU funding to make the trip; Kintisch and Mondschein did not (*NYT*, 21 June 1946, 27). Judge Jonah J. Goldstein, president of the Grand Street Boys, wrote to Charles Diehm, secretary-treasurer of the Metropolitan AAU: "Because of the Jim Crow practices prevailing in San Antonio, Texas, the Grand Street Boys Association is impelled to decline to sponsor that meet in any form" (*NYT*, 20 June 1946, 29). In 1948 the high jumper Irving Mondschein would become the first athlete sent by the Pioneers to the Olympic Games.

The Pioneers objected mainly to the social segregation; black athletes were not permitted to stay at the same hotels as white athletes. Many black athletes, however, did go to the 1946 AAU Nationals, and African Americans won seven of the twenty-one titles (J. Sheehan 1946b). The *New York Times* assured its readers that the black athletes were treated well:

> Negro athletes found conditions beyond their best expectations. On their arrival, they were taken in tow by Valmo Ballenger, millionaire Negro publisher and business leader, who saw that they received

good quarters and entertained them royally. In this respect they fared better than the white athletes, who were on their own. Segregation will end at the meet itself, where all competitors will share common dressing quarters and compete on equal terms without prejudice. (Sheehan 1946a)

For the Pioneers, segregation was unacceptable, regardless of the quality of the accommodations. Ed Levy reiterated the Pioneers' stand:

we refused to go and they sent all kinds of representatives up here to try to get us to come down and wanted us to stay in homes of well-to-do black people in that community where they would put us up. The other athletes, the white athletes, would be able to go to a hotel. But we refused this because we had to go as one, or we just wouldn't go. (Levy 1992)

The problem arose again at the 1950 AAU Nationals, held at the University of Maryland in College Park. By 1950 the Pioneers were a large and very successful team, taking eighty-five athletes to the meet. As an integrated group, the team could not stay together at any hotel in Maryland, nor were they allowed to stay together in University of Maryland dormitories. Roscoe Lee Browne, the Pioneers' 800-meter runner, was then teaching at Lincoln University in Pennsylvania; he later achieved substantial success as a theater and television actor. Browne arranged lodging for the Pioneers at Lincoln University, and the team commuted to the Nationals "for a principle" (Levy 1992).

Racial discrimination had never taken hold in the marathon; the AAU ignored white and black long-distance runners equally. Augustus Johnson, an African American running for the Missouri Valley Association, figured prominently in the Port Chester Marathon since he placed sixth on his first attempt at the race in 1934 (*NYHT*, 13 Oct. 1934, 16). Johnson, third at Port Chester in 1935, was now affiliated with Port Chester's Interstate Sports Club. By 1937, Johnson was a ministry student in Alexandria, Virginia (*NYHT*, 13 Oct. 1937, 30), although he remained a member of the Interstate Club and a top competitor in the Port Chester Marathon. Johnson also competed well in several Boston Marathons and in the 1938 and 1939 Yonkers Marathons.

In 1948, Dietrich Wortmann was elected president of the Metropolitan Association of the AAU, and Charles L. Diehm returned as secretary-treasurer (*NYT,* 16 Oct. 1949, sec. 5, p. 10). Both Wortmann and Diehm had been Nazi sympathizers before World War II. The AAU still maintained close ties with the New York Athletic Club, known to hold anti-Semitic membership policies and to disciminate against African Americans (*NYT,* 26 Aug. 1937, 11). These circumstances promoted cooperation between blacks and Jews that would change the marathon bureaucracy (*NYT,* 5 Mar. 1951, 26).

The Pioneers moved strongly into the long distances in 1946, taking the second-place team trophy in the Yonkers Marathon with the fine performances of Louis White in third place, Harry Murphy in tenth, and Laurence Lesser in twenty-sixth. Born in New Jersey in 1908, Louis White graduated from DeWitt Clinton High School in the Bronx and majored in journalism at New York University. Like others, White chose to take up road racing after seeing runners training in McCombs Dam Park. In 1945 he finished fifteenth in the Yonkers Marathon and joined the Pioneer Club. He began training with Joseph Kleinerman of the Millrose Athletic Association. In 1946, White finished among the top five in national championships at distances from 15 kilometers to the marathon and came in fifteenth at the Boston Athletic Association Marathon. In 1949, White ran 2:36:48 for third place in Boston as a member of the Boston Athletic Association but soon returned to the Pioneer Club. Ted Corbitt has said that Louis White "may have been the fastest black marathoner in history up to that time" (Corbitt 1991, 24).

Theodore (Ted) Corbitt would become the first African American Olympic Marathon entrant. Corbitt joined the Pioneers in 1947 when he was working full-time as a physical therapist to support his family and pay his way through a graduate program at New York University. Corbitt received a master's degree in physical therapy in June 1950, and devoted his newfound spare time to training for the marathon. In four marathons he ran in 1951, his times were under three hours. In 1952 he placed sixth in the Boston Marathon and third in the Yonkers Marathon, performances that earned him a place on the 1952 United States Olympic Marathon Team (Chodes 1974, 4, 13–14, 30–31, 150). All three marathoners were from the East Coast: Victor Dyrgall, a thirty-three-year-old accountant, was a member of the Millrose Athletic Asso-

The New York Pioneer Club marathon team. Left to right: John Sterner, Rudy Mendez, Louis White, Joe Yancey (coach), Ted Corbitt, Howard Jacobson, Gordon McKenzie, Gus Kaligerakis. Kneeling in front: Nat Cirulnick. Photograph courtesy of Edward Levy.

ciation; Thomas Jones, thirty-five years old, was an instructor in English at Lincoln University; and Ted Corbitt, thirty-two, was a physiotherapist running for the New York Pioneer Club (J. M. Sheehan 1952, 24).

Within two years the New York Pioneer Club fielded one of the top national marathon teams, winning the team title in the AAU National Championships at Yonkers in 1954 (*NYT*, 17 May 1954, 29) and 1955 (*NYT*, 23 May 1955, 32). In "Boston Marathon," *Ebony* magazine lauded the three black runners who won the 1955 Boston Marathon team trophy for the New York Pioneer Club: Rodolfo Mendez, Ted Corbitt, and Louis Torres (July 1955, 103–6). Long-distance runners did much of their training apart from most of the team, but they still had an important social function within the New York Pioneer Club. Marathon runners in the 1950s were often in their early thirties, men with families and responsibilities. As Pioneers, the marathoners showed the younger runners what Joe Yancey expected a man to be.

Well into the 1970s men trained for long-distance running under circumstances that severely taxed self-restraint. The sight of a grown man in shorts running through the streets elicited a wide range of taunts, from "There goes bloomer boy" to explicit threats. Hal Higdon's classic *On the Run from Dogs and People*, first published in 1971, documented the problem in great detail and included some humorous examples (1995, 1). But he found no humor in the remarks specifically addressed to African Americans. Lou Scott told Higdon, "I'll be running along and a car will come alongside me. The cat inside will roll down the window and I know what he's going to say: 'Nigger!'" (Higdon 1970, 15). Even today, the African American runner is limited as to where and when he can train. A black athlete training after dark, running through the streets at night, would all too readily be construed a threat.

Racism was rampant among the major white-sponsored track clubs (Higdon 1970, 15) and apparent even in the marathon community. In 1955 the *Saturday Evening Post* ran an article about long-distance runners, then a rather mysterious, small yet disparate group. One runner in the midst of a diatribe against African Americans was reminded that Lou White was African American. "'Oh, that doesn't count,' he said with illogical but obvious sincerity, 'Lou's not really a Negro in my mind. He's a real gentleman, a marathoner!'" (Gray 1955, 100). But, in general, racial integration was part of an ideal toward which the marathon community aspired.

Ted Corbitt had a long and successful career as a marathoner. He won numerous marathons in the 1950s and 1960s, among them Philadelphia's Shanahan Catholic Club Marathon in 1954, 1958, 1959, and 1962. By mid-1966, he had competed in 100 marathons, but his reach now extended beyond 26.2 miles. In the late 1950s, Corbitt had moved up to the "ultras," distance races longer than the marathon, where he achieved even greater success (Chodes 1974, 59, 150–51). The ultramarathon distances had not been contested in the United States since the 1930s. Only South Africa maintained an ultramarathon race, the Comrades Marathon, which had originated in 1921 (Shapiro 1980, 108, 127).

Corbitt's involvement with ultramarathons began in 1959 when he was president of the Road Runners Club of America (RRCA). With the cooperation of Aldo Scandurra, chair of the AAU Long-Distance Committee, Corbitt won sanction for a 30-mile race in the Bronx. He also won the race in 3:04:13. The RRCA raised the funds to send him to England to compete in the 1962 London-to-Brighton run of 52.5-miles, where he placed fourth in 5:53:37. In 1964, 1965, and 1969, Corbitt placed second in this event. He was frequently the winner of ultramarathon races in the United States and his initiative in establishing such events led runners to regard him as the father of American ultramarathoning. In 1973, Corbitt set the American record for a 24-hour run, 134.7 miles, at Walton-on-Thames, England (Chodes 1974, 54–55, 57–58, 151–55).

In 1948 and 1952, Joe Yancey very successfully coached the Jamaican Olympic track team, but in both years the AAU had passed Yancey over in selecting coaches for the United States Olympic teams (*New York Amsterdam News,* 9 Aug. 1952, 7). Nevertheless he continued to coach foreign Olympic teams (Jamaica, Trinidad-Tobago, Bahamas, British Guiana, United States Virgin Islands) through 1968. The State Department sent him overseas to lecture and coach as a goodwill ambassador. And Yancey's work with the New York Pioneer Club continued to send athletes to the Olympics (Corbitt 1975).

Track runners looked down on long-distance practitioners well into the 1960s; "athletes regarded road runners as second-class athletes" (Scandurra 1981, 9). They were stereotyped as blue-collar workers but they actually held white-collar or highly skilled blue-collar positions that placed them securely in the middle class (Lekachman 1955, 132–34). With their maturity and position in the community, the marathon runners could model a campaign of their own after the Pioneer campaigns to change the practices of the AAU.

When the Road Runners Club New York Association, later the New York Road Runners Club (NYRRC), was organized in June 1958, Ted Corbitt became its first president. The Road Runners Club of America (RRCA), the parent association of the NYRRC, had been created in December 1957 to assert the rights of long-distance runners. Because of the Pioneer Club's activities, the conflict between the AAU and the RRCA would center on New York City (NYRRC newsletter, c.

1959, 1). The Pioneers accepted all who wanted to join, and the RRCA continued this policy, seeking strength in numbers as well as bringing the marathon to increasing numbers of people.

The "running boom" of the 1970s and 1980s, which still brings out huge marathon fields in the 1990s, can be traced back to the Pioneer Club's democratic approach to athletics. The Road Runners Club of America also emulated the Pioneer Club in adapting the mass action tactics of the civil rights movement. Women's running was consistent with the RRCA mission, and the struggle for AAU approval of women's long-distance running extended the range of confrontations between the AAU and the RRCA. Integrated but identified mainly with its white founders, the RRCA could accept women without seeming to challenge society's bias against interracial couples.

The paradigm of protest that the Pioneer Club brought to long-distance running continued to evolve in the RRCA. In the process, the relationship of runners to the marathon event changed significantly. Marathoners and the AAU had traditionally had an adversarial relationship, in part the result of class and ethnic conflict. The earlier working-class runners had interpreted the marathon within their own communities to reflect their values and resolve their participation. Now marathon runners were creating an alternative bureaucracy and controlling their own events.

7

Running in the Cold War

As war often unites a people, the Cold War united the American people in a feeling of insecurity (Polenberg 1980, 86). Cold War competition between the West and the communist Eastern bloc effected a reevaluation of many aspects of American life and culture. American military power came under scrutiny, American education came under attack, and American fitness entered the realm of international affairs. In 1960, John F. Kennedy, the president-elect, wrote in *Sports Illustrated* that "physical fitness is as vital to the activities of peace as to those of war, especially when our success in those activities may well determine the future of freedom in the years to come" (Kennedy 1960, 16). When long-distance footracing became part of the competition with the Eastern bloc, the prestige of the marathon increased throughout the United States, most dramatically on the West Coast. The new value placed on track and long-distance athletics led to reconsideration of the amateur ethic and to changes in the rules of amateurism.

A "cult of toughness" precipitated by the Korean War developed to demonstrate the vitality of the American way of life (Mrozek 1995, 257–59). American POWs had been subjected to extreme physical duress and repeated indoctrination, then coerced into public condemnations of the war that were broadcast by North Korea. The prisoners' high rate of mortality, 38 percent, horrified the United States even more than the seeming collaboration; for many prisoners, the precursor of death had been a loss of will, causing them to lapse into an apathetic state and then into coma. A lack of endurance training was particularly blamed for the deaths of American soldiers (Stokesbury 1988, 190–93; Blair 1987, 966).

The American POW experience changed physical training not only in the Army but also in civilian life. Authorities decided that physical stress was an important part of conditioning to resist brainwashing. Physical educators expected that "ethical toughness" could be instilled by subjecting American youth to situations of extraordinary physical hardship. Training for sports now involved stressful—and even painful—routines on the assumption that this conditioning would build moral as well as muscle fiber. Sport had been associated with building character since the nineteenth century; now programs were intended to strengthen the body and the spirit as one, following the behaviorist theory that physical experience can control future behavior. One Air Force survival program, which simulated the environment and experience of torture, received much affirmative publicity, including a photo essay in *Life* magazine (Mrozek 1995, 257–60).

The element of prolonged misery introduced into sport by the cult of toughness (Mrozek 1995, 263–66) found many disciples among long-distance runners. The great Australian miler Herb Elliott in 1956 began to work with the coach Percy Cerutty, who told him, "Thrust against pain. . . . Pain is the purifier. . . . Walk towards suffering. Love suffering. Embrace it" (Elliot 1961, 38). Cerutty called himself a "Stotan" (38), a word he constructed from "stoic" and "spartan." He had begun marathon running in 1943 at the age of forty-eight; he broke three hours for the event within a few years. He honored marathon runners in the introduction to his own book, naming three "gifted 'winners'": Ted Corbitt and John J. Kelley of the U.S.A. and Jim Peters of England. Cerutty compared his training methods to a military breakthrough: "Just as we have grown accustomed to the phenomena of 'going through the sound barrier,' with its involved supersonic speeds, so must the athlete recognise and be prepared to pass through the 'pain barrier'—a phenomena just as remarkable physiologically, emotionally and wonderful to experience" (Cerutty 1964, 154).

During the period immediately after World War II, European runners had dramatically improved their training methods—one factor in the poor placing of the American long-distance runners in international competition. On 13 June 1953, James Peters of England became the first runner to break 2:20 for the marathon, with a 2:18:40.2 at Chiswick, United Kingdom (Martin and Gynn 1979, 377). Peters combined speed with distance, sometimes running a series of workouts totaling over one hundred miles a week at a racing pace (Benyo 1983, 80). Emil Zatopek's most influential contribution to preparation for long-distance racing was the development of "interval training," speed training for long-distance runners (Murphy 1992, 20–21).

Zatopek, a Czech, went to the London Olympics in 1948. Participating just after Czechoslovakia was brought under Soviet rule, he was perceived as an athlete rather than a representative of the Eastern bloc. Zatopek won the 10,000 meter event, and lost the 5,000 meters by only 0.2 second in a dramatic, crowd-pleasing finish (Benyo 1983, 84). The USSR had never entered athletes in the Olympics and as late as 1948 had not even formed a national Olympic committee. But they sent observers to the 1948 London Games and even questioned the motives behind the U.S.A.'s offer to feed all the Olympic athletes (Espy 1981, 28–30).

The USSR participated in the Olympics for the first time at the 1952 Helsinki Games, beginning an Olympic competition between East and West that would continue for the next thirty-six years. At the 1952 Olympics the Soviets provided accommodations for themselves, Hungary, Poland, Bulgaria, Romania, and Czechoslovakia in a separate Olympic Village, reproducing in the Games the alignment of the Cold War. Emil Zatopek won the 5,000 meter race, the 10,000, and then the marathon, becoming the "Man of the Games," the most celebrated athlete of the 1952 Olympics. He had never before attempted the marathon distance, and he was running against England's Jim Peters, the world record holder. But Zatopek won in 2:23:03.2, a new world record for an out-and-back course, and his win brought long overdue respect for the marathon, the so-called endurance event (Wilson 1976, 64–65).

Americans performed poorly in the 1952 Olympic Marathon. Victor Dyrgall, in thirteenth place, was the top American finisher. During the next four years, the marathon made some progress in the United States, but just as many steps back. In 1954, Boston had only 148 starters, the lowest number since 1945 (Martin and Gynn 1979, 172). There were a few new marathons, like that sponsored by the Shanahan

Catholic Club of Philadelphia in 1954 (*Philadelphia Inquirer*, 1 Feb. 1954, 21). Ted Corbitt won the first Shanahan Catholic Club marathon in 1954 and won again in 1959 (*LDL*, 4 Feb. 1959, 24). The Culver City (California) Marathon, first run in 1948, was the only western marathon to become part of the national marathon circuit. Starting in 1950, the AAU championship program included a Junior National Marathon. In 1953, 1954, and 1955, this event was awarded to the Michigan Association of the AAU, bringing a national championship marathon to Detroit and increasing midwestern opportunities to enter the event. But eastern domination of the marathon continued; in 1954, Ted Corbitt of the Pioneer Club won the Junior National and Open Marathon in Detroit, and the Boston Athletic Association took the team prize. In 1956 the Junior National was returned east to Queens, New York (AAU 1953, 17; 1954, 18; 1955, 11).

Vladimir Kuts, representing the USSR at the 1956 Olympic Games, won the 10,000 meters over Britain's Gordon Pirie in a series of breathtaking surges. Kuts also won the 5,000-meter event. American athletes had never performed well in the 5000- and 10,000-meter events, preferring to concentrate on the shorter distances. The glamour of the 1956 Melbourne Games centered on the American sprinter Bobby Joe Morrow, who won gold medals in the 100 meters, in the 200 meters, and as anchor of the 4 × 100 meters relay team. Overall, the United States took fifteen gold medals in men's track and field, with sweeps of first, second, and third in 200 meters, 110-meter hurdles, and 400-meter hurdles. The USSR won three gold medals in men's track and field; Kuts's two, and a sweep of first, second, and third in a new Olympic event, the 20,000-meter walk. Alain Mimoun, an Algerian representing France, won the marathon. Chris Brasher won the 3,000 meter steeplechase for Great Britain (N. Allen 1976, 70–72). From 1912, when the events were first introduced in the Olympic Games, until 1964, the United States achieved only one medal in the 5,000-meters, Ralph Hill's silver in 1932, and one in the 10,000-meters, Louis Tewanima's silver in 1912 (Killanin and Rodda 1976, 230–35).

British runners formally acknowledged road racing as a unique discipline, distinct from track athletics. Recognition of their specialization gave long-distance runners more freedom to develop training and competition to suit their specific needs. Bureaucratic sanction of the separation of long distance from track and field had begun on 16 April 1952, when Ernest Neville formed the Road Runners Club (RRC) of England. The RRC of England comprised serious, highly competitive runners who were unconcerned with the recreational aspects of long distance; the flagship event of the RRC was the 52.5-mile race from Westminster in London to the sea at Brighton. The RRC of England promoted the sport by encouraging long-distance runners in English-speaking countries to share their information and increase their influence by organizing (Scandurra 1981, 9).

American society disapproved of the individualistic long-distance runner who ran along public streets in his shorts no matter what the weather. The long-distance runner stood out in conformist 1950s America. Other white-collar workers rushed to adopt the appropriate corporate persona; long-distance runners clung to their working-class image (Higdon 1979, 57) although now many were college-educated. When Ted Vogel, a junior at Tufts University, overtook Tom Crane of Springfield College in the last mile of the 1947 Yonkers Marathon, William J. Briordy of the *New York Times* noted that Vogel was only the second collegian to win Yonkers and that the event "marked the first time that two college runners have finished one, two in the National AAU grind" (27 Oct. 1947, 30). Charles Robbins later completed medical school and became a physician; Aldo Scandurra, a partner in an electronics firm, earned a doctorate (Chodes 1974, 65).

Long-distance runners generally reached their peak performance in the years after college, but once a runner left college, he had to earn a living—and often support a family—as well as train. For the dedicated runner, marathons were few and far apart, necessitating travel permits and days off from work. Only at Boston could an athlete count on top international competition. And there was no money in long-distance running.

Antagonism between the National Collegiate Athletic Association and the AAU discouraged collegians from marathon running. Of course, the NCAA and the AAU had had conflicts over all shared sports since 1906; the dissension surrounding running had constrained college runners since the 1920s. Runners on college teams, particularly if they were on track scholarships, were required to obtain institutional permission to compete for their schools in AAU events; some college runners were forbidden to enter any AAU events. The exception might be summer, when college runners could keep sharp in AAU races. But overall the rules undercut many AAU club track teams and kept college track runners from long-distance racing and training (Senate 1965, 256–61).

American track coaches objected to road running, believing it would erode the bursting speed necessary for the popular college track distances. John J. Kelley began running in road races at age seventeen; he showed considerable talent and was befriended by Jock Semple of the Boston Athletic Association. Kelley entered Boston University in September 1950 on a track scholarship, training under Doug Raymond, a coach who disparaged both long-distance running and the marathoner, whom he characterized as someone "who passes up college and loses all his speed jogging with a darn fool bunch of road runners" (quoted in Semple 1981, 142). Kelley arranged a compromise, working out with the Boston University track team but incorporating training methods used by long-distance runners (Semple 1981, 132).

The strife between track and road running in the United States had a strong geographical component. Track and field had more status in California than in other areas of the country; Los Angeles was considered the national and perhaps the international capital of track-and-field competition. But the New York–headquartered Amateur Athletic Union, track and field's national governing body, represented the United States on the International Amateur Athletic Federation and on the International Olympic Committee (Senate 1965, 256). The administrative power struggle between the AAU and the National Collegiate Athletic Association, along with the dominance of track and field in California, affected West Coast marathon development; with a few exceptions, such as Jesse Van Zant, marathon runners did not come from California. In 1952 the twenty-sixth annual West Coast Relays included a marathon, the first for that meet. Only seventeen runners started. Aldo Scandurra, a thirty-six-year-old Millrose Athletic Association athlete, won in 3:01:01.2; the second finisher, Won-Ngaw Lou from Culver City, California, had a time of 3:29:42. Scandurra had slowed toward the end of the race, purposely trying to close the gap between himself and the rest of the field. The very slow times may have been due in part to the heat of the day, as well as to the upcoming Olympic Trials marathon, which would have drawn the best runners (*NYT,* 11 May 1952, sec. 5, p. 4). Joseph Brooks of San Diego State College ran a 2:54:30 for tenth place at Yonkers only eight days later (*NYT,* 19 May 1952b, 24). And Jesse Van Zant set a course record of 2:53:25 in the 1952 Petaluma Spartans Marathon (*SFC,* 21 Apr. 1958, 3H). In 1954, Aldo Scandurra and John A. Kelley were among the twenty-seven runners who entered the Culver City Marathon; only twelve finished within the time limit (*NYT,* 20 June 1954, sec. 5, p. 4).

Municipal enthusiasm was responsible for the marathon in Culver City, a western Los Angeles community. Paul Helms, a very successful baker, had worked with the food service for the 1932 Olympic Games in Los Angeles; now the Helms Athletic Foundation promoted sports for Culver City. Helms thought that every major metropolitan area should have a marathon, the most impressive of athletic events. In 1947, William R. Schroeder and Syd Kronenthal joined Helms in an attempt to recreate the 1932 Olympic Marathon, but the tyranny of Los Angeles traffic thwarted many of their plans. They decided to keep the new marathon small and within the confines of Culver City, parameters that made the event an essential part of the municipality. The influence of the directors (Syd Kronenthal was chair of the Long Distance Committee of the Southern Pacific AAU as well as director of the Culver City Parks and Recreation Department) ensured the Culver City Marathon a place in the marathon hierarchy (Kronenthal 1996). As a western marathon, Culver City filled a niche in the region and within the sport bureaucracy as interest in long-distance running grew in California. The race continued, increasing in participants but remaining a relatively small-field marathon.

The 1956 United States Olympic Marathon team included Nick Costes, affiliated with the Finnish-American Athletic Club of Farrell, Pennsylvania, but now teaching school in Natick, Massachusetts, and John J. Kelley and Dean Thackwray, both of the Boston Athletic Association. The three 1956 Olympians had all been students at Boston University, with access to the Boston network of assistance and information about training for the marathon (*Amateur Athlete,* Nov. 1956, 14). All three, however, succumbed to the Australian summer. The Melbourne Olympic Marathon was held on 1 December 1956, when temperatures hit the mid-eighties; Thackwray dropped out, Costes and

Kelley finished twentieth and twenty-first, respectively (Martin and Gynn 1979, 189–91).

In the late 1950s, Fred Wilt, a United States Olympian in 1948 and 1952, synthesized Peters's and Zatopek's methods and added long runs at near race-pace. Leonard (Buddy) Edelen, an exceptionally talented runner from the University of Minnesota, became one of the first to train under Wilt. Edelen and Wilt both took it as a given that no great runner could develop in the United States (Murphy 1992, 21–24). With Wilt's blessing, Edelen went to England to live and train in an environment more hospitable to long-distance runners. In the United Kingdom and on the Continent there were top-level competitors, frequent races, and under-the-table payments of about $500 for a meet. Buddy Edelen never ran the Boston Marathon (Murphy 1992, 21–26).

The Boston Athletic Association was now essentially a single-sport team, self-contained and relatively independent, using the proceeds from its indoor track meet to finance the BAA Marathon. The Boston network was effective in international competition; in 1957, John J. Kelley became the first American to win the Boston Marathon since John A. Kelley in 1945. John J. Kelley followed up his 1957 win at Boston with two second-place finishes, in 1958 and 1959, when the winners were from Yugoslavia and Finland, respectively (Derderian 1994, 212, 257, 260). The international focus of the Boston Marathon left New York as the center of a national marathon network; the Yonkers Marathon, which was the AAU Senior National Championship, more overtly showcased the prowess and potential of United States marathoners (*Yonkers Herald Statesman*, 23 May 1960, 15).

The experiences of the 1960 United States Olympic marathon team illustrate the problems of American marathoners. To choose the team, the track-and-field committee looked at combined performances from Boston and Yonkers. John J. Kelley had dropped out of the 1960 Boston, but his win at Yonkers, 2:20:13.6 over a tough and hilly course, reaffirmed his status as "the strongest United States marathon runner" (White 1960). Gordon McKenzie and Alexander Breckenridge, who finished second and third, respectively, also made the team. They had finished second and sixth at Boston; Paavo Kotila of Finland won. Robert Cons of Culver City, California, who had finished fourth at Yonkers and eighth at Boston, was named alternate. The inclusion of a West

Coast runner on the marathon team indicated that long-distance running was growing nationally and that local marathons were necessary
for developing competitive runners; Cons had won the Culver City
Marathon in 1949, 1953, 1954, and 1955. Gordon McKenzie, a member
of the New York Pioneer Club, went to his second Olympic Games in
1960; he had placed eighteenth in the 10,000 meters in the 1956 Melbourne Olympics (Chodes 1961).

John J. Kelley was the outstanding American marathoner of the
late 1950s. He could have been the best in the world, but he was be-
trayed by the inadequacies of the United States track-and-field bureaucracy, which never provided him with the supplementary support a
world-class marathon runner needs. John is an attractive man with
graying red hair, who still resembles the late Bobby Kennedy; his wife,
Jessie, is strikingly beautiful. If the running boom had only come two
decades earlier, they would have been the favorites of the advertising
industry. But during his most competitive years, John taught high
school English, a very demanding position despite the long vacations.
He later left teaching and became a free-lance writer. Jessie is now a
partner in a running store, Kelley's Pace, and John drives a taxi to aug-
ment their income.

At Rome the indifference of the coaches and the other athletes
so alienated the American marathoners that they trained without
supervision on the outskirts of the city. Kelley remembered the cavalier
attitude of their trainer, Mike Portanova, an ex-marathoner who
was chairman of the Long-Distance Committee; Portanova saw the
Olympic marathon on television in his hotel room. The American
marathoners fended for themselves after the grueling race, while team
officials attended to the other nations' runners. Yet none of the three
complained. "Whether we simply lacked a spokesman capable of De-
Mar's self-righteous rage or whether we expected no more of our officials I can't to this day determine" (Kelley 1984).

Abebe Bikila provided the most dramatic gold medal performance
of the 1960 Olympic Games as he ran the marathon barefoot through
the night over the cobblestone streets of Rome. The performances of
Zatopek, Kuts, and Bikila captivated spectators through the slowly un-
folding drama of their events; long-distance running celebrates the in-

dividual who defies human frailty (Guttmann 1978, 136). Bikila's triumph represented the emergence of black Africa as an international athletics force (Espy 1981, 75–76). Such races assumed heightened significance in the context of the Cold War.

Although enthusiastically engaged in the Cold War, neither the United States nor the USSR really wanted the total nuclear annihilation of humanity; in practice, both favored less-apocalyptic forms of confrontation. So in 1958 the two superpowers began a series of dual track-and-field meets. The American men's team won the first six meets, but the USSR men dominated the long-distance events until 1964, when Gerry Lindgren won the 10,000 meter event (Litsky 1964). Lindgren recalled the track lore of the early 1960s: "For many years, when I was running, I was always told that the Russians were great distance runners and that the Americans were all lazy because they couldn't win a distance race" (quoted in Senate 1965, 27). In context of the cult of toughness, Americans were becoming interested in winning long-distance races and looking carefully at foreign contenders.

The bipolar world of the Cold War had complicated the definition of amateurism with the performances of "state amateurs," athletes who were subsidized by the state (Glader 1978, 74). Emil Zatopek had the military status of subaltern when he won the 10,000 meters and placed second in the 5,000 meters in the 1948 London Olympics; he was then promoted to captain. During the next four years, Zatopek broke a number of middle- and long-distance records and was promoted to major. His three gold medals at the 1952 Helsinki Olympics presaged his elevation to lieutenant-colonel. In 1962, as the debate over amateurism intensified, the German sports historian Walter Umminger questioned Zatopek's military expertise and his ability to legitimately earn such promotions while devoting himself to the intense training his athletic performances demanded (1963, 228–31).

The issue of amateurism became a major point of contention between American athletes and the AAU. The definition of amateurism, and the exclusion of those who did not conform, had been contested since the mid-nineteenth century. The AAU was the standard-bearer for amateurism, and the international sports bureaucracy was modeled after the AAU. Avery Brundage was the "apostle of amateurism"

(Guttmann, 1984, 110) from his appointment as an original member of the American Olympic Association (later the United States Olympic Committee) in late 1921 until his retirement from sports administration in 1972. Brundage had placed sixth in the pentathlon in the 1912 Stockholm Olympics and was U.S. all-round champion in 1914, 1916, and 1918. In 1919 he began an administrative career in the AAU that would lead to seven terms as president of the AAU and twenty-five years as president of the United States Olympic Committee. The environment of Brundage's career included the administrative conflict between the NCAA and the AAU and its repercussions for the athletes (Guttmann 1984, 26, 28–35, 123).

The AAU represented many sports, and because voting in each association was done by member clubs, marathoners had little representation among AAU officers. AAU officers who voted on long-distance running decisions sometimes had not seen a long-distance race all year. Although it was the organization that controlled all marathon running in the United States, the AAU held no marathons, it only sanctioned races held by clubs. In order to compete, marathoners often had to travel to other states, meaning other AAU districts; athletes had to get AAU permission to travel to these races. The AAU did not understand that marathon runners in their thirties had different financial obligations and time constraints than, for example, swimmers in their teens. And the AAU did not appear to select excursion teams and their coaches on the basis of ability or achievement. According to Hugh Jascourt, an attorney who became national president of the Road Runners Club of America, "These trips include athletes picked on a basis which no one has yet been able to rationally explain" (Senate 1965, 521–25).

The world political situation constituted a new threat to amateurism when Brundage was elected president of the International Olympic Committee (IOC) in 1952. Perhaps to ensure continued Olympic participation by the USSR, Brundage accepted the Soviets' denial that their athletes were subsidized, i.e., given phantom occupations that allowed them unlimited time to train at state expense. As the charges against the USSR mounted, the IOC continued to redefine amateurism. At a June 1962 meeting in Moscow, the IOC accepted an elaborate policy refinement that excluded, among others, "Anyone awarded a scholarship mainly for his athletic ability" (Olympic Rules, quoted in Glader 1978, 154–55). Yet the student athletes who received these awards continued to be eligible for the Olympics.

The conflict between the National Collegiate Athletic Association and the AAU, a serious threat to the amateur careers of American track-and-field athletes, intensified in the early 1960s. The NCAA insisted on approving "open" track meets that were accessible to college athletes. The AAU refused to sanction track meets approved by any other organization, on the grounds that the AAU represented American athletes in the International Amateur Athletic Federation. In 1962 the NCAA accused the AAU of incompetence in staging track meets and established the United States Track and Field Federation (USTFF), primarily to conduct open track meets. In theory, the USTFF comprised a number of organizations, most of which were concerned with student athletics—for example, the National Collegiate Athletic Association (NCAA), the National Federation of State High School Associations (NFSHSA), and the United States Track Coaches Association (USTCA). In practice, however, the USTFF and the NCAA were the same organization (Senate 1965, 604).

An NCAA athlete who entered an AAU-sanctioned event not approved by the NCAA was penalized by the NCAA through the affiliated school; an athlete who did not compete in AAU trials for overseas events was ineligible for international competition. Concerned that the squabbling between the NCAA and the AAU might jeopardize the United States' chances in the 1964 Olympic Games, President Kennedy appointed General Douglas MacArthur to mediate between the two. By June 1963, MacArthur had arranged only an uneasy truce to see the athletes through the 1964 Olympics (Senate 1965, 273, 604).

On 25 July 1964, at the sixth United States–Soviet Union dual meet in Los Angeles, Gerry Lindgren, an eighteen-year-old high school student from Spokane, Washington, won the 10,000 meter race. The noted *New York Times* sportswriter Frank Litsky assessed the significance of Lindgren's performance: "His time of 29 minutes 17.6 seconds was only ordinary by international standards. It was miraculous on all other counts" (Litsky 1964). At the Tokyo Olympics in October 1964, Bob Schul of the United States won the 5,000 meters (Bill Dellinger of the United States was third), and Billy Mills of the United States won the 10,000 meters (Killanin and Rodda 1976, 78, 231–32). In the 1964 Olympic Marathon, Buddy Edelen placed sixth in 2:18:12.4; Billy Mills placed fourteenth in 2:22:55.4; and Peter McArdle placed twenty-third in 2:26:24.4 (Martin and Gynn 1979, 232).

The United States was at last coming into its own in the distances. But at the 1965 dual meet in Kiev, the American men lost to the Soviet men for the first time (*NYT*, 2 Aug. 1965, 20). The American women had always lost. A representative of the NCAA, Bill Easton of the USTCA, blamed the AAU not only for generally poor organization before the meet but also for excluding the best college athletes by denying the NCAA right to certification of the AAU national championship meet, on 26 and 27 June 1965 in San Diego, where the selections were made (*NYT*, 2 Aug. 1965, 20).

Risking loss of NCAA eligibility, Gerry Lindgren had gone to the AAU meet in San Diego, where he and Billy Mills broke the world record by running six miles in 27:11.6. On 31 July 1965 in Kiev, perhaps feeling the effects of a cold, Lindgren placed third behind two Russians (*NYT*, 2 Aug. 1965, 20).

On 16 August 1965, Lindgren testified in the U.S. Senate Committee on Commerce hearing on the controversy over track-and-field administration (Senate 1965, 27). The Hon. Warren G. Magnuson, chairman of the committee, had opened the hearing, which was an investigation about the dispute betwen the NCAA and the AAU: "At issue is our administration of amateur track and field events, both at home and abroad. At stake, ultimately, is our continued ability to demonstrate in the Olympic Games that fitness and zest for voluntary competition are the hallmarks of a free and democratic society, in contrast to many others that compete" (Senate 1965, 1).

The most important people involved with track and field testified: Avery Brundage, president of the International Olympic Committee; Kenneth L. Wilson, president of the United States Olympic Committee; Clifford H. Buck, president of the AAU; Everett D. Barnes, president of the NCAA; Jesse Abramson, sportswriter for the *New York Herald Tribune*; and Bill Bowerman, track coach at the University of Oregon. Many others submitted statements, among them Hugh Jascourt, president of the RRCA, and Bert Nelson, publisher of *Track and Field News*.

Jascourt's statement describing the RRCA, its activities on behalf of long-distance runners, and the AAU's neglect of road racing reached this very influential forum (Senate 1965, iii–iv). While the hearings exposed the inadequacies of the AAU, they did little to resolve the dispute. Both organizations agreed to a moratorium, and in December 1965, Vice President Hubert Humphrey appointed a panel of five to continue arbitration (Litsky 1965).

Direct corruption of the athletes made track-and-field headlines after the 1968 Mexico City Olympics. The rival shoe companies Adidas and Puma had paid a number of Olympians to wear their shoes in the Games. Such payoffs, which may have gone on since the 1956 Melbourne Olympics, drew attention once again to the anachronism of amateurism and to the prolix and ineffectual nature of the athletics bureaucracy. Investigating the scandal for *Sports Illustrated*, John Underwood presented a most interesting example of true amateurism: "What must be admitted is that the amateur athlete is an anachronism. An amateur today is the balding accountant who runs laps at the Y and finishes 168th in the Boston Marathon" (Underwood 1969, 23).

The amateur marathoner was more than a metaphor: he was the product of an increasingly important force in American sports, the fitness athlete. Formal athletics and general conditioning programs had become symbols of national strength. In the early 1950s the nation's physical educators claimed that American youth's lack of exercise constituted "a real danger for the country" (*NYT,* 29 Dec. 1954, 15). At this time, when medical authorities had concluded that most people could benefit from exercise, fitness was taken as a demonstration of patriotism, because popular belief held that only a strong citizenry could assure a strong military (Goldstein 1992, 72–73, 83).

In July 1956, President Eisenhower, after attending the Conference on Fitness of American Youth at the Annapolis Naval Academy, had announced the formation of the President's Council on Youth Fitness. The conference recommended that girls' fitness programs, equal to boys', be established and that adults too engage in physical activity (Buder 1956). The adherents of the new fitness movement were mostly educated and middle class, people who read John B. Kelly's grim comparisons in the *Reader's Digest:* "the young people of Italy, Austria, and other nations are in better physical shape than American children"

(1956, 26–29). Kelly had won Olympic gold medals in the single and double sculls in 1920, and again in the double sculls in 1924. His daughter, Grace Kelly, turned to acting but later married Monaco's Prince Rainier, the son of an IOC member. John Kelly, Jr., John B. Kelly's son, took the bronze in single sculls in 1956. In 1985 he became president of the United States Olympic Committee. A few weeks later, while out jogging, he had a heart attack and died at the age of fifty-seven (*NYT,* 4 Mar. 1985, sec. 2, p. 6).

In 1960, President-elect John F. Kennedy expressed concern for American youth's level of fitness because "our increasing lack of physical fitness is a menace to our security" (Kennedy 1960, 16). By 1965 the numbers of both schoolchildren and adults involved in fitness programs had increased (*U.S. News and World Report,* 6 Dec. 1965, 14). Jogging, widely practiced as a suitable exercise, produced a pool of fitness athletes with the potential to run long distances. Liberalized administration and competition policies in running, combined with medical and governmental endorsement of jogging, effectively merged athletics and fitness in one sport, long-distance road racing.

Nationwide, road racing increased in popularity. The Wesleyan University cross-country champion Ambrose Burfoot won the 1968 Boston Marathon (John J. Kelley had been Burfoot's high school English teacher). A Yale runner named Frank Shorter wanted to see if he could run the twenty-six miles at the 1968 Olympic marathon trials; he dropped out and the 1968 Olympic Marathon team comprised Oregonian Kenny Moore, Minnesotan Ron Daws, and George Young of the University of Arizona. Later Frank Shorter went on to win the NCAA six-mile championship as a senior at Yale. After graduating, he won the 10,000 meters in the United States-USSR dual meet in Leningrad in July 1970 (Clarity 1970b). Shorter's victory was particularly important because the United States overall lost the meet for the second time (Clarity 1970a). He remembered this as "the first time any performance of mine was highlighted in the press. The U.S.-Soviet meet was accorded great importance then, and I was credited with 'beating the Russians'" (Shorter 1984, 59).

Jack Bacheler, a graduate student at the University of Florida, convinced Shorter to join the Florida Track Club; Kenny Moore told

Frank Shorter, winner of the 1972 Olympic Marathon. Photograph courtesy of Frank Shorter.

Shorter to consider the marathon. On 5 August 1971, Shorter won the marathon at the Pan American Games a few days after winning the 10,000 meters (Amdur 1971, 21). On 5 December 1971, he won the prestigious marathon in Fukuoka, Japan, in 2:12:50.4 (Martin and Gynn 1979, 292). The 1972 Olympic team of Frank Shorter, Kenny Moore, and Jack Bacheler was arguably the finest marathon team the United States had ever produced.

With his thick dark hair and chiseled features, Frank Shorter presents a neat and well put together appearance. The son of an army physician, Shorter was born in Munich, Germany, in December 1947 and grew up in Middletown, New York. His private school and Ivy

League education imply privilege, but were balanced by his place in a large family and the demands of his father's profession as a general practitioner of medicine (10–12). Shorter's autobiography confirms the legend that his interest in running began in his first year at Mount Hermon School in Massachesetts with the Pie Race. All male finishers under thirty-three minutes for the 4.55-mile course received an apple pie as an award; women had to finish under forty minutes for a pie. In a few years Shorter made a committment to running (18). In his senior year he set school records in the two-mile and a record of 13:40 for the Mount Hermon cross-country course that was not broken until 1982 (20).

At Yale, Shorter's premedical studies became his priority, although he continued to do well under the coaching of Bob Giegengack. As Shorter finished his career at Yale, Giegengack encouraged him to try the marathon (33). "Soon after college, my desire to become the best runner I could superseded all else. I took on the life of a migrant, a migrant runner who lived here and there, earned little money, and survived on the opportunity to excel at running" (Shorter 1984, 45).

On 10 September 1972, at the Munich Olympics, Frank Shorter won the marathon in 2:12:19.8; Kenny Moore was fourth in 2:15:39.8; Jack Bacheler was ninth in 2:17:38.2 (Amdur 1972). Shorter's was a significant win in influencing the way Americans regarded the marathon.

> Winning the marathon in Munich made my running, in the eyes of others, legitimate. Suddenly it was okay *to be a runner*, to train for 2 and 3 hours a day. There was a purpose behind it, something to be gained. My running had been looked upon as a diversion, as a peculiar habit for a grown man. . . .
>
> The victory took the stamp of eccentricity off me. I was a real athlete (Shorter, 1984, 91–92).

The United States produced an unusual number of world-class marathon runners during the 1960s and 1970s. A boom in the economy from the end of World War II to the 1970s enabled young adults to live inexpensively and use their substantial leisure time as they wished—perhaps for long-distance training. In 1972 at least 124 marathons were held in the United States, and six had more than 200 finishers (Martin and Gynn 1979, 294, 298). The marathon now had the heroes to validate it as a spectator sport and the competitive opportunities to extend it as a participant sport. Most importantly, the marathon had achieved national value in the context of the Cold War.

8

The Gentrification of the Marathon

On 10 August 1956 the Pikes Peak Marathon challenged smokers and nonsmokers to compare their stamina in an event that was something between a footrace and a rock climb. The Pikes Peak Marathon was a round trip ascent and descent of Pikes Peak: fourteen started; the four who finished were all nonsmokers. Rudy Fahl, a physical therapist and fitness enthusiast who embraced jogging, vegetarianism, and a number of other health regimens, had helped Dr. Arne Suominen organize the competition (Olsen 1978, 61). In 1959 the race accepted women, and Arlene Pieper completed the round trip in 9 hours, 16 minutes. Nina Kuscsik, the first official women's winner of the Boston Marathon, has called Pieper "the first contemporary woman marathoner" (1977a, 863). Perhaps its hybrid nature freed the Pikes Peak Marathon from social constraints; the race was as much a part of the general fitness movement as of formal athletics.

The marathon increased in importance in the 1960s and 1970s as it became integrated with a number of popular beliefs about Americanism. Since the turn of the century, personal fitness had been considered essential to defend American values, not only in overseas wars but also in maintaining the established culture against the influx of immigrants at home (Goldstein 1992, 78). Recapturing a sense of community was an important component of American nostalgia. After World War II,

H. Browning Ross, founder of the Road Runners Club of America. Photograph courtesy of H. Browning Ross.

Americans sought the small-town sense of community when they moved to the suburbs. Long-distance running also embodied the pastoral ideal of a simple life in harmony with nature. Pastoralism was associated with achievement in the 1950s migration to the suburbs; its appeal continued into the 1970s with the advent of the commune (Berger 1979, 235–40). The image of a runner as a voluntary ascetic drew upper-status individuals to jogging. Marathoners felt a camaraderie in pursuing their unusual sport, gladly accepting into their ranks those willing to put in the long hours on the road (Henderson 1970).

In 1956, H. Browning Ross began *Long Distance Log*, a pulp journal that gave information about training and upcoming races in addition to race results. Ross was the nine-time winner of the Berwick, Pennsylvania, road race (*NYT*, 25 Nov. 1955, 42); an Olympian, he had placed seventh overall, the highest of the Americans entered in the 1948 London Olympic steeplechase. A high school teacher residing in Woodbury in southern New Jersey, Ross, who ran for the Penn Athletic Club, understood the need for a runners' network in the New York City area. He financed *Long Distance Log* himself, doing most of the writing as well as the printing and distribution. According to Aldo Scandurra, "Browning Ross's *Long Distance Log* did more for running than any other publication" (1981, 10, 18).

Long Distance Log: A Publication for Runners by Runners quickly became the voice as well as the advisor of the American marathoner. In 1957, Browning Ross decided that American long-distance runners needed more control of their own sport. Ross was a product of the postwar athletics community that had seen the New York Pioneer Club successfully challenge the AAU; he knew Joe Yancey, having been coached by him during an AAU tour. The organization Ross proposed was modeled on the Road Runners Club of England but went beyond their affirmation of specialization in long-distance running (H. B. Ross 1992). In the Road Runners Club of America, marathoners' dissatisfaction with the AAU would combine with the tradition of protest and mass action that had developed in black Harlem; Joe Yancey influenced the new group far more than did its English model.

In an August 1957 editorial, Ross asked that American long-distance runners begin a club similar to England's Road Runners Club. Although his editorial suggested district representatives, long-distance coaching, and fundraising dinners, Ross's pivotal intention seemed to be the creation of an organization that "could exercise full control of our branch of the sport" (2). On 22 December 1957, Browning Ross organized the Middle Atlantic Road Runners Club in Philadelphia. The New England Road Runners Club started two months later. The national organization, the Road Runners Club of America (RRCA), began on 22 February 1958, when Ross met with nine other runners at the Paramount Hotel in New York City. Shortly after, by mail vote, Ross was elected president and attorney Hugh Jascourt was elected secretary (Williams and Darman 1978, 208).

The support of the New York City marathon culture was vital to the mission of the new Road Runners Club of America. In Scandurra's opinion, "New York City was the key area that gave the RRCA strength [to] bypass the system" (1981, 12). Most of the leaders of long-distance running came from New York City clubs like the Millrose Athletic Association and the New York Pioneer Club. John Sterner of the Pioneers established the Road Runners Club New York Association after some persuading by Browning Ross, who quoted Ted Corbitt to Sterner: "You cannot sit back and complain all the time. Organize and do something about it" (Scandurra 1981, 12). The Road Runners Club New York Association, later called the New York Road Runners Club (NYRRC), was organized in June 1958. Ted Corbitt of the Pioneers was president; Harry Murphy, a former Pioneer member, was secretary-treasurer, assisted by John Sterner. Joe Yancey's example of legal protest served them almost immediately. The NYRRC applied for membership in the Metropolitan AAU; Road Runners Club associations in Philadelphia and New England had already achieved local AAU affiliation. But the Metropolitan AAU refused membership to the NYRRC, citing the problem of dual membership. An athlete could claim membership in only one competitive AAU club, such as Millrose or the Pioneers. But long-distance runners regarded the Road Runners Clubs as an administrative organization that presented races and provided information. In most districts the AAU agreed with this definition and permitted representatives of the RRCA associations to participate in the AAU. The AAU also questioned the NYRRC's right to obtain AAU sanction for "closed" races, open only to RRCA members. The lines had been drawn; the conflict between the AAU and the RRCA would center on New York City (NYRRC newsletter, 1959, 1).

The AAU granted the NYRRC sanction to hold open races that any AAU-registered athlete could enter. On 22 February 1959, the NYRRC sponsored its first marathon at McCombs Dam Park in the Bronx. There were twelve competitors. Corbitt won in 2:38:57; Nat Cirulnick, also of the Pioneer Club, was second in 3:03:06 (*NYT*, 23 Feb. 1959, 29). This event became the Cherry Tree Marathon, precursor of the New York City Marathon.

The RRCA continued to grow at the national level. Hugh Jascourt and Frank McBride started the Michigan Road Runners Club in February 1959, building on the long Detroit road-racing tradition that the AAU had tried to maintain. The RRCA held its next annual meeting on 20 February 1960 in New York City, and New Yorkers assumed leadership of the national organization; Ted Corbitt of the New York Pioneer

Club was elected president, Joseph Kleinerman of the Millrose Athletic Association became vice-president, and John Sterner of the New York Pioneer Club became secretary-treasurer. At the national level the AAU reflected the New York City position, refusing to accept RRCA membership. The struggle for the national Road Runners Club membership in the AAU would not be resolved until the 1960s (Williams and Darman 1978, 208–9). Preparing for confrontations with the AAU over issues important to long-distance runners, Corbitt united the various RRCA districts with a quarterly newsletter, originally titled the *RRC of US Bulletin*. Corbitt was publisher, editor, distributor, and wrote most of the articles.

Jogging would eventually route many Amercans toward the RRCA. The New Zealander Arthur Lydiard, coach of Murray Halberg and Peter Snell, had for years advised relatively slow running or jogging, as part of a training schedule for long distance and as a suitable exercise for middle-aged men, for women, and even for children (Lydiard and Gilmour 1967, 45–46, 114–26). Bill Bowerman, professor of physical education and track coach at the University of Oregon in Eugene, visited New Zealand over the 1962–63 winter holidays and discovered Lydiard's use of jogging for overall conditioning. Bowerman started jogging classes a few weeks after returning to Eugene. Women were early and particularly enthusiastic recruits to jogging regimens, which Bowerman asserted would promote weight loss and endurance as well as increased cardiovascular fitness (Bowerman and Harris 1967, 72–74).

As jogging drew more adherents, the Road Runners Club of America instituted the first joggers' events in 1964. Later called "Fun Runs," these organized jogs were considered an exercise program. Fun Runs conducted by a legitimate sport bureaucracy brought joggers into contact with formal athletics. Because they were not competitions, and therefore outside the domain of the AAU, the Fun Runs were open to both genders and all ages (Williams and Darman 1978, 210–11). Hal Higdon's article, "Jogging Is an In Sport," reached the large, educated audience of the *New York Times Magazine*, popularizing both jogging and the RRCA. The national magazine *Pageant* later reprinted the article. Higdon described the RRCA as an organization of competitive athletes that emphasized Fun Runs "for joggers who want to measure their conditioning against a stopwatch" (1968, 52).

New marathons had appeared, most significantly in the Midwest, in the years since the organization of the RRCA. Among the new annual events were the Labor Day Marathon from Columbia to Fulton, Missouri, begun in 1960 (*LDL*, 8 Oct. 1963, 2); the Windy City Marathon in Chicago, begun in 1962 (*LDL*, 9 Apr. 1964, 19); and the City of Lakes Marathon in Minnesota, begun in 1963 (*LDL*, 16 Oct. 1971, 11). The RRCA now comprised thirteen districts: New York, New England, Michigan, Midwest (Chicago), Middle Atlantic, Maryland, Virginia, Minnesota, District of Columbia, Mid-Pacific (Honolulu), Rocky Mountain (Denver), New Orleans, and South Texas. The RRCA had its own annual Marathon Championship, begun 1 October 1961 in Atlantic City, New Jersey (Williams and Darman 1978, 209–10).

At the RRCA annual meeting in October 1961, Aldo Scandurra convinced Hugh Jascourt that the RRCA needed power, not just representation, in each of the AAU associations. In New York City, the Metropolitan Association AAU finally accepted events sponsored by the Road Runners Club because Scandurra, a competitive marathoner, had become co-chairman of the Metropolitan AAU Long-Distance Running Committee (AAU 1962, 25). Jascourt was elected RRCA national president, and he and Scandurra became a team, spearheading the RRCA infiltration of the AAU. When Jascourt asked the AAU to work more closely with runners in arranging competitions, the AAU set up a subcommittee to coordinate the AAU and the RRCs, and Scandurra chaired the committee. In 1964, Scandurra became chair of the national AAU Long-Distance Running Committee; he held that position through 1967, and for much of that time he was also president of the Road Runners Club New York Association. In 1967, Browning Ross succeeded Scandurra as AAU Long-Distance Running Committee chair. The RRCA had successfully insinuated itself into the AAU hierarchy, and Scandurra earned such appellations as "Macchiavelli" and "the Godfather" (Scandurra 1981, 11, 13).

The Standards Committees of both the RRCA and the AAU also shared many officials. The AAU Standards Committee, created in 1965, used Ted Corbitt's 1964 book, *Measuring Road Racing Courses*, for their guidelines (Williams and Darman 1978, 211). Corbitt had written the thirty-page report that detailed the various systems of course calibration for the RRCA Standards Committee (Chodes 1974, 147–49). The RRCA instituted the bicycle-wheel method of course calibration, raising the level of quantification for road-racing courses all over the United States (Williams and Darman 1978, 211).

As a national organization, the RRCA wielded considerable influence on athletics but was caught along with everyone else in the conflict between the NCAA and the AAU over control of athletes and events. The RRCA favored the AAU; long-distance runners often belonged to both the RRCA and AAU-registered competitive clubs, and RRCA events often were sanctioned by the AAU. The AAU, in turn, officially commended the RRCA for encouraging long-distance running by providing more and increasingly accessible competitive opportunities. But the AAU imposed age limits on racing, medical standards for participants, and restrictions on women's competition. The RRCA could often avert AAU limitations by holding "closed" competitions—those limited to RRCA members, regardless of their affiliations or gender (Williams and Darman 1978, 211).

Testifying as RRCA president in the U.S. Senate hearings about the NCAA-AAU dispute, Hugh Jascourt presented runners' dissatisfactions with the AAU, particularly over the limited opportunities for competition. The AAU, he insisted, must become a promotional organization for long distance. Jascourt decried the NCAA's antipathy toward long distance; NCAA-affiliated schools often refused use of showers or locker facilities to RRCA race participants, on the grounds that long distance was an AAU activity. Jascourt represented the athlete; he asserted that the basic structure of the United States athletics administration must be reoriented around the needs of the athlete; otherwise, "any solution reached will turn out to be a temporary accommodation followed by renewed hostilities with the athlete as the only casualty" (Senate 1965, 525).

A developing bureaucracy specific to long distance accommodated the needs of a wide range of practitioners. Marathon fields swelled after 1963; the number of entrants in the Boston Marathon, for example, climbed from 285 to 369 in 1964, 443 in 1968, and about 500 in 1966. By 1968, Boston Marathon officials expected 1,000 entrants (Derderian

1994, 280, 287, 291, 300). Bill Bowerman and Waldo E. Harris published *Jogging: A Physical Fitness Program for All Ages* in 1967, and the book sold millions of copies (Strasser and Becklund 1991, 76). Hal Higdon, a free-lance writer, had finished fifth, highest of the Americans entered, in the 1964 Boston Marathon. According to Higdon, about three-fourths of the runners in the upcoming 1968 Boston Marathon would be fitness runners who had been jogging for years over increasingly longer distances. Higdon compared joggers to baseball fans; but, while the latter could never play in the World Series, diligent joggers could reasonably aspire to the Boston Marathon. Having developed endurance more than speed, they ran the marathon mainly for the satisfaction of finishing—and yet they were official entrants (Higdon 1968, 42).

Association with well-known upper-status individuals enhanced the social appeal of jogging. In October 1964, an article by Hal Higdon in *Today's Health* cited as joggers the former astronaut John Glenn, *Sports Illustrated* editors Gwilym Brown and Andrew Crichton, the television actor Richard Chamberlain, and Michigan governor George Romney (36–37). In its 25 December 1967 issue, *U.S. News & World Report* documented the popularity of jogging regimens among the nation's political leaders, including Secretary of the Interior Stewart L. Udall, Senator Joseph D. Tydings, Senator William Proxmire, and Representative Henry S. Reuss (49). In 1968, Kenneth Cooper published *Aerobics,* another affirmation of the health-giving properties of jogging.

As upper-status fitness runners entered the marathon, they found suitable heroes in the New England dynasty of John J. Kelley, Ambrose Burfoot, and William Rodgers. Well-educated, literary, introspective, and essentially a loner, yet generous with his running ability and knowledge, Kelley served as the ideal of the marathoner. He had won the Yonkers Marathon, the AAU National Marathon Championship, a record eight straight times from 1956 through 1963. He was nationally respected among track fans, and that was important because many of the new fitness runners had been school competitors and continued to follow the sport. Kelley coached Ambrose Burfoot, the Wesleyan University senior who won the Boston Marathon in 1968, the first American winner since Kelley himself in 1957.

Burfoot's victory reinforced the appeal of the event for upper-

John J. Kelley, winning the 1958 AAU National Championship at Yonkers, New York. Photograph courtesy of John J. Kelley.

status runners. In 1968 both the Boston *Herald Traveler* (Mahoney 1968) and the *New York Times* (Cady 1968) sports page headlines referred to "Burfoot of Wesleyan," connecting the prestigious Wesleyan University and the marathon victory. Burfoot, in turn, encouraged his roommate William Rodgers to run long distances. Rodgers recalls, "After we ran together for a while, Amby started telling me I'd be a good marathoner. . . . His influence on me was really major" (1980, 35). After college, Burfoot served in the Peace Corps in El Salvador. This choice defines his personality: Burfoot is the epitome of the unselfish, caring communitarian. He guided Rodgers's training at Wesleyan, he loaned Frank Shorter a pair of running shoes for the 1968 Olympic Trials mar-

Jock Semple with Amby Burfoot, winner of the 1968 Boston Athletic Association Marathon, in front of the crowd at the finish line. Photograph by Jeff Johnson, courtesy of Jeff Johnson.

athon, and he still maintains a warm friendship with his old coach, John J. Kelley. A former textbook writer, Amby Burfoot is now executive editor of *Runner's World*. Tall and slender, with a mop of curly brown hair, Amby still looks like the college student who won the Boston Marathon. The only difference is the addition of a thick brown beard.

By the late 1960s the presence of fitness runners heightened differentiation in the marathon; the event now comprised two races. In the elite race a group of select runners competed among themselves for the top positions and awards. In the mass race the remainder of the runners tried for more personal goals, such as breaking three hours (Lipsyte 1968). In coming the decades specialization within the marathon would continue to develop. In 1964 women's and masters' road races appeared in Baltimore (Williams and Darman 1978, 211). The concept of masters' events for men over forty years old quickly achieved national acceptance; eventually, marathons would have a masters' category. The RRCA Women's Cross-Country Championship started in 1965 as a closed competition; at 2.5 miles, it was longer than the acceptable AAU distances for women (Williams and Darman 1978, 212). Gradually, more and longer runs for women appeared. When women entered marathons, they would run alongside men over the same course but in their own race.

Beyond the official categories there are infinite possibilities for redefining the parameters of a race around one's own capability. The sociologist Jeffrey Nash has described recreational runners' conversations about differences in course, age, weather, and conditioning, in order to interpret a performance as an "eventful experience" (1979, 207). For example, a runner could hope to complete a race in a faster time this year than last. A slower finishing time did not necessarily mean failure; it could easily be explained by adverse weather conditions, little time to train, or other factors.

Nash stipulated that the staging of a road race should allow for all levels of participation; the bureaucracy must formally acknowledge the more subjective parameters of accomplishment (1979, 207). In the 1960s the Road Runners Club of America established a system of awards based on competition within age groups (Hartshorne 1971, 66). A fifty-year-old runner might finish a race behind the pack of younger runners, but ahead of every other runner over the age of forty-nine. If the race results were compiled by age group, the runner would win in the fifty and older category.

The RRCA designed competitions and programs to give runners at every level a sense of accomplishment. Race officials awarded both trophies and merchandise prizes at gatherings after the race. In races of less than marathon distance, these were often social events where seasoned runners and their families renewed friendships and new participants found conviviality and acceptance. Among Charles Robbins' "Hints for Better Road Races" (1971) was the suggestion that new runners would be drawn to races where, in addition to overall awards, there were special prizes for local runners, for high school runners, and for the lead runner at a certain checkpoint on the course. The RRCA, maintaining a system of standards for the non-elite but competitive runner, awarded certificates in first, second, and veterans' classes, based on three performances at the standard time for each class within twelve months (*RRC Footnotes*, Feb. 1964, 8–9). For beginning fitness runners, the RRCA Personal Fitness Program gave awards based on mileage goals, regardless of speed.

To interpret the race as an eventful experience, the individual runners had to be educated in the environment and mores of running as well as in the techniques of training. This education was first available through *Long Distance Log* and a few basic training manuals: Arthur Lydiard and Garth Gilmour's *Run to the Top* (1967) and Percy Wells Cerutty's *Middle-Distance Running* (1964). "This is the book I grew up with," Amby Burfoot said of Fred Wilt's *How They Train* (1959). Biographies of great athletes provided training schedules and general conditioning advice but were primarily of an inspirational nature; one example is Alan Trengove's *The Herb Elliott Story* (1961).

Inspirational biographies, sports fiction, and the working-class history of the marathon gave rise to a mythology of running in which the long-distance runner symbolized autonomy. Allen Guttmann examines such "Fictive Runners" in *From Ritual to Record*. One of Guttmann's examples is Colin Smith, hero of Alan Sillitoe's 1959 novella, *The Loneliness of the Long-Distance Runner*. Smith is a working-class youth incarcerated in a British correctional institution, where the warden encourages Smith's running ability in the hope he will win a national competition. But Smith stops just before the finish line; according to Guttmann, "He refuses the victory asked of him by his oppressors and he triumphs morally over those who have deprived and injured and humiliated him" (1978, 158). Sillitoe's novella affirmed running as a way to validate personal identity in a mass society.

A new national publication appeared in January 1966: *Distance Running News*, started by Bob Anderson with help from his friend Dave Zimmerman. In an October 1968 editorial, Anderson, a high school senior who had gotten interested in long-distance running, told how he had contacted Ted Corbitt, Arne Richards, and Browning Ross for advice and the names of people who would write articles (3). In 1970, *Distance Running News* became *Runner's World*. *Runner's World* writers encouraged participation in marathoning. The new editor, Joe

Henderson of *Track and Field News*, expected a wide range of ages and abilites among readers: "Five-minute milers and three-hour marathoners, too, have intriguing stories to tell, and they're just as welcome on our stage" (*Runner's World*, Jan. 1970, 1, 7).

Joe Henderson's *Long Slow Distance: The Humane Way to Train* (1969) bridged the gap between fitness joggers and competitive runners by suggesting a training program that emphasized mileage more than speed. Later in the 1970s, George Sheehan (1975) and James Fixx (1977) wrote books that combined sound advice with autogenous inspirational text in the manner of the old biographies of great runners. Sheehan and Fixx were recreational runners; their books sanctioned the serious approach that weekend runners brought to their avocation. Sheehan once wrote, "Give me an hour's run and I can rival Aquinas in contemplation and handle the great Sam Johnson in conversation" (1973).

The RRCA had its own newsletter, which had become a quarterly, *RRC Footnotes*, in 1962. The journal was virtually suspended from 1965 until 1973, when publication resumed with assistance from the United States Track and Field Federation, the NCAA umbrella organization (Williams and Darman 1978, 210, 214–15). By then the RRCA also had received Allied Body status within the AAU. The RRCA policy of cooperation with both the NCAA and the AAU strengthened the long-distance administrative structure. In 1969 the USTFF had taken over publication and distribution of *Long Distance Log*, an arrangement indicative of the importance of the RRCA; Browning Ross was now chairman of the National AAU Long Distance Running Committee and had been offered assistance by Carl Cooper, executive director of the USTFF. *Long Distance Log* ceased publication with its November/December 1975 issue; *Footnotes* continues as the quarterly publication of the Road Runners Club of America.

The number of marathoners grew dramatically because the RRCA provided a meaningful experience for every level of runner, a competition ladder to help recreational runners achieve greater competence, and an information network available to anyone with an interest in running. *Runner's World* identified marathon participants as urbanized, well-educated, and prestigiously employed; the magazine cited New England, California, and Oregon as centers of mass running activity (Cohen 1974; Henderson 1974). Companies began sponsoring road races as a form of advertising (Coleman 1978). The Nike/Oregon Track Club Marathon, sponsored by Blue Ribbon Sports, began September 1972. The Cherry Blossom Ten Mile presented by the District of Columbia Road Runners Club, began in March 1973; financed by an insurance company, the race became a classic event that did not charge entry fees (Krise and Squires 1982, 213–14).

Marathons capitalized on a wide variety of environments. Marathons with splendid natural settings, such as the Avenue of Giants Marathon, run through an ancient redwood forest, provided an important component of satisfaction for recreational runners. The organizers of the Cherry Blossom Ten Mile understood that the beautiful trees lining the course enhanced the sport experience for many runners (Raitz 1995, ix). Marathon runners were part of a generation that yearned not only for the rural past but also for "a sense of ethnic attachment" (Polenberg 1980, 145). In the 1970s many third-generation Americans willingly identified themselves with an ethnic group (243–47). The New York City Marathon wound through old immigrant neighborhoods when the race became a city-wide event in 1976. Within a few years multiculturalism and ethnic awareness distinguished the course. "Bay Ridge spirit, Spanish *salsa*, Greenpoint *gemütlichkeit*, and Harlem soul are highlights marathoners will long remember," asserted an article presenting the history and culture of Brooklyn's Hasidic Jewish community to the New York City Marathon entrants who would run through it (Cody 1982, 24).

Recreational runners wanted to race with the best; world- and national-class runners drew the crowds to enter or watch road races. The cost of underwriting a race included prizes, refreshments, relief stations, and the expenses of the name athletes brought in for the event. Competing for the few top runners, sponsors and race directors inflated athletes' expense money, which was officially intended only to cover the cost of food, lodging, and travel. The excess became "under-the-table" money, payment for appearance, a violation of AAU rules. The clandestine payments undercut the standard of amateurism and the power of the AAU (Krise and Squires 1982, 211–12).

The situation had become so acute by 1971 that Bob Hersh, writing in *Track and Field News*, proposed open payments to United States track athletes. Frank Shorter recalled foreign athletes who anticipated direct payments at European track meets in 1969, the first time he competed abroad. Americans earned a few extra dollars by manipulating travel funds. "I would go out to California, say, from New York for two or three meets, and I would get one or two plane tickets for other meets, and then I would cash these in" (Shorter 1984, 183). The quotation in Shorter's book is taken from his testimony before the President's Commission on Olympic Sports in 1975. Shorter's forthrightness jeopardized his chance to participate in the 1976 Olympics until he received legal assistance to "clarify" his statements (Shorter 1984, 192–94).

Sports equipment and shoe company deals with athletes were rampant by the 1976 Montreal Olympics. According to an unauthorized history of Nike by J. B. Strasser and Laurie Becklund, on 9 June 1976, Frank Shorter signed a $15,000 deal with Blue Ribbon Sports (the corporate name was changed to Nike, Inc., in 1978) to wear Nike shoes (1991, 246). Shorter never found a pair of Nikes that fit quite right; on 31 July 1976, wearing Tiger shoes, he placed second in the 1976 Montreal Olympic Marathon (247). Waldemar Cierpinski of East Germany was first.

The high priority given international sport by other members of the Olympic community, and the entry of many new nations, had pushed Olympic performances by the United States into relative deficiency. Appointed by the President, a Commission on Olympic Sports attended the 1976 Olympic Games as part of their study to determine the causes of steadily declining achievement by the United States in international sports—the United States won six gold medals in track and field in 1976, the same inadequate total as in 1972. The Commission analyzed thirty sports, including track and field, and thirteen multisport organizations. They concluded that poor organization, internecine squabbling, and erratic funding were the major obstacles to optimum performance by American athletes. The Commission also found the lack of programs for athletes not affiliated with colleges led to weaknesses in those sports that are mostly the province of older athletes, such as fencing and long-distance running. As fundamental to improving track-and-field performances, the Commission recommended the establishment of an organization responsible only for track, field, cross-country running, long-distance running, and race walking events (*Final Report* 1977, 11–12, 233–34).

The Amateur Sports Act passed by Congress on 8 November 1978 named the United States Olympic Committee as the central sports organization and created a new, single-sport bureaucracy for athletics (*Amateur Sports Act of 1978*, 371–95). In September 1979, the Athletics Congress (TAC) replaced the Amateur Athletic Union in track and field and related sports. TAC was much the same organization as the AAU, with many of the same people; Ollan Cassell, former president of the AAU, was now both executive director of TAC and the United States representative on the International Amateur Athletic Federation. Both the NCAA and the RRCA were TAC constituencies (*The Athletics Congress/USA Record*, fall 1986, 2). Athletes' funding, both sanctioned and illicit, was the first challenge for TAC.

Road racing had become so popular that long-distance runners now commanded higher appearance fees than track athletes. In 1979 the premier United States marathon runner, Bill Rodgers, along with Greg Meyer and Herb Lindsay, formed the Association of Road Racing Athletes (ARRA). Joan Benoit, Frank Shorter, and other top-level runners joined the group, choosing Don Kardong, fourth in the 1976 Montreal Olympic Marathon, as president. The ARRA wanted a system of direct payments to athletes for performance, rather than "under-the-table" money. TAC suggested a circuit of prize-money races in which athletes' clubs would hold the payments in trust, releasing funds to the athletes as needed for training and living expenses. But the ARRA boycotted the first and only Athletics Congress prize-money race, a 10-kilometer event with $50,000 in prize money, sponsored by Diet Pepsi on 4 October 1980. Athletes wanted more influence in the administration of their sport, and the ARRA set up its own circuit (Rosner 1983, 74; Moore 1981, 40, 43).

The first ARRA event, the 15-kilometer Cascade Run-off on 29 July 1981, subsidized by Nike, also offered $50,000 in prize money (Moore 1981, 43). A number of the top road runners entered the race and finished high enough to receive cash awards. All were notified to appear before a hearing by the Athletics Congress on the revocation of their amateur status. Only Herb Lindsay, the second-place finisher, appeared before TAC. Bob Stone, Lindsay's attorney as well as Frank Shorter's, suggested a trust fund variation, which TAC eventually approved: an agreement between the athlete and any private trustee, such as a bank, that would hold the funds and release them to the athlete in accordance with rules set up by TAC. After approval by the IAAF, the system was enacted in 1982 (Cassell 1984, 4-5).

Road racing athletes had forced the IAAF to redefine amateurism, permitting United States athletes not affiliated with colleges financial assistance comparable to university- and state-funded competitors. The influence of the few top-level athletes had been augmented by the popular backing of the middle-class marathon participants; at this time the RRCA had about 100,000 registered members in 376 clubs in 49 states, and there were approximately 25,000,000 American participant runners overall (Kokesh 1982; Tinsley 1982). Government, medical, and social approbation got them jogging. The Road Runners Club of America brought recreational runners into the administrative structure, involved them in the politics of the sport bureaucracy, and educated them in the needs of athletes who would represent America in international competition. In the words of Aldo Scandurra, "Participation was the foundation of long-distance running" (1981, 17).

9

The "Visible Hand" on the Footrace

On 1 April 1978, Perrier, marketer of bottled water, cosponsored a 10,000 meter Central Park road race with Bloomingdale's department store. Bloomingdale's staff distributed race tank tops and T-shirts at a check-in held in the store's new running wear department. "Can't we get these people to move any faster?" a Road Runners official reportedly asked a Bloomingdale's sales clerk, as runners wavered in their choice between the tank tops and the T-shirts. "How can you possibly give the Bloomingdale's customer a fashion decision to make and expect them to make it quickly?" the clerk replied (Amdur 1978a, C8).

In the 1970s, Bloomingdale's set national trends by serving the interests of young, upwardly-mobile, fashion-conscious New Yorkers, many of whom lived in the Upper East Side neighborhood of the department store. Bloomingdale's chose its merchandise to meet their demands and tailored its marketing strategies to make shopping a leisure-time pursuit. Baby Boomers came to Bloomingdale's on Saturdays to see the newest fashions, furniture, and foods, and to meet one another (Traub 1993, 118–19, 142). By the early 1980s, many of the consumers that Bloomingdale's so assiduously courted would spend Saturday in Central Park running a five-mile race or a twenty-mile training course and socializing. The marketing of the marathon footrace to the people of New York City changed shoppers into joggers, moved affluent young professionals from Bloomingdale's into Central Park, and turned the New York Road Runners Club into a multimillion-dollar business (New York Charities 1985, 1).

During the 1970s innovations and changes in the New York City Marathon served the purposes of managerial capitalism, what Alfred Chandler terms the "visible hand," which used capital and technology to meet a demand that was as much created by road racing administrators and sponsors as determined by the market (1977, 498). The New York City Marathon became a business enterprise, which, Chandler explains, "did not . . . replace the market as the primary force in generating goods and services" but did "take over from the market the coordination and integration of the flow of goods and services" (1977, 11). In the early 1980s, New York State gave the New York Road Runners Club not-for-profit corporation status and registered the club's financial statements, making them public records. These financial statements show "a hierarchy of salaried executives" and indicate the growth and presence of "distinct operating units," both characteristics that Chandler notes in modern business enterprise (1977, 1).

The New York City Marathon led the way for a nationwide change, not only in number of participants but also in restructuring the marathon to validate the presence of many runners of little athletic potential. Before the "marathon boom" of the 1970s, marathoners were competitors who hoped, if not to win, at least to place in the top ten or compete for age-group awards. Marathon courses were often closed after four hours, and the times of late finishers frequently went unrecorded (Higdon 1979, 57). When the New York City Marathon began in 1970, there were 127 starters and 55 finishers, only 40 of whom completed the course in under four hours (Kleinerman 1970). In the 1981 New York City Marathon, about one-third of the field, over 4,000 people, finished after four hours. Race officials stayed to record their times, crowds remained to cheer them, and each finisher was awarded a marathon medal.

The New York City Marathon presented by the New York Road Runners Club, although part of the national RRCA network, derived from specifically local circumstances. Increased accessibility to the Central Park roads had expanded long-distance running in New York

City. The identity of Central Park as public space had been ambiguous for years; in the nineteenth and early twentieth centuries, the working classes were subtly discouraged from using the park by specific rules governing proper behavior and by general inaccessibility. In the 1960s, Thomas P. F. Hoving, Commissioner of Parks, revised park policy to accommodate mass events such as band concerts, artistic "happenings," and political protests. He closed the park drives to automobile traffic on summer Sundays in 1966, to the delight of strollers, joggers, and runners (Rosenzweig and Blackmar 1992, 5–7, 489–94). Recognizing the national trend, the Commissioner of Recreation opened twenty jogging tracks throughout the city in the spring of 1968. The path circling the Central Park reservoir was resurfaced, attracting new joggers from the wealthy neighborhoods surrounding the park (Schumach 1968).

Following the example of open invitation set by the Central Park administration, the New York City Marathon found ways to accommodate and sanction a wide variety of reasons for entering a 26.2–mile footrace. Many people ran for good health or to relieve tension. The New York City Marathon provided a festival atmosphere and symbols, such as finishers' medals and race T-shirts, that assured all who actually completed the course, no matter how slowly, that they were part of an elite group. New marathon runners often perceived the event less as a competition than as a ritual whose subjective reward was spiritual achievement, "a special sensation that attunes them closer to the world yet also raises their consciousness and provides a sense of elation" (Macauley 1976).

A single entrepreneur, Fred Lebow, seized control of the New York City Marathon in the mid-1970s (Milvy 1977a) and enhanced its potential to attract corporate funding by increasing the number of participants, regardless of their athletic ability. A study of the 1980 New York City Marathon showed the runners to be mostly upper-status men and women (Curtis and McTeer 1981, 79). The history of the New York City Marathon from 1970 to 1980 suggests that the marathon's directors consciously sought a comparatively affluent population for the purpose of acquiring corporate sponsors. In creating new services and in presenting the marathon to appeal to upper-status, recreational runners, Lebow changed the nature of the New York Road Runners Club, administrators of the New York City Marathon, from a volunteer organization serving the athletic interests of its members to a business enterprise with a staff of salaried managers (O'Donnell, 1983, 37).

The new upper-status runners were most concerned with personal well-being. Having time and money to expend on their health, they were likely to be informed on the matter. Their interest in marathon running was often ascribed to the marathon's alleged health-enhancing properties (Rader 1991, 258–60). A 1977 article in *Fortune* magazine reported that factors beyond the cardiovascular benefits of exercise stirred the running interest among corporate officers. According to proselytes, "running has improved their sex lives, made them stop smoking, cured hangovers, jet lag, ulcers, constipation, alcoholism, depression, and insomnia, and prevented the common cold" (Wellemeyer 1977, 58).

The association of running with such values as health, fitness, and even feminism made marathoning attractive to upper-status individuals. The positive correlation of health consciousness with social status explains the findings of higher-status backgrounds among marathoners surveyed for a 1981 sociological study of the sport (Curtis and McTeer 1981, 79). The new women marathoners contributed to the overall change in socioeconomic status among runners. Feminism was mainly a middle-class protest movement, concerned with bettering women's educations, opening the professions to them, and protecting their property after marriage. These opportunities were assumed to be for all women, but often only middle- and upper-class women could take advantage of them (Banks 1981, 250). Similarly, upper-status women would be most likely to have the leisure for a time-consuming, financially unproductive pastime such as marathon running. Certainly members of the New York Road Runners Club were predominantly upper-middle class. A 1983 study of its 21,696 members revealed that almost 90 percent were college graduates and that their average income was $40,000 (Litsky 1983, C6).

During the 1960s and 1970s, the New York Road Runners Club became the pivotal section of the Road Runners Club of America by moving into all three of the components that Stephen Hardy identifies as constituting the "sport product": the game form, the goods, and the services. Hardy defines the game form as "the rules defining the way the game is played," adding, "Of course, anyone can make up a game. . . . But this is of little consequence until rule-making is organized and controlled by particular groups" (1986, 17). The New York Road Runners Club was one of those groups. It extended its authority over the game form by standardizing course measurement methods (Scandurra 1981, 12). When Theodore Corbitt, the NYRRC'S first president, published *Measuring Road Racing Courses,* the NYRRC supplied expertise and sanctioning, official confirmation, on course calibration (Chodes 1974, 147).

The second part of the sport product comprises goods. Hardy lists "Balls, goals, sticks, bats, protective equipment and uniforms" as well as facilities, such as running tracks, that are essential to the contest (1986, 19). The New York Road Runners Club was among the pioneers in the use of computerized finish-line equipment for accurately scoring large fields of runners, particularly when several runners would finish at the same time (Milvy 1977, 51–52).

Although sport services are traditionally defined in terms of such social functions as "education, status, military preparation, urban boosterism, political propaganda, and most extensively, entertainment," Hardy adds that special organizations to promote sport and to serve it in ways apart from the game form are also sport services (1986, 18–19). One such special organization was the United States Age Group Competition for boys and girls, originated in the New York City area by Ann and Nat Cirulnick, Barry Geisler, and Joe Kleinerman. This was a significant program for women, because mothers were encouraged to jog with their children in noncompetitive Fun Runs. According to Aldo Scandurra, "This was the breakthrough that led to long distance running scheduled programs for women" (1981, 16).

Women runners may have been the first to present the possibilites of the marathon as a profit-making enterprise. In 1972, Fred Lebow of the New York Road Runners Club was approached by the public relations firm of S. C. Johnson & Son, Inc., about staging a marathon for women. Lebow recognized the attractiveness of a women-only marathon but was also aware of the scarcity of women capable of running 26.2 miles. Instead he suggested, and the sponsor accepted, a women's road race of six miles. Lebow was elected president of the NYRRC in 1972, a position once voluntary but now salaried. He left his career as a

Fred Lebow (left) as president of the New York
Road Runners Club, cheers on former president Ted Corbitt (right). Photograph courtesy
of the New York Road Runners Club.

textile consultant in the late 1970s to devote all his time to directing the
NYRRC (Lebow 1984, 61–62).

Fred Lebow was born Fishel Lebowitz in Arad, Romania, in 1932.
He grew up in a part of Eastern Europe where a number of ethnic
groups had their own enclaves within the national borders created in
the aftermath of World War I. Lebow's family were Orthodox Jews. His
father was a produce merchant, and the young Lebow accompanied
him in dealing with the various communities on his rounds (Lebow
1984, 53). During the Nazi invasion the family split up and was hidden
by friends. When the Soviets occupied Romania, most of the family

went to Israel. Fred Lebow wandered around Europe, became an Irish stateless citizen, and eventually emigrated to the United States. He worked in sales and in improvisational theater, became a United States citizen, and wound up in New York City's garment industry (57–60). In his mid-forties, Fred Lebow was a tall red-haired man with a vaguely Latin accent whose every action, every gesture seemed to come from a need to release energy. No longer a rootless individual, Lebow was totally committed to the marathon. Of his early years, Lebow wrote, "It was challenging, fun in a way, to live by my wits when I was fifteen and sixteen years old. My brother was very studious. But I began to go in other directions" (59). Perhaps that was the appeal of marathon administration for Lebow; the constant crises, the interminable negotiations with sponsors and city departments and elite runners.

In promoting the women's six-mile road race, Lebow handed out entry blanks and flyers all over Manhattan, occasionally taping them to light poles. He encouraged six Playboy Bunnies to run in the race and recruited the patrons of a rock-music nightclub. The public relations firm mailed thousands of invitations to women in local high schools and colleges. The result of all this feverish activity was a field of seventy-eight women (Lebow 1984, 45–46).

This was the first running of what would become a prestigious annual 10,000 meter competition: the women's Mini-Marathon, popularly known as "the Mini." By the late 1970s the event would draw over 6,000 participants to a single 6.2-mile race, but in 1972 it was memorable mainly for its farcical elements. The sponsor insisted that the runners wear identical white T-shirts with their numbers stamped below the name of the product, "Crazy Legs," a women's shaving cream. A male runner decided to pace the first woman, Jackie Dixon, through the race, leading what Tom Derderian (husband of the second woman, Charlotte Lettis) said "looked more like a comic refugee regiment slowly plodding around the park in identical jerseys" (Derderian 1977, 49). Dixon was denied her right to break a tape; instead, she had to burst through a huge paper banner advertising Crazy Legs, her win subjugated to the needs of the sponsor's product (Lettis 1972). Promoting long-distance races for women was going to require even more effort and imagination—or perhaps a little less.

The New York City Marathon received financial support from

Olympic Airways in 1973 and 1974 in return for race-day publicity. In 1975 the marathon lost that sponsor and had to rely on numerous small donations from members. The *New York Times* commented on the incongruity of the loss of corporate sponsorship "at a time when more New Yorkers than ever are embracing a run-for-fun philosophy" (Amdur 1975). In responding to its need to attract sponsorship, the New York Road Runners Club became an entrepreneurial organization, "one with a high motivation," Philip Kotler explains in *Marketing for Nonprofit Organizations,* "and a capability to identify new opportunities and convert them into successful businesses" (1975, 113).

The New York City Marathon had remained an inconspicuous event since it began in 1970. In 1975, although the New York City Marathon was also the Women's National AAU Championship, it still was given very little attention. Horseback riders, bicyclists, pedestrians, and dogs freely crossed the runners' lane during the race. The marathon was a sport eccentricity to the media; marathon coverage on one television station devoted most footage to a chance spectator who shouted, "Look at all these crazy people!" (Ullyot 1976, 145–47). The directors of the New York City Marathon needed some way to enhance the prestige of their event and to associate marathon running with serious achievement.

The New York City Marathon's limited spectatorship and low number of participants (just over five hundred in 1974 and 1975) influenced sponsors' perceptions of the marathon as an event that would have little commercial value. On the other hand, joggers and, increasingly, competitive long-distance runners were already considered upper-status individuals, important as consumers (*U.S. News and World Report,* 25 Dec. 1967, 49). Frank Shorter's gold medal in the 1972 Olympic Marathon was a form of testimonial; the twenty-four-year-old Yale-educated law student provided a role model for young professionals interested in marathoning (Prokop 1976, 46). Affluent earners could, and would, be enticed to recreational running through careful presentation of the services, or benefits, of the sport: cardiovascular fitness, weight control, and the companionship of other upper-status persons (Rosenfeld 1977).

In order to be recruited for the marathon, the well-to-do had to be made aware that it was an attractive, accessible event that offered opportunities for achievement. Two of the recent United States Olympic marathoners competed in the 1976 New York City Marathon. Frank Shorter had won the silver medal in the 1976 Olympics; Bill Rodgers, winner of the 1975 Boston Marathon, had placed fortieth. Both were personable men in their late twenties and graduates of highly-regarded universities—fine examples of marathon runners for affluent earners in their twenties and thirties (Amdur 1976a).

With Bicentennial commemorations under way throughout the country, the New York Road Runners Club proposed that the upcoming New York City Marathon be taken out of Central Park and run on the streets of New York, through all five boroughs, as part of the city's Bicentennial celebration. Abraham Beame, mayor of New York City, and Percy Sutton, president of Manhattan Borough, endorsed the five-borough marathon, and the Rudin family, founders of a major New York City real-estate firm, offered $25,000 to sponsor the race. The event picked up other sponsors through Lebow's promotional efforts, including Manufacturers Hanover Trust Company, *New Times* magazine, Finnair, and Bonne Bell cosmetics. The New York Academy of Sciences' "Conference on the Marathon" was scheduled for just after the marathon, and advertisements for the marathon included announcements of the conference that implied a connection between the New York City Marathon and medical approval. As the race drew near, colorful posters appeared all over the city. Entrants poured in, half of whom had never run a marathon before (Brock 1976, 22).

The success of the 1976 New York City Marathon was to a great extent due to Rodgers and Shorter. The guaranteed appearances of famous, world-class runners attracted the attention of the media that publicized the race and of sponsors who paid for the banners, T-shirts, and other paraphernalia. The acclaim and the spectacle were necessary to draw enough spectators to provide sufficient public relations value to the event's sponsors. "Under-the-table" money underscored the vital role of the top runners (Illingworth 1985, 129).

The payment of athletes by the New York City Marathon during the 1970s is difficult to trace, partly because of the manner in which the payments were made. In 1979, Jon Anderson, 1973 winner of the Boston Marathon, ran in the New York City Marathon and finished ninth. Peter Roth, treasurer of the New York Road Runners Club, arranged for Anderson to receive a $1,500 check from Great Waters of France (Perrier), one of the sponsors of the New York City Marathon. He did not give lectures or appearances; in a January 1982 letter to *Runner* magazine, Anderson wrote that he "simply ran the race and finished ninth" (6). Officially, there was nothing but Anderson's statement to connect the New York City marathon with the payment of an athlete in violation of the amateur code. Bill Rodgers probably received a cash payment in 1976 (Lebow 1984, 15). Rodgers was uncomfortable with the precarious nature of under-the-table payments; in 1977 he and his wife opened a running store and soon after started a clothing line (Rodgers 1980, 285). Both the Bill Rodgers Running Center and the clothing line still provide income to Rodgers (Raia 1997).

Bill Rodgers won the New York City Marathon in 1976, 1977, 1978, and 1979 and won the Boston Marathon in 1975, 1978, 1979, and 1980. Rodgers entered Wesleyan College as a cross-country runner in 1966; his teammate Amby Burfoot introduced him to long distances and essentially became his first marathon coach (Rodgers 1980, 32, 35). But Rodgers quit running in the turmoil of 1970; he was against the Vietnam War, "politically, morally" (32), and concerned with achieving conscientious objector status. After two years of aimlessly marking time, he returned to running and later began a graduate program for a degree in special education (44). Rodgers dropped out of the Boston Marathon in 1973 but finished fourteenth in 1974 and set an American record of 2:09:55 in 1975 (45). He dominated United States marathon running in the late 1970s; his only major disappointment was his fortieth-place finish in the 1976 Olympic Marathon.

Well into his thirties Rodgers appeared to be a boy in repose, and that boyish quality, along with his impressive long-distance performances, contributed to making him the symbol of running for the Baby Boomers in the late 1970s. Rodgers continued to compete through his forties, bringing attention and sponsorship to masters runners. As he aproached fifty, he wrote a book on continuing running throughout life. His last serious attempt to win a competitive marathon was the 1992 Vietnam International Marathon (Raia 1997).

Rodgers was paid $2,000 for the 1976 New York City Marathon, according to Lebow, and Shorter was also "treated . . . fairly" (Illingworth 1985, 129). Although the more than two thousand entrants made the

Bill Rodgers, four-time winner of both the
Boston Athletic Association Marathon and the
New York City Marathon. Photograph by Jeff
Johnson, courtesy of Jeff Johnson.

1976 New York City Marathon the world's largest, in many ways this
race seemed to be aimed at runners who would enter the marathon in
1977 and after. The first five-borough marathon provided a general
awareness of the event to New York City residents whose neighborhoods lined the route, and especially to those with the leisure time to
train for next year's race. The 1976 New York City Marathon attempted
to target the upscale market of health-conscious joggers through the
personal appearances of Shorter and Rodgers; inhabitants of the affluent Upper East Side saw two twenty-nine-year-old Olympians racing,
followed by ordinary, thirtyish men and women much like themselves.

Two days after the marathon, an article appeared in the *New York Times* entitled "Want to Run Marathon? Take It Easy, Doctor Warns Hopeful Novices." The piece contained extensive advice on training and referred to the Academy of Sciences conference. The author concluded with a statement from Fred Lebow that the city would like to continue the marathon as an annual, five-borough event. According to Lebow, "The New York Road Runners Club raised $40,000 from various sponsors, but still will wind up with a $20,000 deficit for the race." This article summed up the situation nicely: Lebow was calling out to next year's runners and next year's sponsors (Amdur 1976b).

Other events surrounding the 1976 New York City Marathon marked a major change in the New York Road Runners Club from a democratic organization to one in which all authority was vested in Lebow. According to Hardy, when a sport is not subsidized by the state or by a philanthropic agency, it is important that the sport have an entrepreneur willing to engage in profit-seeking, risk-taking, and other innovative activity, such as introducing a new service or opening a new market (1986, 20). Lebow fit this description as he guided the New York City Marathon to accepting ever-larger fields and did much of the negotiating himself directly with sponsors and city officials (Lebow 1984, 63, 69). Paul Milvy, a biophysicist affiliated with the Mount Sinai School of Medicine, was a runner who assisted the NYRRC with technical matters. In a letter to the *Road Runners Club New York Association* newsletter, Milvy, then a member of the NYRRC Executive Committee, decried Lebow's administrative practices as undemocratic. Milvy pointed out that neither the president nor the executive board had actually been elected by the membership, that authority to act on matters of NYRRC procedure or race administration was arbitrarily given and rescinded, that "decisions may well be made after careful thought, yet all too likely they are countermanded by the President's personal whim" (1977b).

The 4 June 1977 10,000 meter Women's Mini-Marathon, which increased to 2,000 entrants from 408 in 1976, indicated the direction the marathon and the NYRRC would be taking. First, finish line timing and scoring procedures were computerized to enable the staff to accurately score four or five finishers per second (Milvy 1977a). This 10,000 meter women's race became a test run for the technology that would permit a greatly increased field at the upcoming marathon. The modification had marked commercial value; larger fields were important to sponsors, because they meant that many more people would be exposed to advertising for sponsors' products. Second, the directors of the Mini-Marathon improved public and press relations. According to the *Runner's World* coverage of the event, the 1977 Mini-Marathon's success could be attributed "to a bit of marketing genius" (Derderian 1977, 49). The *Runner's World* article gave an account of Fun Runs and clinics for members of the press, mass mailings of schedules and flyers, and advertisements of the race in upscale magazines such as *Vogue* and *Harper's*, as well as in magazines geared to young adults with significant disposable incomes, such as *Seventeen* and *Glamour*. The April 1977 edition of *Vogue* (136–37) and the May 1977 edition of *Mademoiselle* (92–95) carried articles by doctors explaining the benefits of jogging.

By August five thousand entrants had been accepted for the upcoming 1977 New York City Marathon. The marathon course had been changed slightly so that now the runners would travel up First Avenue past the trendy singles bars. Perrier became a marathon sponsor, and on 23 October 1977, the young, upwardly mobile professionals of the late 1970s became the objects of Perrier's American advertising campaign as they watched Bill Rodgers and Garry Bjorklund struggling for the lead on First Avenue (Lebow 1984, 82–83).

Bill Rodgers won again the next year and appeared on the cover of *Sports Illustrated* on 30 October 1978 during a New York City newspaper strike. His racing number, along with the printed name of a marathon sponsor, Manufacturers Hanover, was clearly visible. *Forbes* magazine quoted Vice President Charles McCabe of Manufacturers Hanover as saying, "You can't buy advertising like that" (O'Donnell 1983, 37). But even without *Sports Illustrated* and the newspaper strike, sponsors like Perrier were reaching a suitable consumer audience through the New York City Marathon. The commemorative T-shirts given to the entrants were ideal for corporate trademarks and other advertising.

The race T-shirts motivated joggers to participate in road events in which they had little chance of winning an award (H. B. Ross 1992). According to the sociologist Jeffrey Nash, "The common practice of awarding T-shirts to all finishers symbolizes the individual conquest of failure" (1979, 212). Running togs became a fashion statement as well, and the commemorative T-shirt implied the wearer was a clean-living individual. While runners and nonrunners alike recognized the social and psychological advantages of wearing a marathon T-shirt (Ullyot 1976, 70), marketing vice-presidents acknowledged the race T-shirt's value as "unsolicited" advertising. "The sight of a smiling corporate vp is not unfamiliar these days at running races," said a 1979 *Advertising Age* article that began with a few paragraphs on the potential of race T-shirts imprinted with a company's name and logo: "All those runners undoubtedly would take those T-shirts home and wear them another day" (Galginaitis 1979).

The journalist Neil Amdur made a connection between the new marathoners and the possibilities for corporate sponsorship. Amdur noted the significance of the New York City Marathon in "changing the image of long-distance running from one of personal struggle to a joyous one shared by an entire city," and, especially, in creating an "expanded constituency" for what was formerly an event of limited participation (Amdur 1978b). Corporations perceived the enormous road racing participant fields as a market comprising middle-class, college-educated consumers who identified with healthy pursuits and the sportsmanship of amateur competition. A 1978 *Runner's World* survey conducted by the market research firm Yankelovich, Skelly, and White indicated that runners were mostly white-collar people with yearly incomes much higher than the national average (*Runner's World*, Dec. 1980, 47). A large part of the sponsoring corporation's image would be determined by the presentation of the New York City Marathon: the overall organization, the facility of procedures, the services offered, and the care of individual runners (Texas 1979, 19; Santry 1979, 12–13).

The New York Road Runners Club was originally concerned with the politics of road racing—developing opportunities for competition, sanctioning races, and representing long-distance runners' interests in a track-dominated athletics culture (NYRRC newsletter [1959?], 1). Administrative and other tasks were carried out through the cooperative efforts of runners and noncompeting members, generally in a private home or temporarily donated office space. When the NYRRC finally obtained its first permanent office in the West Side YMCA, it was intended to be run on a "family basis" with members expected to "drop in to help out" as the need arose (*NYRRC,* spring 1976, 1, 8). But the staging of the first five-borough marathon necessitated the establishment of formal committees, over a dozen of them, each little more than a chairperson dependent on sporadic volunteer help, all under the direct control of Fred Lebow (Milvy 1976). The system was barely viable and often chaotic.

The five-borough marathon required the use of city services, such as police, coordinated by Lebow but clearly under their own direction (Milvy 1976). This set an important precedent as race production became the NYRRC's main product and the various committees achieved increasing autonomy (Lebow 1984, 64, 71). For example, the Medical Committee, chaired by a physician who was a member of the NYRRC, but staffed by volunteer residents, interns, and medical students, was self-contained because of the professional nature of its work. The Medical Committee also filled an important public relations role, as was noted in the minutes of the 25 July 1977 meeting of the Marathon Committee: "If two or three people drop dead then we will be placed in a position of answering a lot of questions. We will have to be able to say that we acted like responsible citizens in allowing people to run twenty-six miles" (Macomber 1977, 3). The Technical Committee, responsible for the finish line structure and timing and recording devices, was another unit that achieved autonomy as a reflection of their highly specialized knowledge and function. As time and road racing progressed, the Technical Committee essentially became "separated from its ownership" (Chandler 1977, 6–10), the members of the NYRRC. By 1980 the NYRRC was renting out its equipment and personnel in consultancy to other races, some far from the area served by the NYRRC. Rather than merely sponsoring an NYRRC race, other organizations could produce their own events by hiring NYRRC technology and expertise (Jahnke 1982; Texas 1979, 16).

A number of established committees shared responsibility for the race within a few years of the first five-borough marathon. Coordinators, salaried managers who developed their own systems of handling different aspects of marathon production and staging, headed the committees. These autonomous units called upon a pool of thousands of NYRRC volunteers for labor. As the systems evolved their own rulebound procedures, the volunteers required formal training for their tasks. In October 1983, *Successful Meetings*, a management periodical, described the bureaucratic experience of volunteering to assist at the New York City Marathon: filling out applications, attending classes, putting in time to gain seniority, and learning new skills required for a promotion. Volunteers received their identification badges, met their supervisors, and mingled with other volunteers at a meeting about two weeks before race day; this social occasion surrounded instructional sessions on race-assistance procedures. Greater responsibility for the volunteer meant additional preparation and education (Adams 1983, 29–30).

In the early days of the NYRRC, members performed race course and finish line tasks, expecting reciprocity when it was their turn to compete as runners. But many of the new volunteers never ran competitively or even assisted in any other NYRRC event. Volunteering became their way of participating in the marathon, a position the NYRRC validated by stressing the "basic, life supportive things" volunteers do for the runners. "How many times do you give someone a drink of water who may get sick or even die without it?" the NYRRC volunteer coordinator asked (Adams 1983, 30). The NYRRC also recognized the volunteers' contributions with awards and small gifts; the most prized were the specially designed "Marathon Volunteer" T-shirts (32).

The New York Road Runners Club now had all the characteristics of a modern business enterprise. As the number of paid employees of the NYRRC grew, the administration of the New York City Marathon became a separate entity that was capable of functioning independently of other NYRRC activities. The New York City Marathon, the NYRRC's state-of-the-art product, could most efficiently be produced by the cooperative effort of a series of autonomous systems run by a professionalized managerial hierarchy using the labor of a controlled work force. Major decisions of the NYRRC, such as the purchase of a building in 1981, promoted the long-term goals of the organization and provided for its stability often before they answered the needs of its athlete constituency (Chandler 1977, 1–10, 107).

Another managerial role of the New York City Marathon, allocating the funds of its wealthy corporate sponsors to the world's greatest runners, was not acknowledged by the city until 1984 (Thomas 1984). Municipal services had been free as long as the New York City Marathon could be considered an amateur event, although the illicit payments that had gone on for years were quite well known; after winning the 1981 New York City Marathon in world record time, Alberto Salazar announced that he made his living from running and preferred under-the-table payments (Amdur 1984). The 1982 New York City Marathon awarded $150,000 in under-the-table payments "with TAC's tacit approval" (Rosner 1983); the men's winner reportedly received $18,000, the women's, $14,000. According to Lebow, Mayor Koch knew of the payments to athletes in 1982: "I even started telling the press off the record that we would probably award between $100,000 and $150,000 in open prize money. But in October [1982] Mayor Koch vetoed the idea. He was worried about appearances of commercialism and wanted to wait and see how the [TAC] plan worked in other places" (Lebow 1984, 150). Race administrators requested TAC sanction for official prize money a few weeks before the 1983 New York City Marathon. The city objected; Henry Stern, the parks commissioner, speaking for Mayor Edward Koch, said, "This is the people's race, the race for everyone. It's a noncommercial event: We don't sell tickets, we don't give prizes, we don't charge for policing it" (Rosner 1983).

New York City could no longer ignore the situation when Fred Lebow's 1984 autobiography revealed that the marathon had paid about $200,000 to athletes in 1983 (Lebow 1984, 192). The City of New York requested $273,800 in payment for the municipal services that supported the marathon in 1984; the amount equaled the total reported prize money, bonuses, and appearance money offered in 1985 (Kardong 1985). The city assessed the New York City Marathon $300,000 in 1985 for services from the Police and Fire Departments; the Departments of Transportation, Sanitation, and Parks and Recreation; the Triborough Bridge and Tunnel Authority; and other municipal entities. Both New York City and the New York City Marathon claimed their services were undercompensated; the New York Road Runners Club hired Economic Research Associates, Inc., to determine the economic benefits of the marathon to New York City (Thomas 1984; Comptroller 1988, p. 5).

In 1988, Economic Research Associates calculated that the New York City Marathon would result in the initial spending of $25,683,530.

This figure reflected expenditures by the runners and their traveling parties on hotels, restaurants, shopping, and entertainment; spectator expenditures; transportation; and advertising and broadcasting fees. As each expenditure prompted additional economic activity, the total economic impact of the 1988 New York City Marathon on the City of New York was calculated to have been $64,208,825. Expenditures by the New York Road Runners Club for the New York City Marathon totaled $3,402,270, offset by revenues from entry and handling fees, bus fees, and sponsors, booth holders, patrons, etc. The marathon budget included $300,000 paid to the city for services estimated at $630,000. The city, having netted $756,000 from various taxes on marathon-generated spending, paid the other $330,000 (Comptroller 1988, 3–4, 16–17). Comptroller Harrison Goldin concluded, "For the 23,000 runners who came from all over the world, the glory of the marathon is unquantifiable; but the race is also a financial boon to the city" (15).

The directors of the New York City Marathon used personal appearances by well-known runners and popular concern with fitness to present their event in a manner that appealed to young, upper-status individuals. Through a change of venue, they modified the game form to make the marathon more accessible. They created auxiliary organizations, sport services, to attract specific groups. They provided sport apparatuses, such as the computerized finish line, which could accommodate the increasing numbers of participants the marathon attracted. As the New York City Marathon grew in size, it became a discrete entity whose continuation was assured as much by its financial contribution to New York City as by the runners, volunteers, and spectators caught up in the once-a-year drama. In the New York City Marathon, managerial capitalism, the "visible hand," united athletic achievement and economic production.

10

Women, the Marathon, and the Corporation

Pikes Peak was the first marathon to have an official women's race. It was held the day before the men's race and consisted only of the 12.5-mile ascent. On 18 August 1962 four women entered, and Mary Guinn, a twenty-nine-year-old physical education teacher in Colorado Springs, won in the record time of 4 hours, 15 minutes. Katherine Heard, age sixty-one, finished second in 5:15:26; Julia Chase finished in 5:46:16; Kathleen Heckt, the 1961 winner, entered but did not finish (*LDL*, Oct. 1962, 12–13; Olsen 1978, 61). The Road Runners Club of America recognized women's right to run long distance at their annual meeting in February 1963 (Williams and Darman 1978, 210–11). On 9 December 1963, two women began the premier West Coast event, the Culver City Marathon, and one of them, Merry Lepper, finished in 3:37:03 (Martin and Gynn 1979, 248).

When Kathrine Switzer challenged the proscription against women in 1967, she ran with a number and tried for an official time in the Boston Athletic Association Marathon. Switzer called media attention to the problem by demanding sanction and equality as a woman marathoner in one of the most prestigious international events. Women were not unwelcome in the Boston Marathon during the 1960s. Back when entrants numbered fewer than one thousand, children and dogs often ran alongside the competitors for a bit; like them, a woman runner would be considered a particularly enthusiastic spectator, carried away by the excitement of the race. As long as she was not an official entrant, as long as her finishing time was not recorded, the woman runner posed no threat and encountered few problems (*NYT*, 19 Apr. 1971, 46).

Switzer first ran the Boston Marathon the year after the founding of the National Organization for Women (NOW) in June 1966. NOW was meant to oppose sexual discrimination in all areas by relying on women's resources and women's potential to effect change (Davis 1991, 66). The movement toward greater athletic opportunities for women derived strength from their need for vocational opportunity. The forces that created NOW would later expand to provide sanction and a pool of potential athletes for the women's marathon (Banks 1981, 212–13). But women came to the marathon for reasons other than athletic competition. The wave of feminism that began in the early 1960s was based in part on the freedom women gained with the birth control pill. Women's insistence on running long distance demonstrated awareness of their physical well-being.

Women's marathoning became part of a feminist attitude toward health care: "self-health," women's assertion of control over their own bodies. In *American Feminism,* Ginette Castro explains that self-health means "unlearning all the distorted truths you have been taught by patriarchal science . . . learning to know your own body through self-examination and self-exploration" (1984, 18–19). In the sense of self-health, the marathon became an opportunity for women to explore their own physical limits of endurance and speed. During the 1970s hundreds of women unlearned the patriarchal belief that they could not run long distances. "A convergence of views occurred in the mid-seventies, as many athletes became feminists and many feminists discovered the importance of sports," according to Allen Guttmann (1991, 209).

Browning Ross and the Road Runners Club of America conducted the first significant bureaucratic advocacy for women's official entry in road races. On Thanksgiving Day 1960, Julia Chase of Groton, Connecticut, was denied entry to the Manchester five-mile road race. Chase was eighteen years old, a first-year student at Smith College, and the New England AAU 880-yard women's champion; John J. Kelley had coached her in the longer distances. In a *Long Distance Log* editorial, Ross said that Chase should have been allowed to run in the men's race if there was no comparable event for women, adding that women in the West competed in such races (Jan. 1961, 22–23). Charles Robbins, now chairman of the Connecticut AAU Long Distance Running Committee, also supported Chase. The next year Chase participated, although she could not officially enter and was not allowed through the finishing chutes (Kuscsik 1977a, 865).

Roberta Gibb Bingay jumped into the field and became the first woman ever to run in and finish the BAA Marathon on 19 April 1966 (Martin and Gynn 1979, 248). Gibb Bingay trained for the 1966 Boston Marathon and ran with the official entrants, but she wore no number and achieved no official time. In a *Boston Globe* interview just before she ran alongside the 1967 Boston Marathon, again without a number, Gibb Bingay was quoted as saying, "The reason I'm running is because a lot of my friends encouraged me to share the feelings of joy I get while running. It's hard to explain. The other runners understand" (18 Apr. 1967, 47). After the race, Gibb Bingay's mother informed the *New York Times*, "Roberta doesn't want to break any barriers. She's not interested in competing against the men. She simply enjoys running with others. I mean, if she were a dancer, she wouldn't want to dance alone in her room, would she?" (20 Apr. 1967, 55).

Kathrine Switzer understood the difference between running alongside the marathon for 26.2 miles and running as an official entrant. Switzer, a journalism student at Syracuse University, entered the 1967 Boston Marathon by sending in an application for "K. Switzer" and having a male runner, her coach and teammate Arnold Briggs, present her health certificate and collect her number. As an occasional runner in the half-mile and mile for the Lynchburg College men's track team, and as an Amateur Athletic Union member, Switzer knew that the AAU prohibited women from competing in any distance over 2.5 miles (Sales 1966). "I think it's time to change the rules. They are archaic. Women can run, and they can still be women and look like women. I think the AAU will begin to realize this and put in longer races for women. . . . I'm glad I ran—you know, equal rights and all" (*NYT*, 23 Apr. 1967b, sec. 5, p. 7).

Tall and beautiful, Kathrine Switzer has fine features and a warm

Kathrine Switzer, who put the power of a transnational corporation behind women's struggle for
their own Olympic Marathon. Photograph courtesy of Kathrine Switzer.

manner that complement rather than contrast with the strength of her
personality. She is a traditionally feminine woman who would have
been successful in any age; in the late twentieth century, her athletic
ability and administrative expertise determined the direction her success would take. In the thirty years following her first Boston Marathon, Switzer continued to compete and to participate in every stage of
the struggle for the highest level of marathon competition, an Olympic
event.

Nina Kuscsik and Sara Mae Berman ran the Boston Marathon for
the first time in 1969, both unofficially. Kuscsik was about thirty, a reg-

istered nurse, the mother of three, and the wife of a financial analyst. She had been an enthusiastic sport participant in roller skating, speed skating, and bicycle racing, activities that were not included, or not included for women, in the Olympic program. Berman, thirty-two, also the mother of three, was introduced to running by her husband, an aerospace engineer (*NYT*, 19 Apr. 1971, 46; Gupte 1971). Berman won the Boston Marathon unofficially in 1969, 1970, and 1971 (Kuscsik 1977a, 868). She also won the first AAU-sanctioned marathon open to women, in Atlantic City on 25 October 1970. Six women members of Road Runners Club of America were allowed to enter because the marathon was a "closed" competition sponsored by the RRCA (Tarnawsky 1971). Sara Mae Berman had drawn up the plans for the women's auxiliary that began in 1965, the same year as the RRCA's first National Women's Cross-Country Championships (Williams and Darman 1978, 208, 211–12). The RRCA also encouraged mothers to run with their young children.

Women runners attracted media attention at the Boston Marathon, but they planned and acted through the New York City Road Runners Club. The feminist movement in New York City was particularly intense and creative (Davis 1991, 6). The New York City Marathon, which has accepted women as official runners since it began in 1970, was held under the auspices of the New York Road Runners Club (a member division of the RRCA) as was a significant "Run for Fun" program. Nat Cirulnick organized the New York area's "Run for Fun" program: "Boys and girls run together, except in championship events, which pleases the girls because they can beat many of the boys" (Cirulnick 1971).

By 1970 women were actively pursuing equal rights at most major races. At the 1970 Bay-to-Breakers, a San Francisco race of approximately eight miles and 1,400 participants, about a dozen women carried placards reading, "AAU Unfair to Women" and "Who Says Women Can't Run?" (Henderson 1971). The next year the AAU raised the distance limit for women to ten miles, and on 23 May 1971, Frances K. Conley won the first Bay-to-Breakers women's division since the race began in 1912 (Wallach 1978, 177, 210). Cheryl Bridges set an American record of 2:49:40 at Culver City on 5 December 1971 (Martin and Gynn 1979, 248). On 17 April 1972, Nina Kuscsik became the first woman officially to win the Boston Marathon. Pressure from runners had convinced the 1971 AAU Convention to allow women to compete in races up to ten miles and to approve the marathon for "selected women." Kuscsik had attended that convention: "Selected women were essentially those who had already run marathons, so in effect they went full circle and now approved what they did not allow" (Kuscsik 1977a, 869–70).

Cross-country running was significant in developing interest among women with the potential for top-level long-distance competitions. Kathrine Switzer, Jacqueline Hansen, Elizabeth Bonner (the first woman to break three hours for the marathon), and Joan Benoit came to long distance from college track and cross-country programs (Benoit 1987, 85–86; Sturak 1993). Women's international cross-country championships had been held regularly since 1967, and the United States won in 1968, 1969, and 1975. An American, Doris Brown-Heritage, won the individual championship from 1967 to 1971; another American, Julie Brown, won in 1975 (Watman 1977, 57). Marilyn Bevans, the first top-level African American woman marathoner, ran on her own through high school and college in Baltimore, finally entering races as a graduate student in Massachusetts (Somers 1976, 39). Athletics teams for women were among the school sports programs affected by a section of the 1972 Educational Amendments Act, Title IX, which prohibited all high schools and colleges receiving federal monies from discriminating against students and employees on the basis of gender. Title IX required "basic equality" in athletic opportunities and facilities for women and men. National interest in women's sports increased with the events leading up to the implementation of Title IX in July 1975 (Davis 1991, 212–17; Hogan 1979).

The first long-distance race for women to attract a sponsor, the 1972 women's "Mini-Marathon," was marred by a number of organizational and administrative difficulties. From 1973 to 1976 "the Mini" was a no-frills event financed by the NYRRC or by Arno Niemand, a NYRRC member (Switzer 1972; NYRRC newsletter, spring 1976, 1; NYRRC newsletter, summer 1976, 1). As an administrator of the Mini in these early years, Kathrine Switzer experienced firsthand the difference a sponsor could make. In 1975, the race had 310 entrants and such stars as Jacqueline Hansen, the top woman marathoner in the world. In a *Run-*

ner's World article Switzer acknowledged the contributions of the sponsor Arno Niemand in bringing this fine field together (Switzer 1975). But women's marathoning had a long way to go; according to Switzer, "an event, or program, exclusively for women, encouraging their humblest beginning efforts and touting their new-found expertise, may be the real secret to creating athletic commitments for them" (1975, 24).

The first National AAU Marathon Championship for women was held in San Mateo, California, on 10 February 1974; there were forty-four finishers, twenty-one under 3:30:00. The 1975 New York City Marathon had thirty-six women finishers, fourteen under 3:30:00 (Martin and Gynn 1979, 307). The slight decrease probably indicated a greater number of women marathoners on the West Coast (Ullyot 1976, 147). Although now any woman theoretically had the opportunity to compete in the marathon, the pool for this event was identified as middle-class, college-educated women. Their appeal to the corporate world as consumers hastened the acceptance of the women's marathon (*U.S. News and World Report,* 25 Dec. 1967, 49).

In 1976 there were 429 starters in the Mini-Marathon, and the race received national recognition. Held in June, the Mini both drew on and contributed to the interest in the upcoming five-borough New York City Marathon. Along with Manufacturers Hanover Trust, *New Times* magazine, and Finnair, the cosmetics firm Bonne Bell became a sponsor of the October 1976 New York City Marathon (NYRRC newletter, summer 1976, 1). Bonne Bell also sponsored the 4 June 1977 Mini-Marathon, which had about 2,000 entrants. The Mini-Marathon was now an important race with a high-quality field that represented women runners nationwide. The directors of the Mini improved public and press relations with informational sessions for members of the press and advertisements in women's magazines (Derderian 1977).

The presentation of information about running in upscale periodicals helped create an economically desirable constituency for women's running as well as a didactic tradition in which women learned from other women. An oral tradition had come to women's running from men. Kuscsik and Berman apparently were influenced by their husbands; Switzer had a male track coach; and Gibb Bingay trained with her husband-to-be, a member of the Tufts University track team (*NYT,* 19 Apr. 1971, 46; Gupte 1971; Ralby 1966, 2). Women also participated in Road Runners Club of America functions; the races were open to women, and there were Age Group Competitions, race-day officiating, even parties that provided a milieu in which women could receive information on training and racing. Along with this they might learn about the benefits of running—that they would feel better with regular exercise and their endurance would be enhanced. Some women were attracted to running as an efficient method of weight control.

Printed information for runners had long been present. Browning Ross had encouraged women's running in *Long Distance Log*. Robert Anderson's *Runner's World* featured columns specifically for women runners. Joan Ullyot's book *Women's Running*, released in 1976 and in its sixth printing by late 1977, encouraged recreational running for its health benefits but assumed that jogging would progress to serious competition (1976, 32, 132).

By 1976 there were about eight hundred competitive women marathoners worldwide and about thirty-nine of them had run the marathon in less than three hours (Kornheiser 1976). The rules of the women's marathon had depended on the circumstances of individual events until 1972, when the AAU permitted women to run marathons officially. According to AAU rules, women who ran in marathons that included men were competing in a separate race if they were separately scored and separately awarded. Some events always had conscientiously recorded women; the Boston Marathon began to record all women's times in 1972. The first International Women's Marathon took place on 22 September 1974 in Waldniel, West Germany (Kuscsik 1977a, 871, 875).

Jacqueline Hansen Sturak had begun running in school mainly to avoid routine physical education classes such as calisthenics and softball; few other sports were available to women in the 1960s. Her talent seemed to be running the half-mile, then the longest distance women were permitted. As the AAU gradually extended the permissible distance for women, Hansen Sturak displayed increasing ability at each stage, eventually setting a world best of 34:34 for six miles on the track. But the farther she ran, the fewer competitive opportunities she found that were available to women. As a track runner, Hansen Sturak was a national collegiate mile champion who qualified for the 1972 Olympic trials in 1500 meters. She trained with the men's track team at Califor-

Jacqueline Hansen Sturak, activist for runners' rights, the first woman under 2:40 for the marathon. Photograph courtesy of Jacqueline Hansen Sturak.

nia State University, Northridge, until she met Laszlo Tabori, a world-class miler who felt that good track performances could translate into excellent performances on the road. Hansen Sturak ran her first marathon in 1972. Overall, the distances at which she competed followed the progress of the AAU's approval (Sturak 1993). Winner of the 1973 Boston Marathon, she was the first woman in the world under 2:40:00, with a 2:38:19 at the Nike–Oregon Track Club marathon on 12 October 1975 (Martin and Gynn 1979, 313, 315). Hansen Sturak continued her career in long distance both as a competitor and as an activist fighting for the women's Olympic Marathon.

On 2 October 1976, fifty-three women representing nine countries assembled at the starting line of the second unofficial International Women's Marathon in Waldniel, West Germany. Seven runners finished under 2:55:00. According to the marathon historians and statisticians David E. Martin and Roger W. H. Gynn, "The quality and international scope of these results served to crystallize in the minds of many a desire to have a women's Olympic marathon" (1979, 325). But women's sport had other, unwritten requirements.

Since the beginnings of modern sport in the nineteenth century, medical opinion held that many activities were dangerous for women. To start their campaign for an Olympic marathon, women first had to have medical sanction. Just as they had once had to convince the AAU to "approve what they did not allow" (Kuscsik 1977a, 869), women now had to prove they could do what they had been doing. From 25 to 28 October 1976, following the first five-borough New York City Marathon, the New York Academy of Sciences held a "Conference on the Marathon." One session of this conference, "Similarities and Dissimilarities among Men and Women Distance Runners," was devoted to determining how the risks of long-distance running differed for men and women. As a result of the papers presented and the literature reviewed, five hundred participants and attendees at the conference passed a resolution stating that, as women athletes "adapt to marathon training and benefit from it," and, as marathon running is in no way "contraindicated for the trained female athlete," it was resolved, "that a women's marathon event as well as other long-distance races for women be included in the Olympic program forthwith" (Milvy 1977c, 819). This resolution influenced the AAU to request that the International Amateur Athletic Federation endorse an Olympic marathon for women (Kuscsik 1977b).

While other sports had professional levels or world championships, the ultimate level of competition for the marathon was the Olympic Games. Adding a new event to the Olympic Games, however, involves meeting requirements at the highest level of the athletics bureaucracy. First, a request from the sport's governing body (such as the Athletics Congress) goes to a National Olympic Committee (the United States Olympic Committee in this case). After that, the request is presented by the National Olympic Committee to the International Federation for that sport. The International Federation for track and field, cross-country, race walking, and long-distance running is the International Amateur Athletic Federation, headquartered in London. Then the International Federation petitions the International Olympic Committee, whose rules stipulate that, for women, only events widely practiced in twenty-five countries and on two continents be included in the Olympic Games; men's sports must be widely practiced in forty countries and on three continents (Killanin and Rodda 1976, 261–62). Women's long-distance running had to develop a wide participant base in order to meet these requirements.

Women's participant sports, while growing and developing, needed more support from all sectors. The *Final Report of the President's Commission on Olympic Sports*, released in early January 1977, assessed women's sports as suffering from decades of neglect, difficulty of access to facilities, inadequate or nonexistent developmental programs, and a general lack of funding (1977, 5–6). Following the Commission's recommendations, the Amateur Sports Act of 1978 stipulated that the United States Olympic Committee "encourage and provide assistance to amateur athletic activities for women" (3046) and provide opportunities for competition without discrimination on the basis of gender (3051).

Popular culture and the commercial sector brought the women's marathon a greater constituency (Switzer 1992). CBS broadcast the television movie *See How She Runs* on 1 February 1978. The protagonist is one Betty Quinn, a woman who is forty, divorced, and coping with two adolescent daughters, an invalid father, and a former husband who is late with child-support payments. The story can be seen as a parable of self-fulfillment: Quinn takes up jogging to lose weight and progresses to the training and accomplishment of marathon running. *See How She Runs* is also a story about women's acceptance of their physical being: a forty-year-old woman acts on her decision to run a marathon; her teen-age daughter proudly announces her menarche (O'Connor 1978).

A mythology of women's running developed around its psychological, health, and cosmetic benefits. The athletic woman had been construed a type of physical beauty for decades. The 1970s' emphasis on a healthful life style as well as a slender appearance led to the association of fitness with attractiveness (Cahn 1994, 77). Popular culture picked up and exploited the connection between fitness and feminist imperatives. Helen Reddy's song "I Am Woman" became the anthem of the women's movement in the 1970s. "It's a chest-beating song of pride," Reddy said of the lyrics that announced, "I am strong. I am invincible. I am woman" (*Newsweek*, 18 Dec. 1972, 68–69). Men's running already had a fine mythology; men knew that, if they took up running, they would be perceived, and would perceive themselves, as having acquired a certain persona (Umphlett 1975, 170). In 1976 an article in *Esquire* magazine stated, "A runner is supposed to be a contemplative, taciturn, vagabond philosopher. Siddhartha in a jockstrap. . ." (Merrill 1976, 87). The woman runner would not see herself as Siddhartha in a jockstrap; she would see herself as Susan B. Anthony in a sweatband.

Kathryn Lance's *Running for Health and Beauty: A Complete Guide for Women* presented noncompetitive participation in the New York Road Runners Club's Mini-Marathon as the culmination of dedicated running. Lance regarded running as neither exercise nor training for competition but rather as a beauty "treatment" that would "help you lose weight, . . . streamline your figure, . . . improve your complexion." Lance's work seemed to veer off into a mythology of women's running as she continued, "If you follow the programs in this book, within three weeks you may begin to notice all the benefits listed above." (1977, xiii–xiv).

Avon Products, Inc., an international cosmetics firm, noticed that women's sports were a suitably feminist advertising vehicle for cosmetics. Avon was already sponsoring sports programs for women when William Corbett, Avon's public relations director, met Kathrine Switzer through the Women's Sports Foundation. Switzer had continued her studies at Syracuse University, earning a master's degree in public relations, and had covered the 1972 Olympic Games for the New York *Daily News*. She was by now a leader in women's running who had not only won the New York City Marathon in 1974 but also organized races for women (Bloom 1981, 196–218). Corbett asked Switzer to suggest a running program for Avon; she responded with a detailed proposal for a series of women's races, a championship, and related advertising themes. Avon liked her ideas and hired her as Manager of Special Promotions (Forkan 1982).

Switzer now had the resources to create a road racing structure that would support petitions for a women's Olympic Marathon. The first Avon Marathon–International Women's Championship was held in Atlanta, Georgia, on 19 March 1978. Twenty-nine states were represented among the competitors, and seven foreign countries: Brazil, Canada, Hungary, Japan, the Netherlands, New Zealand, and West Germany (Avon Products photocopy of demographic details, 1978). The presence of marathoners of many nationalities was of importance to meeting the IOC participation requirements.

Avon was in a unique position to assist with the expansion of women's running. In 1978, Avon was a cosmetics and toiletries company with $1.43 billion in revenue, 26,600 employees, and a strong international presence (*Standard and Poor's* 1977, 197). Founded as the California Perfume Company in 1886, the company was doing business in all forty-eight states and Canada by 1928, when the name was changed to Avon Products, Inc. In 1954, a distribution branch and small sales force became the vanguard of Avon operations in Puerto Rico. From Puerto Rico, Avon moved throughout Latin America; within a decade, Mexico, Venezuela, and Brazil had both distribution and manufacturing facilities. Avon expanded to the United Kingdom in 1959, from there to Belgium and Germany—supplying customers from a manufacturing facility in England—then to France, Italy, Spain, throughout Europe, and on to Africa and the Middle East. In the Pacific, Avon sold its products in Australia by 1964 and in Japan by 1969, then in Thailand and Malaysia (Goldin 1986, 5, 28–31).

Avon's marketing method was well suited to bring long-distance running to lower-middle and working-class women. Avon's hierarchy of personnel is topped by the corporate officers. Just below them are the divisional branch managers, who are assisted by deputies. Among the deputies' responsibilities is the training of the next managerial level, the resident sales managers, each of whom is assigned a sales district. The sales districts are subdivided into territories. The representatives form the base of the pyramid; one specific territory is the primary responsibility of each representative. These representatives are the "Avon ladies" who make household calls (Freedgood 1964, 112, 210). At the "territory-representative" level, the Avon structure essentially followed the wide circle of a woman's friends and casual acquaintances at home or work. From the point of view of the consumer, the

Avon representative was often an integral part of this circle. An Avon executive asserted that Texas customers "feel insulted if our representative doesn't stay for coffee and cake." (Freedgood 1964, 113). In cities, resident sales managers sought representatives who lived in large apartment complexes; integrated projects and neighborhoods included African American and Hispanic American Avon representatives (Freedgood 1964, 113).

The potential to adapt both socially and officially was the key to Avon's success in business and in promoting women's sports. In every country in which it was represented, Avon had a Government Relations Office maintaining communications between Avon and local officials. In Japan the flexible working hours made representing Avon an appealing job for women who wanted to fulfill the traditional roles of wife and mother. When Avon began its series of middle-distance races for women in Japan in early 1979, seven prominent Japanese women were appointed as advisors. Among them was a Japanese American, Michiko Gorman, who had won the New York City Marathon in 1976 and 1977 (Salmons 1979, 43). In Islamic countries Avon products came with a guarantee that they did not violate the Muslim proscription of alcohol. In Guatemala and Honduras, Avon personnel showed educational videos on various aspects of health care, nutrition, pregnancy, and children's needs (Goldin 1986, 26, 29).

The prestige of Avon cosmetics overseas probably influenced many women to accept long-distance running as a pastime. Associated with personal attractiveness and well-being, established as a part of women's lives in many countries and on every continent, with formal lines of communication to foreign governments, and with its own international network, Avon became a route for the institutionalization of the women's marathon at the highest level. The newly created Avon International Running Circuit followed the national and international structure of Avon to bring long-distance running to women all over the world. The Avon International Running Circuit held events in five countries—Australia, Japan, the United Kingdom, the United States, and West Germany—during the 1978–79 season. The circuit itself comprised a yearly series of long-distance races in the participating countries. Each race was preceded by an educational clinic—women were accustomed to receiving advice from Avon personnel. Each series culminated in the Avon International Marathon for the best runners (Marcus 1982, 21).

On 22 September 1979, under the direction of Dr. Ernst von Aaken and Kathrine Switzer, the second Avon International Women's Marathon was held in Waldniel, West Germany. The third Avon International Women's Marathon was held 3 August 1980 in London. The field of approximately two hundred runners included women from twenty-seven countries and five continents. Six hundred thirty-one women competed in the Avon International Women's Marathon held in Ottawa, Canada, on 23 August 1981. By 1982 the Avon International Running Circuit was holding races in Brazil, Canada, Chile, France, Hong Kong, and the Netherlands. In 1983, Argentina, Belgium, Italy, Mexico, New Zealand, Spain, and Thailand joined the Avon circuit (Marcus 1982, 21). By now, other corporations were, like Avon, genuinely interested in training runners and developing opportunities for competition as well as using running as a promotional activity (*Advertising Age*, 23 Mar. 1981, S-18).

Blue Ribbon Sports, a running shoe distributing and manufacturing concern (the corporate name was changed to Nike, Inc., in 1978), supported American track-and-field athletes through its Athletics West Track Club. Athletics West provided equipment, apparel, coaching and medical supervision, travel expenses, insurance, and educational and job placement assistance. Mary Decker (later Mary Decker Slaney) and Joan Benoit (later Joan Benoit Samuelson) were among Athletics West's first women members (Liz Dolan, photocopy of Nike press release, 1989; Nike 1993). Benoit, who lived in Maine, received coaching advice from Bob Sevene of Athletics West; the two had frequent telephone calls to discuss her progress, and Sevene occasionally came to see Benoit in Freeport, Maine. Her autobiography reveals a woman who loves her home state and values her family; Benoit is Down East and down-to-earth, with a mischievous sense of humor. As a student at Bowdoin College, she first won the Boston Marathon in 1979; her time of 2:35:15 was a course record and an American record for women. In 1980, after a demanding temporary appointment as a substitute teacher, Benoit accepted a job at Nike's sports research lab in Exeter, New Hampshire. She found her employers exceedingly sympathetic to her running schedule: "It was understood that I was always free to take

Joan Benoit Samuelson, winner of the first women's Olympic Marathon in 1984. Photograph by Jeff Johnson, courtesy of Jeff Johnson.

off for a race" (Benoit 1987, 142). The tiny, rosy-cheeked, blue-eyed brunette set the world record for women with a 2:22:43 in the 1983 Boston Marathon.

In 1979 a grant from Blue Ribbon Sports (Nike) started the International Runners' Committee (IRC), an advocacy group for elite athletes. The executive board of the IRC comprised fifteen runners, representing all continents; among them were the marathoners Jacqueline Hansen Sturak, Doris Brown-Heritage, Nina Kuscsik, Leal-Ann Reinhart, and Joan Ullyot of the United States; Eleanora Mendonca of Brazil; and Sarolta Monspart of Hungary (IRC newsletter, Feb. 1980, 1; Feb. 1981, 1). Hansen Sturak eventually succeeded Joe Henderson as the IRC's executive director (Sturak 1993). While the Avon Running Circuit ensured a popular base of participation in the sport, the International Runners' Committee worked to secure a place for the elite women. The IRC decided on a full program of distance races for women in the 1984 Los Angeles Olympic Games as their first objective. The IRC did not plan to stage races or govern the sport; rather, they intended to "carry the wishes of the runners to the officials" (IRC newsletter, Feb. 1980, 1). The IRC hoped to increase opportunities for competition and to improve running administration.

Other institutions also acted to promote top-level competition for women long-distance runners. At their August 1979 meeting in Montreal, the IAAF women's committee recommended recognition of women's 5,000- and 10,000-meter records. In November 1979, Adrian Paulen, president of the IAAF, issued a message to the competitors in the Tokyo International Women's Marathon, supporting an Olympic Marathon for women and indicating he would lobby the IOC on behalf of the event for the 1984 Games:

> The world's leading women marathon runners have gathered and surprised us all—not only by the vast number of finishers, but also by the high quality of the leading performers, many of whom would finish high up in any men's marathon race. . . . The athletes running today, by careful preparation and gradual buildup are therefore ready for the challenge which this summit of distance races presents. (IRC newsletter, Feb. 1980, 2–3, reprinted from IAAF Bulletin 28)

In Lausanne, Switzerland, on 16 April 1980, Paulen and General Secretary John Holt presented several new women's track events, including the marathon, to the IOC program committee. The program committee demurred, asking for further studies on the physiological and psychological effects of competitive marathon running on women. "That standard has never been applied to men," retorted Executive Director Joe Henderson of the IRC, and Dr. Joan Ullyot, an IRC member, responded with the extensive, affirmative medical evidence that had been compiled (Cimons 1981, 49–50). Official acceptance of a women's marathon came at the next IOC meeting in Los Angeles; at 6:30 P.M. on 23 February 1981 the executive board of the IOC approved a women's Olympic Marathon to start with the 1984 Games (Cimons 1981, 49–50).

Opposition to a women's Olympic Marathon had come from representatives of the Soviet Union and the countries of Eastern Europe (*NYT*, 24 Feb. 1981, sec. 3, p. 14). These countries' women runners were strongest at the sprint and middle-distance races that were already part of the Games. By not participating in the institutionalization of the women's marathon, the Eastern bloc lagged in creating a pool of potential women long-distance runners and, with a few exceptions such as Sarolta Monspart, in developing many competitive marathoners. Joan Benoit of the United States was the first winner of an Olympic Marathon for women.

The history of the acceptance of an Olympic Marathon for women follows the development of the women's marathon in America until the first National AAU Marathon Championship for women in 1974. In this case, institutionalization was achieved less through group activity and organizations than through individual efforts, such as Kathrine Switzer's daring entry in the 1967 Boston Marathon and the extraordinary athletic performances of Jacqueline Hansen Sturak. Men's athletics had proceeded on parallel tracks of development and institutionalization during the nineteenth century. But because social custom had not accorded women sanction in sport until very recently, the improvements in women's marathon performances during the 1970s outpaced the progress of the institutionalization of the event.

Corporate backing allowed the women's marathon to expand rapidly to meet International Olympic Committee regulations. Avon Products, Inc., by selecting long-distance running, sanctioned the sport as an activity that was compatible with beauty and well-being, and thus fulfilled social functions important to a cosmetics firm. Avon representatives, their friends and acquaintances, and everyone within reach of Avon advertising comprised a pool that could contribute many participants, as the excellent attendance at Avon races proved. Avon had acquired a marathon tradition by hiring Kathrine Switzer, and Switzer assembled a headquarters staff of runners to provide information to race entrants. Avon followed the rules of the existing athletics bureaucracy in staging events at which quantified athletic performances were documented.

A social and competitive structure for women marathoners already existed when Avon first presented its marathon program. But this structure was limited to the United States and a few Western European nations, and even there was further limited to a relatively small number of women. The Avon International Running Circuit, created by Switzer, expanded the existing structure, adding new events and avenues of information. By providing its Running Circuit with an existing international corporate network, Avon Products, Inc., brought long-distance running to women all over the world and endowed the women's marathon with an international cohesion and presence. When the International Runners' Committee began its campaign for a women's marathon in the Olympic Games, it was backed by corporate interest as well as wide participation, corporately provided. In sum, the history of the women's marathon footrace illustrates the importance of corporate support to the institutionalization of a sporting event.

11

Community and Competition

The American marathon footrace has evolved into a cultural performance, a chance for people to tell a story about themselves (Geertz 1973, 448). In late twentieth-century America, that story is about community. On 7 March 1993, the Los Angeles Marathon went on as planned, although riots over issues of racism and police brutality recently had torn the city. The race director had rejected plans to change the marathon course in order to avoid the devastated neighborhoods. He was right; at least for one day, the city of Los Angeles was united over a footrace that functioned as "the city's biggest block party" (Harris and Baker 1993). With the running of the Los Angeles Marathon, hopes for rebirth arose from what had been urban discord.

In its frequent use as a celebration of cities or anniversaries, the marathon constitutes a festival. Joyous by definition (MacAloon 1984, 246), the festival "has boundaries of space, time, and intention" (249), but nevertheless "reaches out to encompass the whole world" (250). Similarly, there is a "theoretical openness" (Guttmann 1978, 107) to the marathon, an event that leaves the stadium for public streets and roads, draws spectators into participation, and does not finish until the last runner comes in.

The marathon runner competes neither in sacred time nor in real time, neither in sanctified nor in vulgar space (Guttmann 1978, 20, 22).

The theoretical openness of the marathon captivates its adherents. It has always been a participant sport in which the assistance of the spectators—whether offers of refreshment or words of encouragement—seemed to have a tangible effect on the official runners. And the marathon in turn affects the spectators, bringing them new respect for human physical potential and pride in national, ethnic, or social community. Most of all, the spectators share in the story told by each marathon footrace (MacAloon 1984, 246).

The setting of the marathon contributes to the many stories and often provides its own drama. The Boston Athletic Association Marathon officially commemorates Paul Revere's ride through the countryside to warn of the approaching British. Begun in 1897, the BAA Marathon starts in traditional New England small towns and finishes in a downtown Boston office complex, recapitulating the turn-of-the-century demographic move from rural to urban living and acknowledging the catalyst of industrial capitalism. The New York City Marathon, held over four loops of the Central Park road when it started in 1970, spread out through the entire city as part of New York's celebration of the American Bicentennial in 1976. Only then did it attract large fields and significant publicity. Years after its first five-borough race, the New York City Marathon still unites a widespread and diverse metropolis in celebration of the city itself.

The city creates the marathon; the marathon serves the city. In the post–World War II era, sports facilities have moved to the suburbs, following the middle-class suburban sports fans (Riess 1989, 258–59). But in the present New York City Marathon, runners travel on foot through the ethnic enclaves and the inner city. Marathoners receive water from the otherwise insular Hasidim of Williamsburg; Harlemites' encouraging cheers are emotionally overwhelming (Cody 1982).

The dynamics of the city determined the nature of the United States marathon from its earliest days. The political and social structure of the city, particularly its ethnic composition, decided the identity of the early marathon runners. New York City athletic clubs and administrative organizations placed the marathon, and marathon runners, in the hierarchy of track-and-field athletics. Once the United States sports bureaucracy acceded to the modifications caused by increasing democratization of the event, the marathon changed, traveling upward across class lines.

The marathon first became popular in New York City as a forum for ethnic identification. Although the marathon officially celebrated national and municipal occasions, ethnic groups also imposed their own meanings on the event. The marathon could be considered a representation of the immigration journey, an experience shared by all the ethnic groups. Enacting the journey as ritual placed it decisively in the past, reaffirming the choice to come to America.

Immigration declined during the 1920s, and ethnicity was submerged in American identity. Athletic clubs accepted runners from all groups, valuing ability over ethnicity. While an important Olympic event, the marathon held a tangential and precarious position in United States athletics. The Depression further depreciated the American marathon; economic difficulties brought out dormant ethnic conflicts, interfering with access to club membership, coaching, and information about long-distance running.

In Harlem the Depression brought not only organized protest against economic discrimination but also a wide range of community programs. The New York Pioneer Club provided guidance and recreation for any male who wanted to join, regardless of athletic ability or race. The continued discrimination that confronted African Americans turned the New York Pioneer Club into an activist association that made substantial contributions to the social integration of track and field. As Pioneer Club runners became an increasing presence in the marathon, they brought with them the legacy of protest that inspired post–World War II marathoners to organize for change in the athletics bureaucracy. In 1957, Browning Ross started the Road Runners Club of America, an organization to advance long-distance running. The RRCA inherited its activist approach and its democratic policy, accepting all who wanted to join, from the New York Pioneer Club.

The Cold War enhanced the RRCA mission by politicizing fitness; conditioning was part of the competition between East and West. Top-level long-distance running increased in importance, particularly when the United States met the USSR in athletics. The climate for long-distance running improved in the United States with the burgeoning of the RRCA and a dramatic increase in the number of marathons in the 1960s and 1970s. The increase in numbers of participants contributed to the growth of marathoning, providing substantial fields and support for the many new races.

The jogging trend started by the RRCA and encouraged by the Cold War affected primarily the middle and upper classes. With RRCA encouragement, many of these joggers became runners and entered long-distance races, changing the image of marathoners from a few athletic eccentrics to a large number of desirable consumers. Corporations sponsored marathons in order to reach this market and beyond; the advertising T-shirts distributed to all finishers were proudly worn on many informal occasions.

The campaign to include a women's marathon in the Olympic Games began in the United States as a corollary to the 1970s running boom. During the course of achieving acceptance in America, the women's marathon attracted industrial and political support that provided financing and power. Corporate backing gave the organizational leaders of women's marathoning the global influence and prestige to challenge a major transnational corporation, the International Olympic Committee, and to bring the women's marathon to the 1984 Olympic Games.

The running boom in the United States had changed by the 1990s. Once the domain of young, upwardly mobile professionals, marathon fields now comprise a more representative cross section of United States society. In July 1993, *Ebony* reported on "The Jogging Craze," saying that jogging had become "a major craze in Black America" (54-57). The health and social benefits attributed to running drew African Americans along with thousands of others into a "second running boom" that may simply be an expansion of the first (Hirsch 1997). By 1997 over one-fourth of United States marathon finishers were women. The sport now spans three generations; mothers and daughters, even granddaughters, enter the same races (Longman 1997, B12). Avon had ended its running program for women in early 1985; in 1997, Avon called upon Kathrine Switzer to reinstate the program with ten major United States races in the first year, as well as events in seventeen foreign countries (Switzer 1997).

For the average runner, the "running boom" participant, the marathon becomes a chance to transcend everyday life. The marathoner races with impunity down the center of a highway, expecting to be regaled with cheers, refreshments, and comfort. Despite the wide range of prices for the various accoutrements of running, almost all marathoners look very much alike in their sneakers, plastic watches, and nylon shorts. Victor Turner's description of the liminal personae of non-Western societies can also be applied to the first-timers at the 1997 New York City Marathon starting line:

> It is as though they are being reduced or ground down to a uniform condition to be fashioned anew and endowed with additional powers to enable them to cope with their new station in life. Among themselves, neophytes tend to develop an intense comradeship and egalitarianism. Secular distinctions of rank and status disappear or are homogenized. (1969, 95)

The parameters of the marathon comprise hours of continual exertion and a distance of 26.2 miles that takes the event away from the track and out into the unpredictable surroundings of the real world. There are three major categories of marathon course: the point-to-point races such as Boston and New York; the loop course that begins and ends in the same place, such as the Olympic Stadium; and the out-and-back course. But even in the out-and-back, where the runner returns over the same roads traveled for the first half of the marathon, the second half of the race differs from the first half.

The time of over two hours for even the fastest marathon allows for drama within the event. The runner, although concentrating on the task at hand, still has time for thought, particularly if the individual is not among the handful of runners who are elite marathoners. There is time to interact with the crowd; time to respond to the environment; most significantly, there is time to reflect on the past and the future.

The marathon provides the space and time for an infinite number of stories. In 1996 over 37,000 runners started the one-hundredth Boston Marathon. Very few of them expected to achieve any distinction in the event. For most of them, running was part of a fitness routine, racing was a social occasion, and finishing a marathon was a personal goal (Longman 1997, B9). These runners were participating rather than competing; they ran 26.2 miles to tell stories other than the winner's. The marathon is run for both private and public reasons, and the history of the marathon footrace reveals many different levels of meaning.

Works Cited
Index

Works Cited

Abramson, Jesse P. 1927. "Indian is First in Marathon to Long Beach." *NYHT*, 16 May, 1.

——. 1930. "DeMar, Never Challenged, Wins Marathon Run to Port Chester." *NYHT*, 14 Oct., 25.

——. 1932. "Lalla, 19–Year Old Caddie Running in First Marathon, Wins." *NYHT*, 17 Oct., 16.

——. 1933. "De Bruyn Wins Marathon to Port Chester." *NYHT*, 13 Oct., 23.

——. 1935a. "AAU Approves Olympics Entry; Mahoney Resigns." *NYHT*, 9 Dec., 1, 20.

——. 1935b. "AAU Defers Fight Over Olympic Issue After Five-Hour Debate." *NYHT*, 8 Dec., sec. 3, p. 1.

——. 1935c. "AAU Elects Brundage Head, No Rival Slate." *NYHT*, 9 Dec., 20.

——. 1935d. "Olympics Ban Tabled in Strife by Met AAU." *NYHT*, 9 Oct., 26.

——. 1936. "Metropolitan Association Drops Kiviat, Silver, Veteran Officials." *NYHT*, 29 Feb., 18.

——. 1945. "Democratic Ideal: The Pioneer Club." *Amateur Athlete* (Sept.): 11, 15.

Adams, Michael. 1983. "The New York City Marathon: How It's Run." *Successful Meetings* 32 (Oct.): 26–32.

Adelman, Melvin A. 1986. *A Sporting Time: New York City and the Rise of Modern Athletics*. Sport and Society Series, edited by Benjamin G. Rader and Randy Roberts. Urbana: Univ. of Illinois Press.

Allen, Neil. 1976. "Melbourne 1956." In *The Olympic Games: 80 Years of People, Events, and Records*, edited by [Michael Morris] Lord Killanin and John Rodda, 69–72. New York: Collier.

Altrocchi, Julia Cooley. 1949. *The Spectacular San Franciscans*. New York: E. P. Dutton.

Amateur Athletic Union. 1908–1970. *Minutes of the Annual Meeting of the Amateur Atheletic Union*.

Amateur Sports Act of 1978. 1978. *Statutes at Large*, 92, sec. 36, 3045–3058.

Amdur, Neil. 1971. "Shorter Wins Marathon for Tough Double." *NYT*, 6 Aug., 21.

———. 1972. "U.S. Wins Its First Olympic Marathon Since 1908, Loses on Basketball Protest; Games Close Today." *NYT*, 11 Sept., 1.

———. 1975. "Area Marathons Feel Money Squeeze." *NYT*, 3 June, 38.

———. 1976a. "New York's First Citywide Marathon Draws Some of World's Top Runners." *NYT*, 25 Oct., 31.

———. 1976b. "Want to Run Marathon? Take it Easy, Doctor Warns Hopeful Novices." *NYT*, 26 Oct., 33.

———. 1978a. "Running Boom: Too Much Too Soon?" *NYT*, 17 Apr., C1, C8.

———. 1978b. "What Makes the Seventies Run?" *The Runner* 1 (Oct.): 14.

———. 1984. "Salazar Prefers Under-Table Payments." *NYT*, 27 Oct., sec. 4, p. 31.

Anderson, Jervis. 1981. *This Was Harlem: A Cultural Portrait, 1900–1950*. New York: Farrar, Straus, Giroux.

Appell, Joseph H. 1930. *The Business Biography of John Wanamaker, Founder and Builder: America's Merchant Pioneer from 1861 to 1922*. New York: Macmillan.

Banks, Olive. 1981. *Faces of Feminism: A Study of Feminism as a Social Movement*. New York: St. Martin's.

Barcus, H. H. 1926. "98-Pound Runner, 40 Years Old, Wins Pontiac-to-Detroit Marathon. *DN*, 4 Apr., sec. 4, p. 1.

Barrett, James R. 1992. "Americanization from the Bottom Up: Immigration and the Remaking of the Working Class in the United States, 1880–1930." *Journal of American History* 79 (Dec.): 996–1020.

Baynes, Ernest H. 1894. "The History of Cross-Country Running in America." *Outing* 23 (Mar.): 484–90.

Bayor, Ronald H. 1978. *Neighbors in Conflict: The Irish, Germans, Jews, and Italians of New York City, 1929–1941*. Johns Hopkins University Studies in Historical and Political Science, Ninety-Sixth Series, 1978. Baltimore: Johns Hopkins Univ. Press.

Benoit, Joan, with Sally Baker. 1987. *Running Tide*. New York: Knopf.

Benyo, Richard. 1983. *The Masters of the Marathon*. With an introduction by Erich Segal. New York: Atheneum.

Berger, Bennett M. 1979. "American Pastoralism, Suburbia, and the Commune Movement: An Exercise in the Microsociology of Knowledge." In *On the Making of Americans: Essays in Honor of David Riesman,* edited by Herbert J. Gans et al., 235–50. Philadelphia: Univ. of Pennsylvania Press.

Bernstein, Irving. 1960. *The Lean Years: A History of the American Worker, 1920–1933.* Boston: Houghton Mifflin.

Berwick Marathon. 1994. *Official Program: 85th Run for the Diamonds,* Berwick, Pennsylvania. 24 Nov., 18.

Black, Jonathan. 1978. "The Private Obsession of Ted Corbitt." *The Runner* 1 (Dec.): 33.

Blaikie, David. 1984. *Boston: The Canadian Story.* Ottawa, Ontario: Seneca House Books.

Blair, Clay. 1987. *The Forgotten War: America in Korea, 1950–1952.* New York: Times Books.

Blodgett, Geoffrey. 1966. *The Gentle Reformers: Massachusetts Democrats in the Cleveland Era.* Cambridge, Mass.: Harvard Univ. Press.

Bloom, Marc. 1981. *The Marathon: What It Takes to Go the Distance.* New York: Holt, Rinehart, and Winston.

Bodnar, John E. 1977. *Immigration and Industrialization in an American Mill Town, 1870– 1940.* Pittsburgh: Univ. of Pittsburgh Press.

———. 1985. *The Transplanted: A History of Immigrants in Urban America.* Interdisciplinary Studies in History, edited by Harvey J. Graff. Bloomington: Indiana Univ. Press.

———. 1992. *Remaking America: Public Memory, Commemoration, and Patriotism in the Twentieth Century.* Princeton: Princeton Univ. Press.

Bogen, Elizabeth. 1987. *Immigration in New York.* New York: Praeger.

Booker, James. 1951. "Joe Yancey, All-American Coach." *New York Amsterdam News,* 3 Mar., 7–8, 16– 17.

Bowerman, William J., and W. E. Harris, with James M. Shea. 1967. *Jogging.* New York: Grosset and Dunlap.

Brandes, Stuart D. 1976. *American Welfare Capitalism, 1880–1940.* Chicago: Univ. of Chicago Press.

Briordy, William J. 1947. "Vogel Takes National AAU Marathon Title at Yonkers." *NYT,* 27 Oct., 30.

Brock, Ted. 1976. "All Around the Town." *Runner's World* 11 (Dec.): 20–22.

Brody, David. 1980. *Workers in Industrial America: Essays on the Twentieth Century Struggle.* New York: Oxford Univ. Press.

Brooks, Thomas R. 1974. *Walls Come Tumbling Down: A History of the Civil Rights Movement, 1940–1970.* Englewood Cliffs, N.J.: Prentice-Hall.

Brown, Richard D. 1976. *Modernization: The Transformation of American Life, 1600–1865.* American Century Series, edited by Eric Foner. New York: Hill and Wang.

Browning, Robert. 1981. *Robert Browning: The Poems.* Vol. 2. The English Poets, edited by John Pettigrew, supplemented and completed by Thomas J. Collins. New Haven: Yale Univ. Press.

Buder, Leonard. 1956. "Eisenhower Acts on Youth Fitness." *NYT,* 20 July, 26.

Cady, Steve. 1968. "Burfoot of Wesleyan is First at BAA Marathon." *NYT,* 20 Apr., 40.

Cahn, Susan K. 1994. *Coming on Strong: Gender and Sexuality in Twentieth-Century Women's Sport.* New York: Macmillan.

Capeci, Dominic J., Jr. 1977. *The Harlem Riot of 1943.* Philadelphia: Temple Univ. Press.

Carens, George C. 1931. "Henigan's Fifteenth Marathon Race is His Greatest." *BET,* 21 Apr., part 2, p. 4.

———. 1932. "De Bruyn Wins Marathon in the Last Mile." *BET,* 19 Apr., 1.

———. 1935. "Kelley Wins BAA Marathon." *BET,* 19 Apr., 1.

———. 1936. "Tarzan Brown Sets Pace to Win Marathon: Kelley Fifth." *BET,* 20 Apr., 1, 4.

———. 1937. "Walt Young Wins BAA Marathon; Kelley is Second." *BET,* 19 Apr., 1.

Cashman, Sean Dennis. 1989. *America in the Twenties and Thirties: The Olympian Age of Franklin Delano Roosevelt.* New York: New York Univ. Press.

Cassell, Ollan. 1984. "History of the Trust Fund." *The Athletics Congress/USA Record* (Feb./Mar.): 4–5.

Castro, Ginette. 1984. *American Feminism: A Contemporary History.* Feminist Crosscurrents, edited by Kathleen Barry. Translated by Elizabeth Loverde-Bagwell. Paris: Presses de la Fondation Nationale des Sciences Politiques.

Cerutty, Percy Wells. 1964. *Middle-Distance Running.* London: Pelham Books.

Chandler, Alfred D., Jr. 1977. *The Visible Hand: The Managerial Revolution in American Business.* Cambridge, Mass.: Belknap Press of Harvard Univ. Press.

Chodes, John. 1961. "Gordon McKenzie's Comments on Olympic Games." *Road Runners Club New York Association* newsletter (winter): 3–4.

———. 1974. *Corbitt: The Story of Ted Corbitt, Long-Distance Runner.* Los Altos, Calif.: Tafnews Press.

Cimons, Marlene. 1981. "How Women Got to Run the Distance: The Olympic Marathon Breakthrough." *Ms.* 10 (July): 47–50.

Cinel, Dino. 1982. *From Italy to San Francisco: The Immigrant Experience.* Stanford, Calif.: Stanford Univ. Press.

Cirulnick, Nat. 1971. " `Run for Fun' Program." In *Guide to Distance Running*, edited by Bob Anderson and Joe Henderson, 42. Mountain View, Calif.: World Publications.

Clarity, James. 1970a. "Soviet Conquers U.S. in Track, 200–173, as Its Men Post for 2d Series Victory." *NYT*, 25 July, 17.

———. 1970b. "Soviet Gains 103–78 Over-All Edge in Track; U.S. Men Trail by 3 Points." *NYT*, 24 July, 22.

Clogg, Richard. 1992. *A Concise History of Greece.* Cambridge, U.K.: Cambridge Univ. Press.

Coben, Stanley. 1964. "Nativism and the Red Scare of 1919–20." *Political Science Quarterly* 79 (1): 59–75.

Cody, Joe. 1981. "The Yonkers Marathon: The Golden Years." *New York Running News* (Aug./Sept.): 15–19.

———. 1982. "The View From Williamsburg." *New York Running News Special Marathon Issue* (24 Oct.): 24–25.

Cohen, Martin. 1974. "The Next Running Boom." *Runner's World* 9 (May): 16–17.

Cole, William T. 1910. *Motives and Results of the Social Settlement Movement.* Publications of the Department of Social Sciences in Harvard University, No. 2. Cambridge, Mass.: Harvard Univ. Press.

Coleman, Joseph K. 1978. "Sports Grow as Promotion Arena." *Advertising Age*, 16 Oct., P12.

Considine, Bob, and Fred G. Jarvis. 1969. *The First Hundred Years: A Portrait of the NYAC [New York Athletic Club].* Toronto, Ontario: Macmillan.

Conzen, Kathleen Neils, et al. 1992. "The Invention of Ethnicity: A Perspective from the U.S.A.." *Journal of American Ethnic History* 12 (fall): 4–41.

Cooney, Terry A. 1995. *Balancing Acts: American Thought and Culture in the 1930s.* Twayne's American Thought and Culture Series, edited by Lewis Perry. New York: Twayne.

Copland, Al. 1911. "Little Tewanina Wins Marathon." *NYT*, 7 May, sec. 4, p. 1.

Cooper, Kenneth H. 1968. *Aerobics.* New York: Bantam.

Corbitt, Theodore. 1975. "Testimonial to a Pioneer: Joseph J. Yancey." *Road Runners Club New York Association* newsletter (fall): 10.

———. 1991. "Lou White, 1908–1990." *New York Running News.* (Feb./Mar.): 24.

Coubertin, Pierre de. 1896. "The Olympic Games of 1896." *Century* (Nov.): 39–53.

Crider, John H. 1934. "Westchester Folk Decry Annexation." *NYT*, 25 Nov., 7.

Cumming, John. 1981. *Runners and Walkers: A Nineteenth Century Sports Chronicle.* Chicago: Regnery Gateway.

Curtis, James, and William McTeer. 1981. "Toward a Sociology of Marathon-ing." *Journal of Sport Behavior* 4: 67–81.

Daley, Arthur J. 1930. "Koski Wins Title in AAU Marathon." *NYT,* 24 Mar., 18.

———. 1931a. "Komonen is First in Marathon Race." *NYT,* 13 Oct., 31.

———. 1931b. "Michelson Victor in Title Marathon." *NYT,* 6 Apr., 30.

———. 1932. "Steiner Victor in Metropolitan Title Marathon, De Bruyn Second, Far Behind." *NYT,* 9 May, 22.

Daniels, Roger. 1990. *Coming to America: A History of Immigration and Ethnicity in American Life.* New York: Harper Collins.

Davis, Flora. 1991. *Moving the Mountain: The Women's Movement in America since 1960.* New York: Simon and Schuster.

DeMar, Clarence. 1981. *Marathon.* Brattleboro, Vt.: Stephen Daye Press. 1937. Reprint. Shelbourne, V.: New England Press.

Derderian, Tom. 1977. "Women's Day in Central Park." *Runner's World* 12 (Aug.): 48–50.

———. 1994. *Boston Marathon: The History of the World's Premier Running Event.* With forewords by Joan Benoit Samuelson and Bill Rodgers. Champaign, Ill.: Human Kinetics.

Donovan, Wally. 1976. *A History of Indoor Track and Field.* El Cajon, Calif.: Edward Jules.

Dubofsky, Melvin. 1975. *Industrialsim and the American Worker, 1865–1920.* American History Series, edited by John Hope Franklin and Abraham S. Eisenstadt. Arlington Heights, Ill.: Harlan Davidson.

Edwards, Harry. 1973. *Sociology of Sport.* Homewood, Ill.: Dorsey Press.

Edwards, Richard. 1979. *Contested Terrain: The Transformation of the Workplace in the Twentieth Century.* New York: Basic Books.

Effrat, Louis. 1934. "Marathon Crown Kept by Steiner." *NYT,* 26 Mar., 25.

Eisenstein, Louis, and Elliot Rosenberg. 1966. *A Stripe of Tammany's Tiger.* New York: Robert Speller.

Eisinger, Peter K. 1980. *The Politics of Displacement: Racial and Ethnic Transition in Three American Cities.* New York: Academic Press.

Elliott, Herb, as told to Alan Trengove. 1961. *The Herb Elliott Story.* New York: Thomas Nelson.

Espy, Richard. 1981. *The Politics of the Olympic Games.* With an epilogue, 1976–1980. Berkeley: Univ. of California Press.

Ewen, Stuart. 1976. *Captains of Consciousness: Advertising and the Social Roots of the Consumer Culture.* New York: McGraw-Hill.

Federal Writers' Project of New York. 1938. *The Italians of New York.* New York: Random House.

Field, Bryan. 1927. "Michelson Victor in Marathon Here." *NYT*, 8 May, sec. 9, p. 8.
———. 1928. "Wilson Wins Run; 3 Hurt in Traffic." *NYT*, 6 May, sec. 11, p. 1.
Fixx, James F. 1977. *The Complete Book of Running*. New York: Random House.
Flath, Arnold William. 1964. *A History of Relations between the National Collegiate Athletic Association and the Amateur Athletic Union of the United States, 1905–1963*. Champaign, Ill.: Stipes.
Flynn, William J. 1955. "Costes Clips Record in Taking National AAU Marathon Championship." *NYT*, 23 May, 32.
Forkan, James P. 1982. "Out as Tennis Sponsor, Avon Bolsters Support of Women's Running, Bowling." *Advertising Age*, 12 Apr., 41.
Frank, Stanley B. 1935a. "Flipping Pages of Brightest Chapters with Crescents." *NYP*, 2 Jan., 18.
———. 1935b. "German-American Athletic Club Heils Athletes but Not Hitler: Jewish Members Play a Big Part." *NYP*, 3 Jan., 20.
———. 1935c. "Irish-American Athletic Club Gave Workingman a Break." *NYP*, 5 Jan., 17.
———. 1936. *The Jew in Sports*. New York: Miles.
Freedgood, Seymour. 1964. "Avon: The Sweet Smell of Success." *Fortune* 70 (Dec.): 108–13, 238, 240.
Galginaitis, Carol. 1979. "To Corporations, Name's the Game." *Advertising Age*, 27 Aug., S-2.
Gavrin, Arthur J. 1948. *The Snapeasy Bulletin*. Dec., 1.
Geertz, Clifford. 1973. *The Interpretation of Cultures*. New York: Basic Books.
Gitlin, Todd. 1987. *The Sixties: Years of Hope, Days of Rage*. New York: Bantam.
Glader, Eugene A. 1978. *Amateurism and Athletics*. New York: Leisure Press.
Glazer, Nathan. 1984. "Jews and Blacks: What Happened to the Grand Alliance?" In *Jews in Black Perspectives: A Dialogue*, edited and with an introduction by Joseph R. Washington, Jr., 105–12. N.J.: Fairleigh Dickinson Univ. Press.
Goldaper, Sam. 1985. "John B. Kelly Jr. Dead at 57; Olympic Committee Leader." *NYT*, 4 Mar., sec. 2, p. 6.
Goldin, Bobbi. 1986. *The Greatest Beauty Story Ever Told: Avon, 1886–1986*. New York: Avon Products.
Goldstein, Michael S. 1992. *The Health Movement: Promoting Fitness in America*. New York: Twayne.
Gordon, David M., Richard Edwards, and Michael Reich. 1982. *Segmented Work, Divided Workers: The Historical Transformation of Labor in the United States*. New York: Cambridge Univ. Press.

Gorn, Elliott J. 1986. *The Manly Art: Bare-Knuckle Prize Fighting in America.* Ithaca, N.Y.: Cornell Univ. Press.

Gray, J. M. 1955. "I Love to Run and Run and Run." *Saturday Evening Post,* 16 Apr., 42–43, 100.

Greenberg, Cheryl Lynn. 1991. *"Or Does It Explode?" Black Harlem in the Great Depression.* New York: Oxford Univ. Press.

———. 1992. "The Politics of Disorder: Reexamining Harlem's Riots of 1935 and 1943." *Journal of Urban History* 18 (Aug.): 395–441.

Gupte, Pranay. 1971. "Housewife Runs, Too." *NYT,* 7 Nov., sec. 15, p. 13.

Gurock, Jeffrey S. 1979. *When Harlem Was Jewish, 1870–1930.* New York: Columbia Univ. Press.

Guttmann, Allen. 1978. *From Ritual to Record: The Nature of Modern Sports.* New York: Columbia Univ. Press.

———. 1984. *The Games Must Go On: Avery Brundage and the Olympic Movement.* New York: Columbia Univ. Press.

———. 1986. *Sports Spectators.* New York: Columbia Univ. Press.

———. 1988. *A Whole New Ball Game: An Interpretation of American Sports.* Chapel Hill: Univ. of North Carolina Press.

———. 1991. *Women's Sports: A History.* New York: Columbia Univ. Press.

———. 1992. *The Olympics: A History of the Modern Games.* Illinois History of Sports Series, edited by Benjamin G. Rader and Randy Roberts. Urbana: Univ. of Illinois Press.

Hallahan, John J. 1932. "Bill Kennedy Promises to be in Prize Winners." *BG,* 18 Apr., 18.

Halttunen, Karen. 1982. *Confidence Men and Painted Women: A Study of Middle-Class Culture in America, 1830–1870.* New Haven: Yale Univ. Press.

Handlin, Oscar. 1973. *The Uprooted.* 2d ed., enlarged. Boston: Little, Brown.

Hardy, Stephen. 1982. *How Boston Played: Sport, Recreation, and Community, 1865–1915.* Boston: Northeastern Univ. Press.

———. 1986. "Entrepreneurs, Organizations, and the Sport Marketplace: Subjects in Search of Historians." *Journal of Sport History* 13 (spring): 14–33.

Hargreaves, John. 1986. *Sport, Power, and Culture: A Social and Historical Analysis of Popular Sports in Britain.* New York: St. Martin's.

Harris, Scott, and Chris Baker. 1993. "L.A. Marathon Makes Strides for Harmony." *LAT,* 8 Mar., sec. 1, p. 1.

Hartshorne, James. 1971. "Masters Mile Comes of Age." In *Guide to Distance Running,* edited by Bob Anderson and Joe Henderson, 66–67. Mountain View, Calif.: World Publications.

Hayes, John J. 1908. "How I Won the Marathon Race." *Cosmopolitan* (Dec.): 113–18.

Hemmingway, William. 1909. "How Canada Started the Marathon Craze." *Harper's Weekly*, 1 May, 24.

Henderson, Joe. 1969. *Long Slow Distance: The Humane Way to Train.* Mountain View, Calif.: World Publications.

———. 1970. "Editorial." *Runner's World* 5 (Jan.): 1, 7.

———. 1970. "The Relevance of Running." *Runner's World* 5 (Nov.): 18.

———. 1971. "Women Take Their Place." In *1971 Marathon Handbook*, edited by Bob Anderson and Joe Henderson, 28. Mountain View, Calif.: World Publications.

———. 1974. "An Honest Day's Work." *Runner's World* 9 (Oct.): 18–19.

Henry, Bill. 1948. *An Approved History of the Olympic Games.* New York: G. P. Putnam's Sons.

Herodotus. 1954. *The Histories..* Translated by Aubrey de Selincourt. Baltimore: Penguin Classics.

Hersh, Bob. 1971. "A Solution: Open Track." *Track and Field News* 24 (Dec.): 4–5.

Higdon, Hal. 1964. "Run for Your Health." *Today's Health* (Oct.): 36–37.

———. 1968. "Jogging is an In Sport." *NYT Magazine*, 14 Apr., 36–52.

———. 1970. "On the Run." *Runner's World* (Jan.): 15.

———. 1979. "The AAU: Kingdom in Crisis." *Runner* 1 (September): 54–65.

———. 1995. *On the Run from Dogs and People.* Chicago: Henry Regnery. 1971. Reprint. Michigan City, Indiana: Roadrunner Press.

Higham, John. 1984. *Send These to Me: Immigrants in Urban America.* Rev. ed. Baltimore: Johns Hopkins Univ. Press.

Hirsch, George. 1997. "The Second Running Boom." *Runner's World* 32 (Apr.): 12.

Hobsbawm, Eric, and Terence Ranger. 1983. *The Invention of Tradition.* New York: Cambridge Univ. Press.

Hogan, Candace Lyle. 1979. "Shedding Light on Title IX." In *Out of the Bleachers: Writings on Women and Sport*, edited by Stephanie L. Twin, 173–82. New York: McGraw-Hill.

Hopkins, C. Howard. 1951. *History of the YMCA in North America.* New York: Association Press.

Hudson Guild, a Neighborhood Guild. 1933. New York.

Illingworth, Montieth M. 1985. "Run for the Money." *Manhattan, Inc.* 2 (Oct.): 124–32.

Jacoby, Sanford M. 1985. *Employing Bureaucracy: Managers, Unions, and the Transformation of Work in American Industry, 1900–1945.* New York: Columbia Univ. Press.

Jaher, Frederic C. 1982. *The Urban Establishment: Upper Strata in Boston, New York, Charleston, Chicago, and Los Angeles.* Urbana: Univ. of Illinois Press.

Jahnke, Art. 1982. "The Boss." *Running* 8 (Sept./Oct.): 34–40.

Kardong, Don. 1985. "Star Wars II." *The Runner* 8 (Oct.): 40–46.

Kaups, Matti. 1979. "Finns in Urban America: A View from Duluth." In *Finnish Diaspora II: United States,* edited by Michael G. Karni, 63–86. Papers of the Finn Forum Conference, vol. 2, held in Toronto, Ontario, November 1–3.

Kelley, John J. 1984. "A Wee Bit of History Helps Pass a Runner's Afternoon." *New London (Conn.) Day,* 22 Jan., C-7.

Kelly, John B. 1956. "Are We Becoming a Nation of Weaklings?" *Reader's Digest,* July, 26–29.

Kennedy, John F. 1960. "The Soft American." *Sports Illustrated,* 26 Dec., 15–17.

Kennedy, Rose Fitzgerald. 1974. *Times to Remember.* Garden City, N.Y.: Doubleday.

Kieran, John, and Arthur Daly. 1965. *The Story of the Olympic Games, 776 B.C. to 1964.* New York. J. B. Lippincott.

Killanin, Lord [Michael Morris], and John Rodda, eds. 1976. *The Olympic Games: 80 Years of People, Events, and Records.* New York: Collier.

Kleinerman, Joe. 1970. "Gary Muhrcke Wins First Annual New York City Marathon." *LDL* 15 (Sept.): 7.

Kokesh, Jerry. 1982. "President's Column." *Footnotes* 10 (summer): 2.

Kornheiser, Tony. 1976. "Marathon Woman: She Runs with Pride and Pain." *NYT,* 16 Apr., 29.

Korsgaard, Robert. 1952. "A History of the Amateur Athletic Union of the United States." Ed.D. diss., Columbia Univ.

Kotler, Philip. 1975. *Marketing for Nonprofit Organizations.* Englewood Cliffs, N.J.: Prentice-Hall.

Krise, Raymond, and William Squires. 1982. *Fast Tracks: The History of Distance Running since 884 B.C.* Brattleboro, Vt.: Stephen Greene Press.

Kronenthal, Syd. 1996. Telephone conversation, 14 Nov.

Kuscsik, Nina. 1977a. "The History of Women's Participation in the Marathon." In *The Marathon: Physiological, Medical, Epidemiological, and Psychological Studies,* vol. 301 of *Annals of the New York Academy of Aciences,* edited by Paul Milvy, 862–76. New York: New York Academy of Sciences.

———. 1977b. "Resolution for a Women's Marathon in the Olympics Passes." *Road Runners Club New York Association* newsletter, no. 72 (summer): 23.

Lagerquist, Walter E. 1910. "Social Geography of the East Side." *NYT Magazine,* 8 Apr., 1.

Lance, Kathryn. 1977. *Running For Health and Beauty: A Complete Guide for Women.* New York: Bobbs-Merrill.

Lebow, Fred, with Richard Woodley. 1984. *Inside the World of Big-Time Marathoning.* New York: Rawson Associates.

Lekachman, Robert. 1955. "Our 'Revolution' in Income Distribution: An Appraisal." *Commentary* 20 (Aug.): 132–40.

Leonard, "Lank." 1928. "60 year Old Veteran One of Harriers." *PCDI,* 12 Oct., 1, 17.

Lettis, Charlotte. 1972. "Promoting Women's Running?" *Runner's World* 7 (Sept.): 44.

Levine, Peter. 1992. *Ellis Island to Ebbets Field: Sport and the American Jewish Experience.* Sport and History Series, edited by Peter Levine and Steven Tischler. New York: Oxford Univ. Press.

Levy, Ed. 1992. Manager of the New York Pioneer Club. Interview by author. Tape recording. New York City, 15 Jan.

Lewin, Warren J., Historical Collection. 1938. "History of Port Chester Marathon." Port Chester Public Library, Port Chester, New York.

Lewis, Frederick. 1992. *Young At Heart: The Story of Johnny Kelley—Boston's Marathon Man.* Edited by Dick Johnson, with a foreword by Kenneth H. Cooper. Waco, Texas: WRS Publishing.

Lipsyte, Robert. 1968. "Pride Goeth Before Heartbreak Hill." *NYT,* 20 Apr., 40.

Litsky, Frank. 1964. "U.S. Sets Two World Records to Lead Soviet in Track." *NYT,* 26 July, sec. 5, pp. 1, 3.

———. 1965. "Kheel Heads 5-Man Panel to Arbitrate Track Dispute." *NYT,* 15 Dec., 61.

———. 1983. "A Second Wind in the Running Boom." *NYT,* 16 Apr., C1, C6.

Longman, Jere. 1997. "Catching a Second Wind: New Running Boom is Much More Low Key." *NYT,* 28 May, B9, B12.

Lucas, John. 1980. *The Modern Olympic Games.* New York: A. S. Barnes.

Lucian. 1954. Translated by K. Kilburn. Loeb Classical Library. Cambridge, Mass.: Harvard Univ. Press.

Lydiard, Arthur, and Garth Gilmour. 1967. *Run to the Top.* Rev. ed. Auckland, New Zealand: Minerva, Limited.

MacAloon, John J. 1981. *This Great Symbol: Pierre de Coubertin and the Origins of the Modern Olympic Games.* Chicago: Univ. of Chicago Press.

———. 1984. "Olympic Games and the Theory of Spectacle in Modern Societies." In *Rite, Drama, Festival, Spectacle: Rehearsals Toward a Theory of Cultural Performance,* edited by John J. MacAloon, 241–80. Philadelphia: Institute for the Study of Human Issues.

Macauley, Ian T. 1976. "Marathon Men and Women on Their Marks." *NYT,* 22 Oct., C22.

Macomber, Kathleen. 1977. *Minutes, 25 July 1977 Meeting, Marathon Committee, New York City Marathon for the Samuel Rudin Trophy.*

Mahoney, James. 1968. "American Victor in Marathon." *Boston Herald Traveler,* 20 Apr., 1, 14, 17.

Mandell, Richard D. 1976. *The First Modern Olympics.* Berkeley: Univ. of California Press.

Mandle, W. F. 1979. "Sport as Politics: The Gaelic Athletic Association, 1884–1916." In *Sport in History: The Making of Modern Sporting History,* edited by Richard Cashman and Michael McKernan, 99–123. Queensland: Queensland Univ. Press.

Marcus, Susan. 1982. "Avon Sets Off Explosion in Women's Running." *New York Marathon Magazine,* 24 Oct., 20–21.

Marsh, Margaret. 1988. "Suburban Men and Masculine Domesticity, 1870–1915." *American Quarterly* 2 (June): 165–86.

Martin, David E., and Roger W. H. Gynn. 1977. "Development of the Marathon from Pheidippides to the Present, with Statistics of Significant Races." In *The Marathon: Physiological, Medical, Epidemiological, and Psychological Studies,* vol. 301 of *Annals of the New York Academy of Sciences,* edited by Paul Milvy, 820–61. New York: New York Academy of Sciences.

––––––. 1979. *The Marathon Footrace: Performers and Performances.* Springfield, Ill.: Charles C. Thomas.

McCaffrey, Lawrence J. 1976. *The Irish Diaspora in America.* Bloomington: Indiana Univ. Press.

McElvaine, Robert J. 1984. *The Great Depression: America, 1929–1941.* New York: Times Books.

McGeehan, W. O. 1909. "Marathon Race Is an Inspiring Spectacle." *SFC,* 23 Feb, 10.

McNab, Tom. 1976. "Athletics." In *The Olympic Games: 80 Years of People, Events, and Records,* edited by [Michael Morris] Lord Killanin and John Rodda, 89–94. New York: Collier.

––––––. 1980. *The Complete Book of Track and Field.* New York: Exeter.

Melnick, Murray. 1994. Letter to author, 10 Aug.

Menke, Frank G. 1977. *The Encyclopedia of Sports.* 6th rev. ed., with revisions by Suzanne Treat. Garden City, N.Y.: Doubleday.

Mercer, Sid. 1944. "Yankee Doodle Went to Town." In *Sports Extra: Classics of Sport Reporting,* edited by Stanley P. Frank, 219–25. New York: A. S. Barnes.

Merrill, Sam. 1976. "Running in Packs." *Esquire,* Oct., 87, 143–44.

Meyer, Stephen, III. 1981. *The Five Dollar Day: Labor Management and Social Control in the Ford Motor Company, 1908–1921.* SUNY Series in American Social History, edited by Elizabeth Pleck and Charles Stephenson. Albany, N.Y.: State Univ. of New York Press.

Meyers, Charles Lee. 1889. "The Jersey City Athletic Club." *Outing* 13 (Feb.): 445–51.

Mezo, Ferenc. 1956. *The Modern Olympic Games.* Budapest: Pannonia Press.

Miller, Kerby A. 1985. *Emigrants and Exiles: Ireland and the Irish Exodus to North America.* New York: Oxford Univ. Press, 1985.

Milvy, Paul. 1976. "The Definitive Short History of the New York City Five-Borough Marathon." Typescript. NYRRC library.

———. 1977a. "How the Mini Kept Score." *Runner's World* 12 (Aug.): 51–53.

———. 1977b. "Milvy to Lebow." Letter from Paul Milvy to Fred Lebow. *Road Runners Club New York Association Newsletter,* no. 71 (spring): 6.

———. 1977c. "Similarities and Dissimilarities among Men and Women Distance Runners." In *The Marathon: Physiological, Medical, Epidemiological, and Psychological Studies,* vol. 301 of *Annals of the New York Academy of Sciences,* edited by Paul Milvy, 725–819. New York: New York Academy of Sciences.

Montgomery, David. 1977. "Immigrant Workers and Managerial Reform." In *Immigrants in Industrial America, 1850–1920,* edited by Richard L. Ehrlich, 96–110. Charlottesville.: University Press of Virginia.

———. 1979. *Workers' Control in America: Studies in the History of Work, Technology, and Labor Struggles.* New York: Cambridge Univ. Press.

———. 1987. *The Fall of the House of Labor: The Workplace, the State, and American Labor Activism, 1865–1925.* New York: Cambridge Univ. Press.

Moore, Kenny. 1981. "Dawning of a New ARRA." *Sports Illustrated,* 6 July, 40–45.

Morris, Aldon D. 1984. *The Origins of the Civil Rights Movement: Black Communities Organizing for Change.* New York: Free Press.

Mrozek, Donald J. 1983. *Sport and American Mentality, 1880–1910.* Knoxville: Univ. of Tennessee Press.

———. 1995. "The Cult and Ritual of Toughness in Cold War America." In *Sport in America: From Wicked Amusement to National Obsession,* edited by David K. Wiggins, 257–67. Champaign, Ill.: Human Kinetics.

Murphy, Frank. 1992. *A Cold Clear Day: The Athletic Biography of Buddy Edelen.* With a postscript by Hal Higdon. Kansas City: Windsprint.

Nash, Jeffrey E. 1979. "Weekend Racing as an Eventful Experience: Understanding the Accomplishment of Well-Being." *Urban Life* 8: 199–217.

Nelli, Humbert S. 1983. *From Immigrants to Ethnics: The Italian-Americans.* New York: Oxford Univ. Press.

Nelson, Daniel. 1975. *Managers and Workers: Origins of the New Factory System in the United States, 1800–1920.* Madison: Univ. of Wisconsin Press.

New York, N.Y., Office of Policy Management. Office of the Comptroller. 1988. *The Economic Impact of the 1988 New York Marathon.*

New York State Department of State. Office of Charities Registration. 1982. *New York Road Runners Club, Inc.— Financial Statements for the Year Ended 31 December 1982.*

————. 1985. *New York Road Runners Club, Inc.— Financial Statements for the Year Ended 31 December 1985.*

Nike, Inc. 1993. "Timeline." Promotional material.

Noel-Baker, Philip. 1976. "Stockholm 1912." In *The Olympic Games,* edited by [Michael Morris] Lord Killanin and John Rodda, 40–44. New York: Collier.

O'Connor, John J. 1978. "TV: Joanne Woodward, Forty, 'Sweet,' and Running." *NYT,* 1 Feb., sec. 3, p. 23.

O'Donnell, Thomas, with Jinny St. Goar. 1983. "Marathon Money Matters." *Forbes* 24 (Oct.), 37–38.

Olsen, Eric. 1978. "A View from the Top." *The Runner* 1 (Dec.): 57–63.

Orsi, Robert Anthony. 1985. *The Madonna of 115th Street: Faith and Community in Italian Harlem, 1880–1950.* New Haven: Yale Univ. Press.

Osofsky, Gilbert. 1963. *Harlem, the Making of a Ghetto: Negro New York, 1890–1930.* New York: Harper and Row.

Polenberg, Richard. 1980. *One Nation Divisible: Class, Race, and Ethnicity in the United States since 1938.* New York: Viking.

Porter, Glenn. 1973. *The Rise of Big Business, 1860–1910.* New York: Thomas Y. Crowell.

Postal, Bernard, Jesse Silver, and Roy Silver. 1965. *The Encyclopedia of Jews in Sports.* New York: Bloch.

President's Commission on Olympic Sports. 1977. *The Final Report of the President's Commission on Olympic sports, 1975–1977.* Washington, D.C.: Government Printing Office.

Prokop, Dave. 1976. "Frank Shorter." *Runner's World* 11 (Jan.): 46–48.

Rader, Benjamin G. 1977. "The Quest for Subcommunities and the Rise of American Sport." *American Quarterly* 29 (fall): 355–69.

————. 1991. "The Quest for Self-Sufficiency and the New Strenuosity: Reflections on the Strenuous Life of the 1970s and the 1980s." *Journal of Sport History* 18 (summer): 255–66.

Raia, James. 1997. "Still Leading the Pack." *Footnotes* 25 (spring): 13.

Raitz, Karl B. 1995. "Preface" and "The Theater of Sport: A Landscape Perspective." In *The Theater of Sport,* edited by Karl B. Raitz, viii–x, 1–29. Baltimore: Johns Hopkins Univ. Press.

Ralby, Herb. 1966. "Girl Finishes Marathon." *BG,* 20 Apr., 2.

Redmond, Gerald. 1971. *The Caledonian Games in Nineteenth-Century America.* Rutherford, N.J.: Fairleigh Dickinson Univ. Press.

Riess, Steven A. 1989. *City Games: The Evolution of American Urban Society and the Rise of Sports.* Sport and Society Series, edited by Benjamin G. Rader and Randy Roberts. Urbana: Univ. of Illinois Press.

Robbins, Charles. 1971. "Hints for Better Road Races." In *Guide to Distance Running,* edited by Bob Anderson and Joe Henderson, 41. Mountain View, Calif.: World Publications.

Rodgers, Bill [William], with Joe Concannon. 1980. *Marathoning.* With a foreword by Amby Burfoot. New York: Simon and Schuster.

Rosenfeld, P. 1977. "Cooper's Cohorts Run Down Heart Disease." *Saturday Evening Post* 249 (Sept.): 18–20.

Rosenzweig, Roy. 1983. *Eight Hours for What We Will: Workers and Leisure in an Industrial City, 1870–1920.* Interdisciplinary Perspectives on Modern History, edited by Robert Fogel and Stephan Thernstrom. New York: Cambridge Univ. Press.

Rosenzweig, Roy, and Elizabeth Blackmar. 1992. *The Park and the People: A History of Central Park.* Ithaca, N.Y.: Cornell Univ. Press.

Rosner, Dave. 1983. "They'll Take the Money and Run." *Sport,* Aug., 73–81.

———. 1983. "N.Y. Marathon Wants to Pay Cash in Open." *Long Island (N.Y.) Newsday,* 14 Oct., 134.

Ross, Carl. 1972. *The Finn Factor in American Labor, Culture, and Society.* With an introduction by Rudolph Vecoli. New York Mills, Minn.: Parta Printers.

Ross, H. Browning. 1957. "Editorial." *LDL* 2 (Aug.): 2.

———. 1969. "Memo from the Editor." *LDL* 14 (July): 2.

———. 1992. Interview by author. Tape recording. Woodbury, N.J., 16 Jan.

Ross, Jay. 1959. "Marathon Falls Prey to an Era." *PAC,* 2 Apr., 4.

Rotundo, E. Anthony. 1993. *American Manhood: Transformations in Masculinity from the Revolution to the Modern Era.* New York: Basic Books.

———. 1983. "Body and Soul: Changing Ideals of American Middle-Class Manhood, 1770–1920." *Journal of Social History* (summer): 23–38.

Ryan, Dennis P. 1989. *Beyond the Ballot Box: A Social History of the Boston Irish, 1845–1917.* Rutherford, N.J.: Fairleigh Dickinson Univ. Press, 1983. Reprint. Amherst: University of Mass. Press.

Sales, Bob. 1966. "Has Marathon Become Battle of Sexes?" *BG,* 20 Apr., 52.

Salmons, Sandra. 1979. "Japan Changes Avon's Make-Up." *International Management,* July, 42–43.

Santry, David G. 1979. "The Business of Running." *New York Running News* 21 (Dec.): 8–13.

Scandurra, Aldo. 1981. "History of Long Distance and Road Racing." *Long Island Running News* 1 (May): 9–18.

Schmertz, Fred. ?1967. *The Wanamaker Millrose Story: History of the Millrose Athletic Association, 1908–1967.* Yonkers, N.Y.: Millrose Athletic Association, c/o John Wanamaker Westchester.

Schroeder, W. R. 1961. "The AAU: A History of Achievement." *Amateur Athlete*, Oct., 12–13, 36–37.

Schumach, Murray. 1968. "Jogging Picks Up its Pace Here as 20 Tracks Open on Ideal Day." *NYT*, 21 Apr., 66.

Seller, Maxine. 1977. *To Seek America: A History of Ethnic Life in the United States.* New York: Jerome S. Oser.

Semple, Jock (John), with John J. Kelley and Tom Murphy. 1981. *Just Call Me Jock: The Story of Jock Semple, Boston's Mr. Marathon.* Waterford, Conn.: Waterford Publishing Co.

Shannon, William V. 1966. *The American Irish.* New York: Macmillan.

Shapiro, James E. 1980. *Ultramarathon.* New York: Bantam.

Sheehan, George A. 1973. "To Think and Talk." *Runner's World* 8 (Apr.): 13.

———. 1975. *Dr. Sheehan on Running.* Mountain View, Calif.: World Publications.

———. 1977. "Fitness Rx." *Vogue* 167 (Apr): 136–37.

Sheehan, Joseph M. 1946a. "Strand Beats MacMitchell: AAU Title to NYAC." *NYT*, 30 June, sec 5, pp. 1, 3.

———. 1946b. "300 Stars in Texas for AAU Events." *NYT*, 28 June, 25.

———. 1952. "Dyrgall Captures Marathon Honors." *NYT*, 19 May, 24.

Shorter, Frank, with Marc Bloom. 1984. *Olympic Gold: A Runner's Life and Times.* Boston: Houghton Mifflin.

Simons, William. 1986. "Abel Kiviat: Interview." *Journal of Sport History* 13 (winter): 235–66.

Simpson, Vyv, and Andrew Jennings. 1992. *Dishonored Games: Corruption, Money, and Greed at the Olympics.* New York: Shapolsky.

Smith, Ronald A. 1988. *Sports and Freedom: The Rise of Big-Time College Sports.* Sport and History Series, edited by Peter Levine and Steven Tischler. New York: Oxford Univ. Press.

Somers, Ron. 1976. "Black Distance Runners: Minority within a Minority." *Runner's World* 11 (Jan.): 37–39.

Sparrow, E. Edward. 1926. "DeMar Captures Marathon; Michelson Finishes Second." *Baltimore Sun*, 10 May, sports sec., p. 3.

Spitz, Barry. 1993. *Dipsea: The Greatest Race.* San Anselmo, Calif.: Potrero Meadow Publishing.

Stack, John F. 1979. *International Conflict in an American City: Boston's Irish, Italians, and Jews, 1935–1944.* Westport, Conn.: Greenwood.

Standard and Poor's Register of Corporations, Directors, and Executives. 1977. New York: Standard and Poor's Corporation.

Stokesbury, James L. 1988. *A Short History of the Korean War.* New York: William Morrow.

Strasser, J. B., and Laurie Becklund. 1991. *Swoosh: The Unauthorized Story of Nike and the Men Who Played There.* New York: Harcourt, Brace, Jovanovich.

Sturak, Jacqueline Hansen. 1993. Telephone conversation, 10 May.

Sullivan, James E. 1909a. "The Marathon Craze." *Harper's Weekly*, 15 May, 6.

———. 1909b. *Marathon Running.* Spalding Athletic Library, no. 317. New York: American Sports Pub. Co.

Switzer, Kathrine. 1972. "Leaving the Side-Show Era." *Runner's World* 8 (Aug.): 27.

———. 1975. "The 'Mini' Marathon and How it Grew." *Runner's World* 10 (July): 24–25.

———. 1992. Telephone conversation, 24 Oct.

———. 1997. Telephone conversation, 20 June.

Tarnawsky, Pat. 1971. "What's This? Women Welcome!" *Runner's World* 6 (Jan.): 22.

Texas, James. 1979. "Take the Money and Run." *The Runner* 2 (Jan.): 16–21.

Thernstrom, Stephan. 1973. *The Other Bostonians: Poverty and Progress in the American Metropolis, 1880–1970.* Harvard Studies in Urban History, edited by Stephan Thernstrom and Charles Tilly. Cambridge, Mass.: Harvard Univ. Press.

Thomas, Robert McG. 1984. "Marathon Payment Revealed." *NYT*, 4 Oct., B27.

Tinsley, Harold. 1982. "Where We Have Been, Where We Are Going." *Footnotes* 10 (summer): 5.

Torliatt, Lee. 1952. "Marathoners Off and Running at Petaluma Today." *Santa Rosa (Calif.) Press Democrat*, 6 Apr., 25.

Traub, Marvin, and Tom Teicholz. 1993. *Like No Other Store . . . The Bloomingdale's Legend and the Revolution in American Marketing.* New York: Times Books.

Trengove, Alan. 1961. *The Herb Elliott Story: The Dramatic Struggle of the Greatest Runner of Our Time.* New York: Thomas Nelson.

Trout, Charles H. 1977. *Boston, the Great Depression, and the New Deal.* Urban Life in America Series. New York: Oxford University Press.

Tsuchiya, Hiroko. 1986. "The Making of Hard-Playing Americans: The Legitimization of Working-Class Leisure, 1890–1929." Ph.D. Diss., Columbia Univ.

Turner, Victor W. 1969. *The Ritual Process: Structure and Anti-Structure.* Chicago: Aldine.

Ullyot, Joan. 1976. *Women's Running.* Mountain View, Calif.: World Publications.

Umminger, Walter. 1963. *Supermen, Heroes, and Gods: The Story of Sport through the Ages.* Translated by James Clark. New York: McGraw-Hill.

Underwood, John. 1969. "No Goody Two Shoes." *Sports Illustrated,* 10 Mar., 14–23.

Umphlett, Wiley Lee. 1975. *The Sporting Myth and the American Experience.* Studies in Contemporary Fiction. New York: Bucknell Univ. Press.

University Settlement Society. 1893. *Report and Plans for the Winter's Work of the University Settlement Society.* New York: Concord Printing.

Union Settlement. 1970. *There May Be More Interesting Communities than East Harlem but If So It Is Hard to Imagine Them.* New York: Martin Printing.

U.S. Bureau of the Census. 1913. *Thirteenth Census of the United States, Taken in the Year 1910,* vol. 1. Washington, D.C.: Government Printing Office.

———. 1922. *Fourteenth Census of the United States, Taken in the Year 1920,* vol. 3. Washington, D.C.: Government Printing Office.

U.S. Senate. 1965. Committee on Commerce. *NCAA-AAU Dispute: Hearing before the Committee on Commerce.* 89th Cong., 1st sess., 16–27 August.

Wallach, Len. 1978. *The Human Race.* With a foreword by Joe Henderson. San Francisco: A California Living Book.

Warner, Sam B. 1976. *Streetcar Suburbs: The Process of Growth in Boston, 1870–1900.* Cambridge, Mass.: Harvard Univ. Press, 1962. Reprint. New York: Atheneum.

Watman, Melvyn. 1977. *Encyclopedia of Athletics.* With a foreword by Harold Abrahams. New York: St. Martin's.

Weigold, Marilyn E., ed. 1983. *Westchester County: The Past Hundred Years, 1883–1983.* Valhalla, N.Y.: Westchester County Historical Society.

Wellemeyer, Marilyn. 1977. "Addicted to Perpetual Motion." *Fortune,* June, 55–68.

White, Gordon S. 1960. "Kelley Wins National AAU Marathon Run for Fifth Straight Time." *NYT,* 23 May, 42.

Whitfield, Stephen J. 1991. *The Culture of the Cold War.* Baltimore: Johns Hopkins Univ. Press.

Williams, Gar, and Jeff Darman. 1978. "History of the Road Runners Club of America." In *The Road Runners Club of America Handbook: A Guide to Club and Race Administration,* edited by Gar Williams, 208–18. Alexandria, Va.: Road Runners Club of America.

Willis, J., and R. Wettan. 1976. "Social Stratification in New York City Athletic Clubs, 1865–1915." *Journal of Sport History* 3 (spring): 45–63.

Wilson, Peter. 1976. "Helsinki 1952." In *The Olympic Games: 80 Years of People, Events, and Records,* edited by [Michael Morris] Lord Killanin and John Rodda, 64–69. New York: Collier.

Wittke, Carl. 1939. *We Who Built America.* New York: Press of Western Univ.

Worner, Ted. 1936. "Mel Porter of Newark Wins Twelfth Renewal of Yonkers Marathon Classic." *Yonkers Herald Statesman,* 9 Nov., 10.

———. 1938. "Pat Dengis of Baltimore Repeats in Yonkers Marathon Championship." *Yonkers Herald Statesman,* 7 Nov., 17.

———. 1939. "Pat Dengis Shatters Record to Win Marathon for Third Year in a Row." *Yonkers Herald Statesman,* 13 Nov., 13.

Index